D0770962

HOW WE FOUND THE
MARY ROSE

HOW WE FOUND THE
MARY ROSE

by

Alexander McKee

ST. MARTIN'S PRESS
NEW YORK

HOW WE FOUND THE MARY ROSE
Copyright © 1982 by Alexander McKee
All Rights reserved.
Printed in Great Britain.
No part of this book may be used without
written permission except in the case of brief
quotations embodied in critical articles or reviews.
For information, address St. Martin's Press,
175 Fifth Avenue, New York, N.Y. 10010

ISBN 0–312–39630–9

First published in Great Britain by Souvenir Press Ltd.

First U.S. Edition
10 9 8 7 6 5 4 3 2 1

Contents

Acknowledgements

During the years 1965 to 1978, when we were still a small and mostly local organisation, at least a thousand people helped us in one way or another. I should like to thank them, *en bloc*, for there are too many to name. Above all, my gratitude must go to that tiny, dedicated minority who stayed with the project for year after year of unrewarding, unregarded effort. Most of us are still together as the Mary Rose Special Branch of the British Sub-Aqua Club, diving for clues to other sites offshore which may one day rank with the *Mary Rose*.

I must also thank the wives and sweethearts who put up with so many lonely weekends for up to seventeen years. The *Mary Rose* proved to be a fascinating rival!

In particular I must mention those members of the diving team who contributed original material to this book, so that this is not just my story, but theirs as well. Thank you: Percy Ackland, Tony Barber, Douglas Barnard, Don Bullivant, George Clark, John Cleaver, Reg Cloudsdale, Tony Glover, Albert Kirby, N. Q. Knights, Ray McLaren, Dick Millerchip, Geoffrey Morgan, N. C. Robinson, Mick Russell, Eric Sivyer and Maurice Young.

I must also express my gratitude to Dr. Harold E. Edgerton of the Massachusetts Institute of Technology, Boston, for allowing me to quote from an article originally intended by him for an academic publication; and to two other Americans, both long-standing students of ship construction—Raymond Aker of Palo Alto, California, and Edward Von der Porten of Santa Rosa, California—for their assistance in reconstructing the lines of the *Mary Rose*, based on the small amount of evidence available to date. In this respect I am also grateful to Pino Dell 'Orco of Rome, who has studied the carrack for more than twenty years; and to Maurice Young (a second time), who helps to build modern warships as well as diving to old ones. Finally, my thanks to Gaile Matchan and Colonel Wendell Lewis for their memories of the recovery, and to Pete Smith and the Portsmouth *News* for allowing me to quote from Pete's report of the events of 10 October, 1982.

Without you all, the *Mary Rose* would still be lying buried at the bottom of the sea.

Alexander McKee
Hayling Island,
June, 1982.

Note: The poem on page 27 is from 'Mary Rose (1545)' by Jeremy Hooker, part of a sequence called *Solent Shore* (Carcanet New Press, 1978).

Prologue

'Could you tilt the model a little more?' asked Paul Armiger, the photographer from the *Daily Telegraph*.

Dutifully I heeled the *Mary Rose* back towards his camera and, trying to look natural, continued my conversation with John Grace. We were standing in a room at the headquarters of the Mary Rose Trust, discussing a new method of salvage he had proposed. The 'locked box' solution would still be used, but we were planning to alter the method of attaching the hull of the ship to the prefabricated lifting frame standing above it—for the better, in my opinion. Paul Armiger was there to record the new developments for his paper.

The frame, the cradle and pontoon, which were to contain the *Mary Rose*, were also modelled to the same scale, but they were masking the reconstruction of what we now knew to be left of the great carrack.

'Shall we try a picture without the lifting frame?' I asked, moving the yellow-painted grid to one side.

The frame before us was only about a foot long. The real thing—117 feet long and 49 feet wide—was at that moment standing on its 32-foot legs above the opened grave of the real *Mary Rose* and her long-dead crew. It was June, 1982, and the preliminaries for the final stages of the multi-million pound excavation and recovery operation were now set in motion. Fancy was becoming fact.

Seventeen years ago, in April, 1965, I had set out from Portsmouth with four companions in a tiny open boat to make my first dive at Spithead—the first of more than six hundred dives I was to make in a bid to find King Henry VIII's lost flagship. Now, the dream of discovering and then raising that key ship of history seemed to be coming true.

Holding the model in my hands, I found myself imagining the ship as she must have looked on that day in July, 1545, when she went down. Even then she was an old ship, the veteran of several engagements since her launching in 1510. This date, which I had worked out from Tudor documents, had been confirmed only a few days before, when one of her watch bells had been dug out of the mud. Paul Armiger had just been photographing it against a blue-green background, and embossed clearly upon it was the year of her launching—1510.

But for the accident that sank the *Mary Rose*, she would in all probability have been broken up after forty or fifty years of service, and so lost forever. Her dramatic sinking, under the very eyes of Henry VIII, had been a disaster at the time, but paradoxically it had preserved her for immortality. Now, after the long years of searching and digging, she was rising again, delivering up the secrets of her hidden past and of the men who had sailed in her; perhaps to reveal at last the true story of those final, fatal moments when she heeled and sank before the aghast Royal gaze.

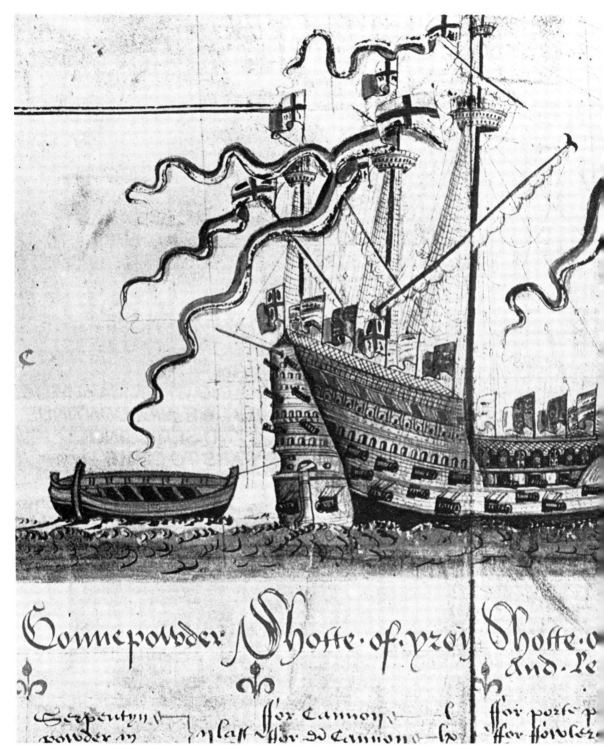

The only authentic picture of the *Mary Rose*, taken from the Anthony Roll inventory of the King's Ships. For the first time, complete batteries of heavy siege guns have been mounted, but the overhanging fighting castle at the bow has been retained. Note the boarding netting rigged in the waist and over the stern castle. Photo: Reproduced by permission of the Masters and Fellows of Magdalene College, Cambridge.

Chapter 1

The End of the Mary Rose

Portsmouth, 1509–1545

THE THUNDER of the guns came rolling in from seaward. Thud on distant thud, like the slamming of heavy doors.

The fighting galleys of the invaders came forward towards the motionless English fleet like giant waterbeetles, their long rows of oars rising and falling in unison. The still, blue water, the current almost slack, was perfect for them; and with their shallow draft the shoals where the English lay becalmed held no hazard. Bright yellow flame stabbed out from their bows where their heavy guns were mounted, and great clouds of smoke gushed out. For long seconds there was silence, as the beakheads of the galleys drove forward into their own gunsmoke. Then it came again. *Duf, duf, duf.* Thud upon thud of cannon and culverin, hammering at the helpless English ships.

In any ordinary summer the south coast of England is neither very wet nor very calm; often sunny but usually windy, gusting sometimes to near gale force. The very conditions for which Henry VIII had built his royal fleet, and especially the battleships, those towering carracks heavily freighted with guns and armed men. But now, in this unseasonable summer of 1545, when a few miles to seaward the French invasion fleet—235 ships in all, some 30,000 men—lay assembled in full sight of the shore, there was no wind; a hot breathless calm held the great ships of the English navy motionless, at the mercy of the French galleys. To repulse the enemy forces, Henry had been able to muster around him here at Portsmouth a mere 60 ships and fewer than 10,000 men: an unequal battle in which the very elements seemed arrayed on the opposing side.

King Henry himself, his privy councillors, his commanders, even some of their gentlewomen and the foreign ambassadors to his court, all were there that day. Under the gleaming white walls of the artillery castle that he had built at Southsea a year

9

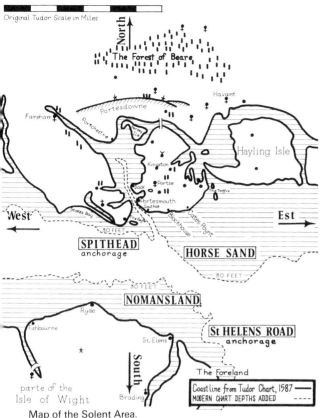

North

The Forest of Beare

Havant

Portesdowne

Fareham

Portchestra

Hayling Isle

Kingston

Portse

Dock

The Triffrs

Portsmouth
Southse

West

Est

Gates Point

Stokes Bay

Blockhouse

30 FEET

SPITHEAD
anchorage

HORSE SAND

30 FEET

30 FEET

NOMANSLAND

Ryde

Fishbourne

St. Elens

St HELENS ROAD
anchorage

South

The Foreland

parte of the
Isle of Wight

Brading

Coastline from Tudor Chart, 1587 ———
MODERN CHART DEPTHS ADDED   - - - -

Map of the Solent Area.

before to command the main channel into Portsmouth Harbour, the Tudor monarch had set up his battle headquarters. From that vantage point on a day such as this one could look right across the blue waters of Spithead and the Solent to the Isle of Wight and see the hills, some 16 miles away, that marked its southern shores. The entire battleground, land and sea alike, was open to view.

For an hour, under the royal gaze, the deadly pageant was played out on the still water, the French galleys manoeuvring to fire at best advantage, the English often unable to reply with more than their lighter guns. *Tirduf, tirduf, tirduf, tirduf,* came the crack of the smaller weapons. And now and then arose the chatter of the swivels, handguns and hailshot pieces, *tik-tak, tik-tak, tik-tak,* like a woodpecker knocking on wood.

Then came a breeze from off the land. The blue water broke up, lost its calm, ceased to reflect the white clouds of July. The sea, now turned bronzegreen, began to move and ripple past the heavy rope cables of the anchored English ships. Whistles shrilled along their decks. The capstan parties began their chant—'Haul! Haul! Haul one and all! Haul!' The

yardmen loosed the sails. As the anchors came home and the main sails billowed out, the great English ships heeled to the wind and moved remorselessly towards the galleys. Suddenly the balance had swung: so quickly had the breeze sprung up that the enemy's oared vessels were caught far from their main fleet; it was the moment the English commanders had been waiting for.

Ports open, the muzzles of bronze and iron guns run out and ready, the two English flagships led the charge. Lord Lisle, the senior of the two admirals, commanded the fleet in the giant carrack *Great Harry,* named for the king. Sir George Carew was his viceadmiral, riding to battle in the *Mary Rose,* named for Henry's younger sister, Mary Tudor, with under him as captain Roger Grenville. Lady Mary Carew, Sir George's wife, stood beside Henry VIII, watching her husband go into battle.

But there was something wrong with the *Mary Rose:* she was heeling over, with her gaping ports dangerously near the waves. The other ships began to pass the stricken vessel, one of them commanded by Sir Gawen Carew, uncle of the vice-admiral. He called across the water to his kinsman, asking, what was the matter with the *Mary Rose?* And Sir George shouted back, 'I have the sort of knaves I cannot rule.'

Slowly the great carrack lay down on her side and hung there a moment, with one great wailing cry coming out from her flooding decks. For the hundreds of men penned on her main gundeck, low down the hull near the waterline, there was no escape at all; they were trapped inside a solid cage of timber. Nor was there any hope for the hundreds more on the gundeck above their heads; although this deck in the waist was open to the sky, the boarding netting had been rigged above, strong ropes intended not only to keep boarders out but to catch any falling spars shot away by the enemy. They too were caged and helpless. And as the ship turned right over, everything loose on the high side of her hull, men and gear alike, slid down to the low side to be engulfed by the chill green seas roaring onto the decks, shutting out their light forever.

The king screeched like any maid, it was said, crying: 'Oh my gentlemen, Oh my gallant men!' Then it was all over, with one great cry to heaven. 'Drowned like rattens,' wrote a poet, 'drowned like ratten.'

Lady Carew, who had just seen her husband perish before her eyes, little more than a mile away, half-swooned. The king tried to comfort her, saying he thanked God there was a younger brother, Sir Peter, to carry on the Carew line. Then to the other shocked members of his court he expressed the hope that out of such a hard beginning there might follow a better ending.

The two tallest masts of the sunken carrack, heeled crazily, reared out of the water to mark the site of the tragedy. Some men, presumably sailors, were still clinging to the rigging; and a few more, lightly clad, were swimming in the disturbed eddies and bursts of compressed air above the wreck. Boats were already coming in to pick them up, but there seemed pitifully few survivors, less than three dozen out of possibly as many as 700 seamen and soldiers.

In the French fleet there was satisfaction. Their galleys had been firing at the English carracks for the last hour or more; now one of the enemy flagships had gone down, proof of the power of French gunnery. The rest of the battle might be just as easy.

Henry VIII came to the throne of England, Wales and Ireland in June, 1509, at the age of eighteen. The Venetian ambassador was most impressed, reporting that:

His majesty is the handsomest potentate I have ever set eyes on, above the usual height . . . his complexion very fair and bright, with auburn hair, combed straight, and short, in the French fashion, and a round face so very beautiful, that it would become a pretty woman, his throat being rather long and thick. He speaks French, English, and Latin, and a little Italian; plays well on the lute and harpsicord, sings from book at sight, draws the bow with greater strength than any man in England, and jousts marvellously. Believe me, he is in every respect a most accomplished prince.

Henry had a passion for music. He not only sang and played, he was a composer as well; and he was fond, too, of dancing. But he was trained to be a king in a time of turmoil. A leading continental thinker of the time, Niccolo Macchiavelli, studying modern war as practised by France and Spain, much greater powers than England, concluded that, 'The main foundations of every state are good laws and good arms. A Prince should have no other object or thought except war, its organisation and its discipline.'

The young Henry's father, on winning the English throne by force of arms in 1485, had almost immediately begun a naval rearmament programme to up-date the outmoded English fleet. He ordered the construction at Portsmouth of the first dry dock in the kingdom and built two new, four-masted carracks, the 1,000 ton *Regent* in 1486 and the 800-ton *Sovereign* in 1488. The *Regent* was certainly a copy of a foreign model, ordered to be built 'like unto a ship called the *Columbe* of France' and made by a 'novel construction with ordnance and fittings'. And that is all we know about her. We know even less about the *Sovereign*. Apart from an inventory, there is only a mention in 1525 that she is in bad condition but worth repair because 'the form of which ship is so marvellously goodly that great pity it were that she should die.'

Henry inherited these two ships, now in their turn out-dated by technical progress on the continent, and almost the first act of his reign was to order the rebuilding of the *Sovereign* and the construction of two new carracks to the latest European designs; all this work to be done at Portsmouth, the best anti-French naval base in the kingdom. The report of a Royal Commission on the Navy, dated 1618, a little over a century later, noted:

. . . but since the change of weapons and fight, Henry the Eighth, making use of Italian shipwrights, and encouraging his own people to build strong ships of war to carry great ordnance, by that means established a puissant Navy. . . .

The decision to build two new ships to take the new weapons and use them in the new way must have been taken in 1509. The earliest surviving warrant, which is from the King to John Dawtrey, is dated 29 January, 1510. In its first paragraph it authorises the spending of £700 for

tymber, ironwerk and workmanship of twoo new shippes to be made for us, and the oon shipp to be of the burden of 400 tonnes, and the other ship to be of the burdeyn of 300 tonnes.

The second paragraph authorises the expenditure of £316. 13s. 4d.

for all maner of implements and necessaries to the same twoo shippes belonging, for sailes, twyne, merling, ropes, cables, cabletts, shrowds, hawsers, boye ropes, steys, shells, boye lines, tacks, lists, toppe armers, stremers, standerd, compasses, ronnyyng glasses, tankerds, bolles, disshes, lanterns, shevers of bras and poleys, vitaills and wages of men for setting up theyr masts, shrowds and all other taclyng.

Another warrant went from Henry to Hans Poppenreuter of Malines (in what is now Belgium) for

Fighting Ships: The Vikings to the *Victory*. Drawings: Maurice Young.

Viking longship, 850–900 AD. A large, light open boat with auxiliary oar propulsion. Many examples known.

Mid-13th century English cog. A ship rather than a boat, with temporary castles built on in time of war. No plans exist.

Late 14th century 'nef' with permanent built-in castles. No plans exist.

Grace Dieu, a huge early 15th century carrack built by Henry V after Agincourt. Remains of lower hull can still be seen in Hamble River.

Mid-16th century carrack. A four-master with heavy guns as main armament. No plans exist.

English galleon of about 1586. Still a four-master, but the towering castles have been reduced. Result: improved sailing qualities. A few plans exist.

Swedish galleon *Wasa* of 1628. Deliberately discovered by Anders Franzén in 1956 and salvaged intact in 1961.

First rate line-of-battle ship HMS *Victory* as she appeared in 1805. A giant headquarters ship for an Admiral.

the latest ordnance from that famous gun foundry in Flanders—a dozen heavy brass curtows of 40 cwt., a dozen lesser brass curtows of 28 cwt., and two dozen brass serpentines of 11 cwt.

By the late summer of 1511 the two battleships had been completed for sea and were taken through the Channel to the Thames, where they received their guns from the royal armouries at the Tower of London. Both were four-masted carracks and as the personal property of the king had received royal names. The larger, now rated as 600 tons, was named the *Mary Rose*—'Mary' for the king's strikingly beautiful younger sister, 'Rose' for the Tudor emblem. Spelling, probably based on local dialects, was free and easy, and in Tudor documents *Mary Rose* is spelt in eight different ways—*Mary Rose*, *Mare Rose*, *Marye Rose*, *Marye Rosse*, *Marie Roos*, *Mary Roos*, *Mary Roose*, *Mary Roase*. The smaller ship now bore the name *Peter Pomegranate* (or *Petyr Pomie Garnade* or *Peter Pome Garnett*), as a compliment to Henry's Spanish wife, Katherine of Aragon, the pomegranate being part of the arms of Granada, recently liberated from the Moors.

By January, 1512, England was at war with France, and within six months of receiving her guns at the Tower, the *Mary Rose* was appointed flagship of the Lord Admiral. There were 25 ships fitted out in all, but only three—the newly-built pair and the recently rebuilt *Sovereign*—seem to have been given modern weapons, which were scarce and expensive. A great gun of brass could cost £35, a great gun of iron about £12. It is doubtful whether the decks of the older ships could take the weight, plus the stress of recoil. But any monarch whose armies and ships did not possess such weapons was not of European stature. There had been a revolution in warfare as a result of rapid technological changes in gun-founding; the new muzzle-loading guns, cast usually in brass, were far more powerful than the old 'built-up' breech-loading guns made of wrought-iron. As Shakespeare was to write in Henry V:

> . . . the nimble gunner
> With linstock now the devilish canon touches,
> And down goes all before him!

This was not in fact true in Henry V's time, when the Welsh longbow proved supreme both on land and at sea; but at Formigny in 1450 and at Castillon in 1453, the new French artillery had out-ranged the massed English archers and destroyed them. By the

Detail of a 16th century ship at Plymouth, showing the beamy hull with flat transom stern and two gunports, and above the curving 'tumblehome' of the hull to the stern castle. The fighting castle at the bow is obscured by the huge mainsail. Photo: Cotton Mss, British Library.

1490s heavy artillery had so developed in power and mobility that it made lightning war possible; stone walls and armoured horsemen alike could not stand against it. In 1494 the French invaded Italy and swept on to Naples, castles and citadels going down like ninepins before them. The stronghold of Monte San Giovanni had once withstood a siege of seven years; in 1494 the walls lasted eight hours and for the crime of resisting the French King, the garrison were massacred. Guicciardini, an Italian witness, wrote that the new cannon were

> planted against the walls of a town with such speed, the space between the shots was so brief, and the balls flew so speedily, and were driven with such force, that as much execution was inflicted in a few hours as used to be done in Italy over the same number of days.

It was guns such as these, together with the supporting arms—archers and pikemen—which ambitious monarchs wanted to put into their ships, so that they could fight at sea with the same advantages as on land. Up to now, the archers had been the primary arm and—supported by both small guns and pikemen—had been dominant in sea battles. Great fighting castles to house them had been built in the ships, so that an infantry-armed carrack looked not unlike a swan or a duck, with a disproportionately lofty fortress overhanging the bow. Now, it was the archers who would support the guns, provided that the shipwrights could solve the problems of installing them. The only name which has come down to us is that of Descharges of Brest, who in 1501 is supposed to have introduced some method of making water-tight ports in the hull of a great ship, so that the weighty new ordnance could be stationed low down in the hull. To mount it in the castles or entirely in the waist would have made a ship liable to capsize without warning. Of course, the safest place for heavy weights in a ship is as near the keel as possible, but provided the ports could be closed and made watertight, then the ship could heel over in a strong wind or rough sea without harm, because the buoyancy of her high-built sides would bring her back again. If the ports were left open, however, and the ship should heel very much, the water would not merely enter but by its weight further press down the deck, so that with frightening rapidity a moderate heel could become a fatal capsize. That hazard would have to be accepted, because to continue with the old system of armaments was to invite defeat at sea.

13

B.P. commissioned this theoretical model of the *Mary Rose* to be made in the early days of the project as an aid to understanding the Anthony Roll picture over which experts were divided. Photo: BP Chemicals International Ltd.

There had been other changes recently in ship construction, for instance from the clinker method of overlapping planks to the carvel form, where the planks were butted up against each other; and from the rounded stern to the square, transom stern. The latter was probably in order to give space for the mounting of heavy stern guns and so eliminate a weak spot which invited attack by galleys. However, we know very little about all this. There are no builder's plans or builder's models of any ship of the period, and all we can be sure of is that the *Mary Rose* was a 'key' vessel in the development of the warship—the first English ship to be specially built to mount the new ordnance and fight at sea by the new methods. She had hardly been built before she was put to the test of a full scale sea battle.

Chapter 2

Fair Stood the Wind for France

The King's First French War, 1512–1514

IN HENRY VIII's time there was no conscription in the modern sense, no call-up, no draft. There was no standing army or network of depots, not even a state police force. Government was local and the only regular soldiers were the few hundred men of the royal bodyguard. The officers had to go out and find men to man the ships. Thomas Spert, the master of the *Mary Rose*, the senior professional mariner on board, had to make journeys of up to 150 miles. Mr. W. Forde, one of her 'lodesmen' or navigators, spent 40 days in the great port of Bristol recruiting seamen. Some of the soldiers were recruited in Norfolk, 100 miles from London.

There was one great difference between the English system and that used on the continent. Continental armies relied heavily on the mercenary, whereas Henry employed part-time soldiers enrolled in a national militia. Many of these men were armed with what foreigners would regard as outdated weapons—bill, lance and longbow. Abroad, they used the long pike and the new handguns, which the continentals called the hakbutt or arquebus.

However, the English had time for preparation. The war of 1512 was planned by the King of Aragon and the Pope in 1511, and Henry decided to join their 'Holy League'. They were to invade France in April, 1512, and the task of the English fleet under Sir Edward Howard was to dominate the Channel. With eighteen warships plus two crayers as waterboats and supply vessels, and victualled for three months at a time, Howard was to cruise the 'Trade'—as the main sea routes between Brest and Calais were known. Henry had mobilised with such 'wonderful speed' (considering that shanks's pony was the principal means of transport), that hardly a shot was fired by the English fleet. The only ships in the Channel were those of merchants and fishermen; many French, some Flemish, a few Spanish. The English warships made a clean sweep of them all, foe and friend alike.

They returned to Portsmouth having seen nothing either of their French enemies or their Spanish allies. On 31 July Henry VIII rode down to Portsmouth to relish the spectacle of his war fleet gathered together—there were now 25 ships with Howard—and to offer their captains 'a banquet before their setting forward' for the second time.

Louis XII of France had levied a tax for the war, appointed agents to collect victuals, and ordered a fleet fitted out. In Normandy, 14 ships were being prepared, in Brittany, eight ships; five of them belonged to the King, four to the Queen, the rest were hired. René de Clermont was appointed Vice-Admiral to command them. More significantly, Louis gave up Lombardy and Genoa which he had conquered in 1499, in order to free for battle against the English his Mediterranean fleet consisting of the galleys commanded by a famous admiral, Prégent de Bidoux, Knight of Rhodes. When the Levant galleys arrived, Sir Edward Howard's ships would be at a serious disadvantage. Louis had also begun a blockade and commerce war against England as well as Spain and Portugal. It became impossible to insure cargoes from Crete or the Greek islands, and trade stopped.

From Portsmouth to the French naval base at Brest, menacing the western end of the Channel, was 250 miles against the prevailing winds. Howard sighted the enemy ships on the morning of 10 August, and found them completely unprepared. Captain Hervé de Portzmoguer, a noted privateer, was entertaining 300 local dignitaries and their wives in a famous raider, the 700-ton carrack *Marie la Cordelière*; while Vice-Admiral René de Clermont was host to many more in his 790-ton flagship *Grande Louise*. Both these great carracks were of fairly recent design, having been built about 1498-9. The *Cordelière* was formidably armed with fifteen 'gret brasyn cortauds' and 'other gunys of every sorte' and packed

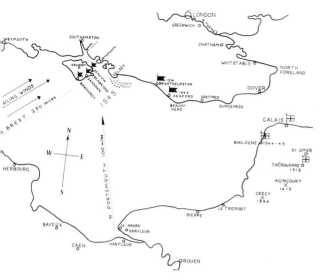

Map showing the geography of King Henry VIII's French wars.

with men—800 soldiers and sailors, 400 crossbow-men, plus 50 to 100 gunners, it was reported, under the command of 'four lords'. The men wore uniforms consisting of red jackets with blue or black breeches. The castles and fighting tops of the ships were pavesaded with shields bearing either the ermine of Brittany or a black cross on a white ground. Taken by surprise, some of the French ships had no time to raise their anchors and were forced to cut their cables; others were brought to action before they could even unfurl their fighting sails.

The English had the advantage of preparation. They had rigged their waist cloths and top armings—long strips of stiff, painted canvas to hide their crews from view. Darts and stones had been taken up to the tops for hurling down onto the enemy's decks. Shot had been placed beside the guns: iron shot and stone shot for smashing or penetrating the enemy ship's sides or castles; crossbar shot for tearing rigging and weakening masts, hollow incendiary shot containing 'wyldefyre', and for the lighter guns, bags of rounded lead pellets or square iron dice to spread like hail from the muzzles.

A seaman's clothes cost only 20d, whereas the green-and-white uniforms of the soldiers were 4s. each, the principal item being a 'jack', a stiff leather sleeveless jerkin probably capable of giving some protection against spent arrows and weak or glancing blows from pike or sword, while still permitting

freedom of movement. The soldiers were divided into pikemen and bowmen. The archers were mostly equipped with the powerful Welsh longbow which combined great range with rapidity of fire. The archers would have already selected the shafts they were going to use—rough ones for volley fire, more perfect arrows for individual shooting, with a few incendiary shafts to hand, equipped with hooks to catch in the enemy's sails or rigging; and they had a choice also in shaft heads—some were armour-piercing.

The *Mary Rose*, not the largest ship on the English side, but the most lethal, chose the enemy flagship *Grande Louise* for her opponent, opening fire first. The great brass curtalls of the main muzzle-loading battery thunder-cracked out their heavy shot, run-ning back with the shattering recoil of the explosions, to be swabbed out and reloaded in the swirling reek of black powder smoke, the guns' crews hardly able to see their own length before them. The breech-loading murderers, big guns of brass or iron, belched yellow flame before the recoil; as they came to rest at the end of their ropes, the crew whipped out the expended gunpowder chamber, ready to replace it with a new one as soon as fresh shot and wadding had been thrust into the smoking, reeking breech. The other guns added their voices to the din: the cast pieces, the slings, the stone guns, the top guns, the serpentines. The decks stank of gunpowder, wreathed in smoke like a fog which only slowly cleared through the gratings. Men's ears were numb with noise. This was the new way of war, the fire-fight which preceded the assault with cutting or stabbing weapons.

Within an hour, 300 men were dead or wounded on the decks of the French flagship, and her main mast was gone. Painfully, she turned away from the shore, trying to escape capture.

Elsewhere, the English were concentrating super-ior numbers against the most important ships of the enemy. The nef of Dieppe, of which Rigault de Barquetot was captain, had a seven-hour-long fight to hold off five English ships which were trying to board and take his vessel; he had 32 men killed, many more wounded. Then some ships from Guernsey came to his aid. De Barquetot was so bitter about being abandoned by his admiral—for that was how he saw the retreat of the *Grande Louise* before the guns of the *Mary Rose*—that he challenged René de Clermont to a duel.

The other great French ship almost overwhelmed

by the English was Hervé de Portzmoguer's Breton carrack *Marie la Cordelière*, of 700 tons. She was attacked at once by a much smaller ship, the *Mary James* of 400 tons, commanded by Captain Anthony Ughtred, who had closely followed the *Mary Rose* into action. He brought the *Cordelière* to a standstill in the water by bodily ramming her, and then firing his battery guns into her hull point-blank. Portzmoguer replied with his much heavier armament and hurt Captain Ughtred's ship very badly; but Ughtred had held the Frenchman long enough for the 1,000-ton *Sovereign*, rebuilt and rearmed in 1509, to join the fight. She was commanded by Sir Henry Guildford and Sir Charles Brandon, who was soon to marry the King's sister for whom the *Mary Rose* was named. Their attack miscarried, however. The *Sovereign* 'lay stem to stem with the great carrack of Brest,' wrote the Tudor historian Holinshed. 'But by the negligence of the master, or else by smoke of the ordnance, or otherwise, the *Sovereign* was cast at the stern of the carrack, with which advantage the French shouted for joy.'

It was then that the great 1,000-ton *Regent* entered the battle. She carried 700 men but retained the old-fashioned armament consisting of hundreds of mainly light long-guns—brass and iron serpentines. As she drove alongside the *Cordelière*, already trying to escape from the *Mary James* and the *Sovereign*, hooks and grapnels hurled down from the *Regent* onto the Breton carrack and held her fast. Sir Thomas Knyvett and Sir John Carew of the *Regent* had given up their fight with another great French ship in order to make sure of this one, and rightly so, for Portzmoguer was a hero of France and the *Cordelière* a most formidable battleship. And now they had got her. Giving up his attempt to escape, the French captain let go an anchor and the two great towering hulls turned slowly with the run of the tidal stream so that they lay across the wind, the English ship in the lee of the French one.

A blizzard of arrow shafts and crossbow bolts poured down from the high tops and castles onto the fighting men on the decks below; Briton and Breton in bitter combat. 'The fight was very cruel, for the

French assault on Brighthelmstone (Brighton) in 1514. The galleys, acting as landing craft, have put the soldiers ashore. They are covered by the guns of the great carracks lying off in deeper water. Photo: British Library.

Detail of a French carrack taking part in the landings at Brighton in 1514. It is almost identical to the *Mary Rose* in design but appears to have only one gun deck. Photo: British Library.

archers of the English part, and the crossbows of the French part, did their uttermost,' wrote Holinshed. 'But for all that, the Englishmen entered the carrack.' Sir Thomas Knyvett was already dead, slain by a gunshot, when 400 English fighting men poured over the bulwarks of the *Regent* and into the *Cordelière*. At point of pike, they forced their way forward over splintered decks and heaped corpses. Wrote Cardinal Wolsey to the Bishop of Winchester:

> Our men so valyently acquyt themselfe that within one ower fyght they had utterly vanquyshyd with shot of gonnys and arrows the said caryke, and slayne moste parte of the men within the same. And sodenly as they war yelding themsylf, the caryke was one a flamyng fyre, and lyke wyse the Regent within the turning of one hand . . . So bothe in fyght within three owrys war burnt, and most parte of the men in them.

From tarred rigging to powder-strewn decks, these ships were fire hazards, and with their gunports open for battle, they generated a tremendous draught. Giant flames roared out, red points of fire raced up the rigging, trapped men hurled themselves into the cold waves. The two great fighting ships, side by side, belching flame and smoke up to the heavens as if they

were one mighty furnace, made a spectacle which stilled the battle. Even the sorely battered *Mary James* stopped trying to kill Frenchmen and started trying to save some.

When the two great ships had gone from sight and only the wind-blown smoke and the drifting debris marked the scene of mutual disaster, more than 2,000 men had died. They included all the leaders, Knyvett, Carew, Portzmoguer. An early report gave the number of survivors from the 1500 men in the *Cordelière* as 20, later reduced to a mere six (perhaps some had died of burns in the interval); while 180 English had survived out of the *Regent* which had lost some 600 men.

The *Mary James* had suffered heavily from the *Cordelière*'s fire; some 60 of her wounded had to be permanently pensioned off from sea service. The *Grande Louise* had suffered worse from the guns of the *Mary Rose*, and the crippling of the French flagship by the English flagship may have helped persuade the French to give up. They retired into Brest, while Howard in the *Mary Rose* cruised for two days afterwards outside the port, burning or taking 32 French vessels and capturing 800 men.

The war went on into 1513. The Holy League now consisted of Spain, Venice, the Papal States, the German Empire and England allied against France, the major military power of Europe. A combined offensive in France was planned for the summer; an English army was to be ferried across the Channel into the existing English bridgehead around Calais, covered by Henry's new royal navy. He had now added more ships to it, including two recently-purchased foreign-built carracks, the 800-ton *Gabryell Royall* from Italy and the 700-ton *Kathereyn Fortaleza* from Spain. The 600-ton *Mary Rose* was still the flagship under the command of Sir Edward Howard. Henry wanted comparative sea trials carried out before the campaigning season began, so after a royal review at Greenwich on 19 March, Howard led the fleet towards the Channel and then ordered all ships to make full sail simultaneously and race each other through the tricky waters of the Straits of Dover.

Some of the smaller vessels, which drew less water, cut the corner by sailing close inshore off the Foreland, but the *Mary Rose* drew ahead of all the others. The race ended with the *Mary Rose* leading the *Sovereign* by half a mile, with half a mile behind that a group of smaller ships, followed by the main body of the battleships trailing a full three miles behind their flagship. Howard wrote to the King; describing her as 'your good shipp, the flower, I trow, off al ships that ever saylyd.'

A dangerous situation, caused by the wind changing when the fleet was racing through the narrow channels between the deadly sandbanks, forced the ships to tack time after time in rapidly shallowing water among steep, short seas. As Howard told Henry, this was the best trial of their sailing qualities it was possible to have, and few ships did not take in water over their lee gunwales as they heeled to the breeze.

A few vessels performed badly. The 300-ton *Christ* 'was one of the wurst that day ... overladen with ordnance, beysyd her hevy toppes, which are byg inough for a shipp of 8 or 900 (tons).' Generally, Howard was pleased with his force. 'In Christendom owt of one realm was never seen such a flete as this.'

The best of them all was his own flagship, the *Mary Rose*. 'Sir, she is the noblest shipp of sayle and grett shipp at this hour that I trow be in Christendom. A shipp of 100 ton wyl not be soner at her ... abowt than she.'

So as a replacement for the burnt *Regent*, a scaled-up version of the *Mary Rose* was ordered. At first called the 'Gret carrik' *Imperyall*, she was later named the *Henry Grace de Dieu*, more commonly the *Henry Grace á Dieu* or *Great Harry*, listed usually at 1,000 tons, sometimes as 1,500 tons. The figures are useful only as a comparison between like ships of the period, for the exact meaning of the Tudor 'tun' is doubtful, particularly when applied to warships, a 'tun' being a cask of ale or wine, not a good measure for cargoes of guns, ammunition and armed men. She was armed with 184 guns, no fewer than 24 being listed as 'grete', and one 'grete bumbarde of brass apon iiii trotill wheles' can hardly have been less than a 10-inch or 12-inch gun. However, this giant battleship was not ready in time to help Howard wage the fatal campaign of 1513.

For the 1513 campaign there were some changes to the crew numbers actually aboard the *Mary Rose*. The theoretical complement was always 400 plus the captain or admiral, but the actual strengths tended to be higher, which affected the pay and rations. During April to July 1512 there had been two very senior officers, paid out of all proportion to the rest: Sir Edward Howard, 'chief capeteyn and admyrall of the fleet', at 10s. per day, and Sir Thomas Wyndeham, 'treasurer of the army by sea', at 18d. (1s. 6d.) per day. Much lower down the scale were the two 'lodesmen alias pylotts' (i.e., navigators) at 20s. a month; the 251 'souldiours', the 120 'maryners', the 20 'gonners' and the 20 'servitours', all at 10s. a month (compared to Howard's 10s. a day). In October, a list shows that Wyndeham's staff then numbered 26, and there were also five trumpeters.

The returns for 1513 show 200 soldiers, 180 mariners, 20 gunners; plus Howard and the master, Thomas Spert—402 in all. The campaign stores included many items for the archers—350 bows, 700 bowstrings, 700 sheaves of arrows, 200 stakes for the field (for making a defensive hedge when fighting ashore). For the men-at-arms there were 300 bills, 300 morris pikes, and 220 sets of 'harness' (armour). And three lasts of gunpowder for the ordnance.

The list shows clearly what the great ships were intended for: to land troops on an enemy coast and give them covering fire—what would now be called a combined operation. The best way of dealing with an enemy naval base is not to bomb it or bombard it, but to capture it. And this is what Howard was commanded to perform against the French port of Brest.

An English four-masted carrack, similar in design to the *Mary Rose*, at Dover in 1520. Photo: Science Museum.

At the very least, he had to keep the French bottled up or too busy to get out into the Channel where they might cut the English ferry and supply route to the Calais bridgehead, and might even kill the King himself, for Henry intended to go over and command the campaign personally.

Sir Edward Howard reached Brest even before the galleys of the French Mediterranean fleet, led by Prégent de Bidoux. He had his great ships anchored close in, right in the harbour mouth. Beyond, protected by a floating barricade of two dozen hulks chained together and covered by the fire of land batteries on one side, the French northern fleet lay penned like cattle in a semi-open stall. For Howard had landed soldiers who had taken a position covering part of the harbour; however, they were not in sufficient strength to capture Brest and burn it. Further, the supply arrangements had broken down and the English were on short rations.

On 19 April a convoy of supply ships led by Sir Edward Echyngham in the 100-ton *Germyne* slipped past the patrolling French galleys and delivered the victuals, Sir Edward reporting personally to Howard on board the *Mary Rose*. The admiral told him that for the last ten days his force had been existing on one meal a day, and one drink of beer. Echyngham could testify to the fear inspired in his Spanish crew by the sight of Prégent's galleys in the far distance. They had begun muttering: 'Now is the day comyng that we shal be fayne to go to the hospital.' Scare stories about the gun power of the galleys had been reported for some time by English agents in the Mediterranean: four of them were 'fitted with three Venetian basilisks; one shot of these guns can strike through any ship!' The latest situation report from Italy was that Prégent was on his way with '6 gallioni, 2 nave, 2 barze'—six galleys accompanied by four supply and support craft which the English called 'foysts'.

On 22 April the galley force and its supply train tried to break the English blockade and join up with the French fleet in Brest. Sir Edward Echyngham wrote that they

> came through part of the Kynges navie, and there they sanke the ship that was maister Compton's, and strake through oone of the Kynges new barkes, the which sir Stephen Bull is capiteyn of, in 7 placys, that they that was within the ship hide much payne to hold her above the watre.

Compton's vessel seems to have been a smallish merchantman of 160 tons, but Sir Stephen Bull's command was a minor warship, the *Lesse Bark* of 240 tons and 201 men. Even so, Prégent did not break through into Brest; but he did lose one of his foysts, taken by boats from the English ships.

Keeping to the shallows where the English carracks could not go, Prégent led his shallow-draught force to a rocky bay near Conquet, covering the northern approach to Brest, and put his guns ashore to command the narrow entrance. Howard's first idea was to disembark 6,000 men just out of the range of Prégent's batteries, and then take them and his ships from the rear by infantry assault. But aggressive counter-action by the French land forces in Brest pinned down too many of his troops on the main objective.

His second plan was to attack the bay head on, sending in six small, shallow-draught oared vessels packed with soldiers, but lacking in fire power. To impart the necessary dash and decision, he decided to lead the strike in person, accompanied by a group of chosen noblemen as commanders under him. The attack went in with reckless impetuosity through the narrow mouth of the bay, flanked by bulwarked French batteries on both sides. In them were so many guns and crossbowmen 'that the quarrelles and the gonstones came together as thick as it hade be haylestones.'

Howard's small oared vessel broke through to board Prégent's great flag galley, a formidable warship. An English grapnel anchor went soaring across the waves, lodged on the French vessel, and held. This time, it was attached to a capstan, so that the line could be veered or cut, to avoid the fate of the *Regent*, consumed by a beaten opponent. Howard jumped the bulwarks onto the enemy vessel, closely followed by a Spanish officer and 16 men. Then, before a second wave of attackers could follow, the grapnel line parted and open water appeared between the two ships. Howard beckoned to his own vessel to close the gap, shouting 'Comme aborde agayne! Come aborde agayne!' But it was too late. In overwhelming numbers, the French pikemen advanced across the deck and pinned him up against the rail with the glittering points of steel. At the last, he was seen to take off the golden whistle which was an English admiral's insignia, and throw it into the sea.

The *Grande Louise*, French flagship at the Battle of Brest, which was defeated by the *Mary Rose*.

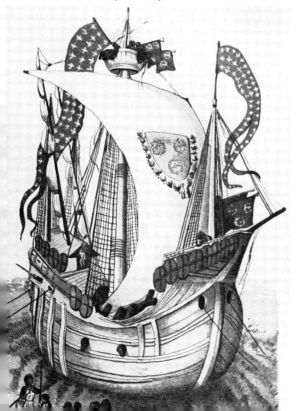

Only one man of that 18 who had boarded was rescued by his comrades. That man had received 18 wounds, but was still alive. Sir Edward Howard, however, was certainly dead, forced overboard in armour, still bearing his gilt shield.

Without orders, the whole fleet abandoned the blockade and sailed back to England, echoing a similar mutiny which had occurred in the army sent to Spain in 1512. Henry was choleric but cunning. He sent his fleet a new commander. The man he chose was Sir Thomas Howard, later Earl of Surrey, a field officer with recent battle experience. He was also the elder brother of the drowned admiral from the *Mary Rose*. He reached Dartmouth in Devon on 6 May and next morning took over not only his dead brother's fleet but his brother's ship, to which all the noblemen, captains and ship-masters who had survived the clash at Conquet were summoned.

> At oon of the clock I assembled in the *Mary Rose* my lorde Ferres and all oder noblemen and capetynes and most expert masters of your army, and ther rehersed unto them your commandment yeven unto me, and after that I enquired of them the cause of their comyng from the parties of Breton without your commandement. Unto which they answered with oon hole voyce and all in oon tale they did it upon dyverse and resonable grounds.

Howard was told that in the fleet there had been food for less than three days—with the next supply convoy pinned in English ports by unfavourable winds. Such winds would take them home easily, but they had left Brest only when there was virtually nothing left to eat on board.

The second point they made was one which was to plague Henry VIII in the future and was never to be satisfactorily solved in his lifetime. It concerned the modern Mediterranean galley armed with modern muzzle-loading guns of bronze. If the ordinary Channel breezes died away to give a completely calm day, then the great ships were at the mercy of heavily-armed oared vessels which could still manoeuvre at will. 'If the galyse being within 3 myle of them, they shuld not a fayled to have sonke such of your ships as they list to have shot their ordnance unto; which ordnance, if it be such as they report, is a thynge marvelous.'

Howard then asked, could not the two small English galleys of the fleet, the English rowbarges, together with the boats of the fleet, have attacked the French galleys? The unanimous reply was that, in a calm, a single galley could take on the lot of them. No

The *Cordelière* and the *Regent* locked together and burning during the Battle of Brest in 1512.

doubt it was true, but Howard's suggestion was to be seized on and developed by the King. The germ of an answer might be there.

Then, in his brother's ship, in his brother's cabin, the elder Howard put the delicate question. Had these officers left their admiral to be butchered?

A single crayer, it was true, had suffered no casualties at all; but that was not because she had faltered; she had attacked, closed, and boarded. Her crew had survived by a fluke of battle. All the other vessels had taken heavy losses; indeed one which had never even reached the galleys had every man on board killed or wounded to no avail whatever. In Howard's own galley only 56 men remained alive out of the 175 who had gone into battle with him. Two-thirds of her crew had been killed in action in the course of a few hours. The men had not failed their admiral; the fault lay in the admiral's plan, a fact tacitly admitted in a fighting instruction issued about 1530 by Sir Thomas Audley, forbidding affairs like Conquet to be carried out on the admiral's order alone; the captains, masters and pilots had to approve.

The defeat had had a shattering effect. Howard reported to Cardinal Wolsey (who could be held responsible for the supply failures):

> I have here fowned the worst ordered armye and furthest owte of rewle that ever I saw. . . . Ther is a grete number stolen away. . . . Never man saw men in greater fere then all the masters and maryners be off the galies, insomoche that in a maner they had as leve go into Purgatory as to the Trade.

Howard soon restored discipline and confidence; under him, the fleet covered first the crossing of the main English army into Calais and then went north to Scotland, which had entered the war on the side of France. That was the year of Henry's triumph, after a bad beginning: the year of fallen French towns, of fleeing French cavalry, of the bloody defeat of the Scots at Flodden Field where Howard led the van. The Tudor king had helped humble the great power across the Channel and beaten down unaided his pugnacious northern neighbour.

The war ended the following year, in March, 1514, but in April the truce was broken by Prégent, whom the English called Prior John because he was an officer of that military order, the Knights of Rhodes, soon to be the Knights of Malta. First he threatened to burn the English fleet in Calais harbour and then:

> With his galleys and foists, charged with great basilisks and other artillery, he came on the borders of Sussex in the night season, at a poor village there called Brighthelmstone, and burnt it, taking such goods as he found. When the people began to gather, Prior John sounded his trumpet to call his men aboard, and by that time it was day. Then certain archers that kept the watch followed Prior John to the sea, and shot so fast that they beat the galley men from the shore, and wounded many in the foist to which Prior John was constrained to wade, and was shot in the face with an arrow, so that he lost one of his eyes, and was like to have died of the hurt.

Prégent lived, and thanked Our Lady of Boulogne for the miracle. The English avenged the burning of what is now the fashionable town of Brighton by sending a small fleet to the French coast on a punitive expedition; in revenge, they burnt 21 towns or villages.

'Prior John' had given the English an unwelcome taste of galley warfare, while the English archers had left him something to remember them by. Those events were to be repeated on a giant scale when next the French galleys came out of the Mediterranean, this time as part of an immense invasion armada which was to attempt at Portsmouth in 1545 what the English had failed to do at Brest in 1513.

Chapter 3
'Drowned Like Rattens'

The King's Last French War, 1544–1545

IN JULY, 1514, the fleet came into the Thames to be paid off from the war and a full inventory was taken. Masts, yards, sails, all the rigging down to the pulley blocks and parrells; all the anchors and kedges; the ship's boats and everything in them; the ordnance great and small, the spare chambers for the breech-loaders, and their gear—forelockes, myches, hammers, picks, sponges, leather bags, charging ladles; and the shot of iron, of lead, of stone; the buckets, the bolts, the long streamers for the tops, the silk flags large and small, the top armers, the standards; the gunpowder; the bills, the morris pikes, the stakes for the field, the arrows of wyldfyre—93 pages of it, carefully inscribed in Tudor copperplate. There is nothing theoretical about it; this is what was actually in the ships that summer day more than four-and-a-half centuries ago.

Of the ships themselves, however, almost nothing has come down the years; no shipwright's plans, no builder's models, often not a single authentic picture. The *Mary Rose* in 1514 is a shadowy ship. Even the names of many of her guns are merely names—and no more. We might guess that the five 'grete curtalles of brass' and the 'grete murderer of yron' were heavy guns, and sometimes a useful statistic slips through elsewhere—from a land campaign, a note of how many horses must be had to pull a gun of a certain type, for instance.

In 1517, the *Mary Rose* had a maintenance crew of five men, compared to 12 men for the *Great Harry* and three or four men for the other ships. Then, from 1523 to 1525 there is another French war; the fleet is needed to protect the convoys for the Calais bridgehead. There are lists of stores embarked and paid for; and lists of crews. Thomas Howard is still Lord Admiral, but his flagship is the *Great Harry* now. The *Mary Rose* is only the second ship of the fleet, the flagship of the Vice-Admiral, Sir William Fitz-William (at 6s. 8d. per day), and housing the fleet treasurer, Sir William Sydney (who is paid 2s. per day). The master is John Browne (at 5s. a month). There are 126 soldiers, 244 mariners, 30 gunners; and 2 'surgeons' at 23s. 4d. the pair of them. In 1526 the *Mary Rose* is in reserve again, with 8 mariners for 'kepars'.

Then in his search for a wife who might give him a son to carry on the Tudor dynasty (it was thought impossible for a female to be a successful ruler in such warlike times), Henry broke with the Papacy. In doing this, he risked his former allies joining with his former enemies; so he paid his insurance policy. Around 1536 the fleet was rebuilt and rearmed. The *Mary Rose* went into dock at Portsmouth in 1536 and emerged as a 700-ton ship. Instead of the heavy but hotch-potch armament of 1514, a more regular, standard armament of more modern type was put on board—91 guns as against 78—but many of the names convey very little to us. The 'grete murderers' have been replaced by 'port pieces', the 'stone guns' by 'fowlers', the 'serpentines', by 'slings'; 'bases' and 'hailshot pieces' have appeared, and only the 'top pieces' remain from the old lists. However, some perfectly comprehensible gun names now appear—cannons, demi-cannons, culverins, demi-culverins, sakers, and falcons. These are all modern muzzle-loading guns of brass, the cannons being heavy, short-ranged battering pieces, the culverins being long-ranged (but small-shotted) counter-battery guns. The sakers and falcons are small long-guns of the secondary armament. Also, in addition to the bows, 50 handguns appear.

Encouraged by Henry, British gun foundries had been set up and were rivalling the best of the German and Italian masters; as new weapons became available, they went to the ships and the shore forts. Castles had undergone a complete change. The old high square walls defended by infantry were gone. The new fortifications were low, rounded gun platforms; shortly to be succeeded by the angled bastion plan with concealed gunports giving interlocking flanking fire across the walls at any attacker. From 1539, when the crisis deepened, a rash of new artillery forts appeared in the area of Portsmouth and the Isle of Wight, some designed by the Bohemian engineer, Stephan von Haschenberg. By 1544, a formidable gun fort was under construction at Southsea, covering the deep water ship channel into Portsmouth harbour. Another was built at Sandown Bay in the Isle of Wight, dominating a vulnerable beach.

In diplomacy, there are no permanent friends or foes. By 1544 Henry was allied again with Charles V, the German Emperor, in a combined campaign directed at the French capital and called the 'Enterprise of Paris'. Henry's part was to advance southward from the cramped English bridgehead around Calais and pinch out the French salient around Boulogne which fell to the English besiegers on 18 September, but the Imperial attacks had been fatally slowed by other French fortresses, and on that same day, 18 September, Charles V came to terms with Francis I of France. Henry VIII was left to fight on alone.

In 1545, Francis decided to deal with him. By the summer he had gathered immense forces for a double blow: Marshal du Biez was to be given an army of 14,000 men with which to retake Boulogne, while Claude D'Annebault, Baron de Retz, was to be given 30,000 men and an armada of 235 ships with which to destroy both the English fleet and its main base at Portsmouth. Du Biez would press in on the bridgehead, D'Annebault would cut that bridgehead's communications with England. The English foothold in France would be eliminated.

Henry VIII did not wait to be attacked. Two disruptive strikes were made, aimed at the French fleet gathering at Le Havre and other Norman ports, but both failed. An attempt to burn the French with 30 fire-ships turned into fiasco as a result of a gale and the death of the English leader from a bursting gun. All attempts to go in and do the job by gunfire proved unsuccessful: if there was a gale, the English ships were endangered on that treacherously shallow coast; but if there was a calm, the great force of Mediterranean galleys which the French now had prevented all but the most distant shooting.

On 6 July the King of France sat down to dine aboard Admiral D'Annebault's flagship, the splendid

Claude D'Annebault, Baron de Retz, the Admiral of the French invasion fleet of 1545. From a painting in the Musée de Versailles. Photo: Giraudon.

800-ton *Carraquon* which carried 100 bronze guns ready for battle. Around them off Le Havre lay the bulk of the fleet, which consisted of 150 large 'roundships', 60 'flutes', and no less than 25 Mediterranean galleys of the largest and latest type. After the banquet the King and his court went ashore and rode up to Caux Head to watch their ships sail to the capture of Portsmouth. What they saw was spectacular but terrifying.

No doubt the oven was down below in the hold, fire-proofed with bricks; perhaps the cooks were tired and flustered after the work of preparing a meal for the King and his ladies; anyway, there was an accident. The flames spread with unbelievable speed. When they reached the gundecks above, the open ports acted like so many chimneys; the flames roared with fierce energy around the lashed artillery, the guns heated up, and then they began to fire of themselves, so that it seemed as if the flagship had declared war on her fleet. The galleys had to shift anchor and some vessels were sunk. A few men and the fleet treasury were saved.

D'Annebault transferred to the next greatest of the carracks, *La Maistresse*; but on moving out into the roadstead she struck one of the many sandbanks and was damaged. However, the leaks could be got under control, and *La Maistresse* put to sea at the head of the invasion force, course being set for the Isle of Wight.

On Saturday, 18 July (which would be 28 July by the modern calendar), another pre-battle banquet was held in another flagship, the *Great Harry*, on the opposite side of the Channel. The English fleet of about 60 ships (with 40 more to join) were gathered at Portsmouth. When up to full strength they would carry some 12,000 men, less than half the numbers of the French. However, the King could call on 140,000 men of the part-time militia and, although they could not be gathered together in one great army and some must be withheld to ward off the Scots, French landings would not go unopposed. Any success the French had was likely to be local—unless the English made a rash move at sea. This Henry was determined not to do, so he came down to Portsmouth in person with his court to command even the anchoring positions for each ship in a defensive battle, making as sure as was humanly possible that no over-eager subordinate would be likely to lose his fleet for him.

At the King's table were Sir John Dudley, Viscount Lisle, who had been Lord Admiral of England for the past two years; Sir George Carew, Lieutenant-General of the Horse, whose appointment as vice-admiral in the *Mary Rose* had been made on this day; his uncle, Sir Gawen Carew, who commanded the 600-ton *Matthew Gonson*; and his younger brother, 31 year old Sir Peter Carew, captain of the 700-ton *Great Venetian*. Probably present was the captain of the *Mary Rose*, Roger Grenville, who was related to the Lisles. His youngest son, Richard Grenville, at this time a child of three, was in 1591 to take Drake's galleon *Revenge* into a suicidal fight against an entire Spanish fleet off the Azores.

After the meal the King spoke secretly to his two admirals, Lisle and Carew. No doubt he stressed discretion, because the fleet was full of fire-eaters like the unfortunate Edward Howard; the young Carew was just such a one. Judging by what his force subsequently did in action, Henry must have said something like this: We are not at our full strength yet and are gravely outnumbered. We have an excellent defensive position here; the risks are for the French to take. If they choose not to take them, or try and fail, it is all one; to win, we merely have to stay here.

New fighting instructions were issued in written form a month later, so these too were probably discussed. The old code used off Brest in 1512–1513 required amendments; the King had many more ships now than he had had then, and so they were to be sub-divided into three—a Van, a Battle, and a Wing. The Wing was a new concept—an anti-galley screening force of fast, light vessels which could operate independently of the wind, as the galleys did. Henry had added three new classes of such vessels to his fleet—fifteen 'galleasses' of 140 to 450 tons, ten 'pynasses' of from 15 to 80 tons, and thirteen 'roobaergys' (rowbarges) of 20 tons each. Flush decked, or nearly so, they lacked the fighting castles necessary for a close fight with the towering carracks. Their role was 'the better beate off the gallies from the great ships'. In 1513, the French had had four galleys. Now they had 25.

The German Emperor's ambassador, Van der Delft, was waiting on board the *Great Harry* for an interview; which he got—if receiving a blistering torrent of Tudor invective regarding his master's lack of faith can be so considered. The diplomat had hardly left the ship before Henry ordered a lookout to be sent up to the maintop. A contemporary biographer, John Hooker, wrote:

> The word was no sooner spoke but that Peter Carew was forward, and forthwith climbeth up to the top of the ship, and there sitting, the King asked him what news, who told him that he had sight of three or four ships, but as he thought, they were merchants. But it was not long but he had espied a great number, and then he cried out to the King there was, as he thought, a large fleet of men-of-war. The King supposing them to be the French men-of-war, as they were indeed, willed the board to be taken up, and every man to go to his own ship, as also a long boat to come to carry him to land.

A French eyewitness, Martin du Bellay, described the scene from the opposite side, as the French fleet entered the deceptively wide gulf of water between the Isle of Wight and Portsmouth.

> The admiral sent for the Baron de la Garde to go with four galleys, both to reconnoitre the Island as far as St. Helen's Point, and to judge the strength of the enemy. The enemy's force consisted of sixty picked ships well arranged for war, fourteen of which, helped by a land breeze, came out of Portsmouth with great haste and in such fine order, that one would have said they were calmly waiting for our force to engage it. But when our

S G.Carow Knigh

Sir George Carew, Vice-Admiral of Henry VIII's fleet in 1545, who went down with the *Mary Rose.* From a drawing by Holbein. Photo: Reproduced by gracious permission of Her Majesty the Queen.

> admiral moved against them with the rest of our galleys, then the rest of their force, too, came out of Portsmouth harbour to meet him. After a long fight with cannon balls, the enemy began to slip to the left to the shelter of the land, where it was defended by a few forts which stood on the cliff and on the other side by shoals and rocks covered by water which bar the way, leaving only a narrow channel for a few ships to pass abreast. This withdrawal, and the approaching night, put an end to the first day's fighting without our having suffered notable loss from the cannon balls and other shot.

The galleys retired to the St. Helen's anchorage only to discover that the flagship of the carracks was sinking. *La Maistresse*, the best and largest ship of the French force, had suffered greater damage in her grounding off Le Havre than the French had at first thought; now she had to be unloaded and run ashore in the shallows. Admiral D'Annebault had to find himself a new flagship and then give out battle orders for the next day, 19 July. The best ships were to be divided into three divisions: the centre of 30 ships in front of two flanking wings of 36 ships each. This was to form the trap, with the galleys as bait, as Du Bellay explained.

> Because of the advantage of place which the enemy had, it was arranged that early in the morning the galleys would go and find the enemy ships where they lay at anchor, to engage them in as fierce a gun-fire skirmish as possible; and while they were fighting, the galleys would withdraw towards our warships, in order to lure the enemy into the open sea.

On 19 July, Henry's Privy Council dictated four urgent letters 'signifying that 22 galleys were anchored on this side St. Ellen's Point, and over 100 sail in sight behind them.' Soon, the thunder of gunfire came rolling in from seaward. *Duf, duf, duf, duf, duf.* Thud on distant thud, like the slamming of heavy doors.

At dawn, the weather had brought unexpected good fortune to the French. It was perfect for galleys. Du Bellay continued:

> In the morning with the help of the sea which was calm, without wind or force of current, our galleys could be steered and manoeuvred at will to the detriment of the enemy, who, not being able to move through lack of wind, lay openly exposed to the fire of our artillery, which could do more harm to their ships than they could to the galleys, more so because they are higher and bulkier, and also by their use of oars, our galleys could run away, avoid danger, and gain the advantage. Fortune supported our force in this way for more than one hour. During this time, among other damage suffered by the enemy, *la Marirose*, one of their main ships, was sunk by gunfire, and out of five or six hundred men who were on it, only thirty-five were saved. *Le Grand-Henry*, which carried their admiral, was so damaged that had she not been supported by ships close to her, would have suffered the same fate. Other more memorable losses they would have suffered, if the weather had not changed in their favour, which not only freed them from this danger, but was favourable for attacking us, for there rose a land breeze, which together with the current bore them down under full sail upon our galleys.

Edward Hall, the Tudor historian, describing the scene three years later, wrote:

> But one day of all other, the whole navy of the Englishmen made out, and purposed to set on the Frenchmen; but in their setting forward, a goodly ship of England, called the *Mary Rose*, was, by too much folly, drowned in the midst of the haven, for she was laden with much ordnance, and the ports left open, which

were very low, and the great ordnance unbreached, so that when the ship should turn, the water entered, and suddenly she sank.

John Hooker, the contemporary biographer of young Sir Peter Carew wrote:

Sir George Carew being entered into his ship, he commanded every man to take his place, and the sails to be hoisted; but the same was no sooner done, but that the 'Mary Rose' began to heel, that is to say, lean on the one side. Sir Gawen Carew being then in his own ship, and seeing the same, called for the master of his ship, and told him thereof, and asked him what it meant, who answered that if she did heel she was like to be cast away. Then the said Sir Gawen passing by the 'Mary Rose', called out to Sir George Carew, asking him how he did, who answered that he had a sort of knaves whom he could not rule. And it was not long after but that the said 'Mary Rose', thus heeling more and more, was drowned with seven hundred men which were in her, whereof very few escaped. This gentleman . . . had in his ship a hundred marines, the worst of them being able to be a master in the best ship within the realm; and these so maligned and disdained one the other, that refusing to do that which they should do, were careless to do that which was most needful and necessary, and so contending in envy, perished in frowardness.

The German Emperor's ambassador, Van der Delft, who had been aboard the *Great Harry* the previous day, also heard the story of the tragedy at first hand:

I was told by a Fleming among the survivors that when she heeled over with the wind the water entered by the lowest row of gunports which had been left open after firing. All the 500 men on board were drowned save about 25 or 30 servants, sailors and the like.

The numbers said to be on board vary greatly— 500, 600, 700—and it is possible that, fighting so close to land and fresh supplies, an extra company or two of soldiers was embarked in the great ships; but concerning the survivors there is no dispute—35, 25-30, or 'very few'. The *Mary Rose* carried down with her many hundreds of terrified, living men—all trapped under deckheads or netting and pinned there by their own buoyancy. As a later versifier wrote:

Sunk by her own guns
cannoning to leeward,
gunports open to the sea

The King he screeched
like any maid:
'Oh my gentlemen
Oh my gallant men'

Sir Gawen Carew, uncle of Sir George, who commanded the *Matthew Gonson* on 19 July, 1545. As the *Mary Rose* heeled dangerously, he called across to his nephew, enquiring what was amiss with the ship. From a drawing by Holbein. Photo: Reproduced by gracious permission of Her Majesty the Queen.

All over. The cry of mun,
the screech of mun, Oh sir,
up to the very heavens.

The very last souls I seen
was that man's father,
and that man's.

Drowned like rattens,
drowned like ratten.

There were to be parallels in future. In 1593, Sir Richard Hawkins found that his own ship had been nearly cast away in the same manner, and not in the sea but in the River Thames.

The wind being east north east, when they set sayle, and vered out southerly, it forced them for the doubling of a point to bring their tack aboard, and looffing up; the winde freshing sodenly the shipp began to make a little hele; and for that she was very deep loaden, and her ports open, the water began to enter in at them, which no bodie having regard unto, thinking themselves safe in the river, it augmented in such manner as the waight of the water began to presse down the side, more than the

Sir Peter Carew, younger brother of Sir George, was present at the battle in 1545 and later described the sinking of the *Mary Rose* to his biographer, John Hooker.

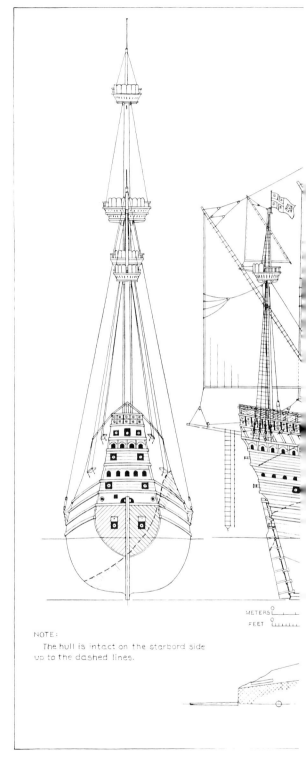

NOTE:
The hull is intact on the starbord side up to the dashed lines.

winde; at length when it was scene and the shete flowne, shee could hardly be brought upright.

Hawkins referred to three other cases known to him where the ship did not recover, one of them being the *Mary Rose*,

which was overset and suncke at Portsmouth, with her captain, Carew, and the most part of his company drowned in a goodly summers day, with a little flawe of wind; for that her ports were all open, and making a small hele, by them entred their destruction; where if they had been shut, no wind could have hurt her, especially in that place. In the river of Thames, Master Thomas Candish had a small ship over-set through the same negligence. And one of the fleet of Syr Francis Drake, in Santo Domingo harbour, turned her keele upward likewise, upon the same occasion.

Hawkins, Cavendish, Drake—three great names of Elizabethan exploration, all suffering the same type of accident. It seems as if the French claim to have sunk the *Mary Rose* by gunfire was simply the natural conclusion which would follow when one fired at a ship and then saw her heel over and go down. Du Bellay's was an honest opinion, although almost certainly mistaken.

While the boats were still picking up survivors from

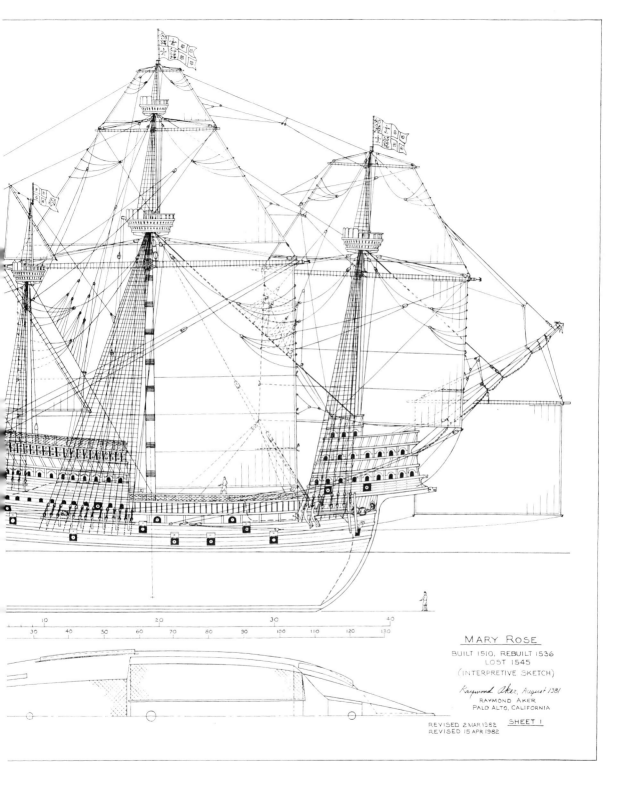

MARY ROSE

BUILT 1510, REBUILT 1536
LOST 1545
(INTERPRETIVE SKETCH)

Raymond Aker, August 1981
RAYMOND AKER
PALO ALTO, CALIFORNIA

REVISED 2 MAR 1982   SHEET I
REVISED 15 APR 1982

the *Mary Rose*, the feigned attack of the galleys and the limited counter-thrust by the English fleet developed like a delicate duel. Slowing the oar strokes to disguise their true speed, the galleys dragged their coats to the edge of risk, and when the English suddenly came at them with wind and tide behind, were nearly caught and driven under the heavy bows. They extricated themselves by a brilliantly executed battle turn, but as they fled at speed were chased and hit by the new oared vessels the English had. Then the English turned away and made back to their main fleet, and Admiral D'Annebault knew that his first ploy had failed. The English were not to be tricked out of their strong position.

So ended the second day of cautious skirmishing, with each side having lost a flagship by accident and inflicted some gunfire damage on the other. However, while the French were able to pump out and refloat *La Maistresse* behind the cover of their great fleet, the English could not attempt the same for the *Mary Rose* until the enemy had been driven off, because to raise such a weight required the lifting power of two other ships of equal size; these could not be spared until the crisis was past. And far from ending, the French effort was now intensified, as Du Bellay wrote.

> Our Admiral had had news that the King of England had come to Portsmouth, and he thought that if we made a landing on the Isle of Wight and fired the countryside in the sight of the King, and killed his people only a handsbreadth from him, then the indignation he would feel at such an insult, the pity he would have for the wounding and death of his subjects, and the spectacle of the wasting and burning of his realm, would make him send his ships to the rescue, especially as they were barely two cannon shots away. . . . Our Admiral ordered the invasion to take place in three different areas simultaneously, so as to divide the enemy's forces.

On the right, the galleys of Pietro Strozzi landed men to take a small but annoying English artillery fort near St. Helen's; and then went on to burn Barnsley and destroy its manmade harbour so thoroughly that it disappeared from the map of England (until I recognised its remnants in the 1980s).

In the centre was vulnerable and vital Sandown Bay, covered by a new artillery fort Henry had built. Led by two galley captains, Marsay and Pierrebon,

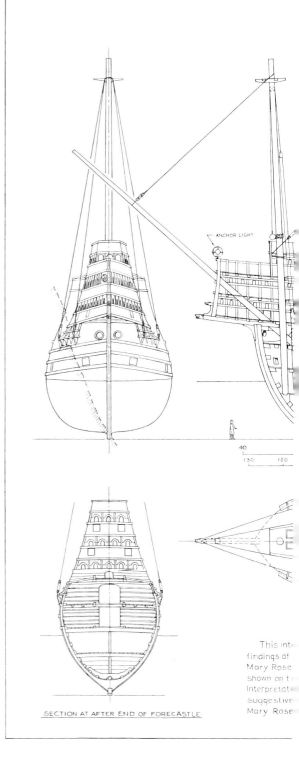

ANCHOR LIGHT

40
130   120

SECTION AT AFTER END OF FORECASTLE

This int
findings of
Mary Rose
shown on t
Interpretat
suggestive
Mary Rose

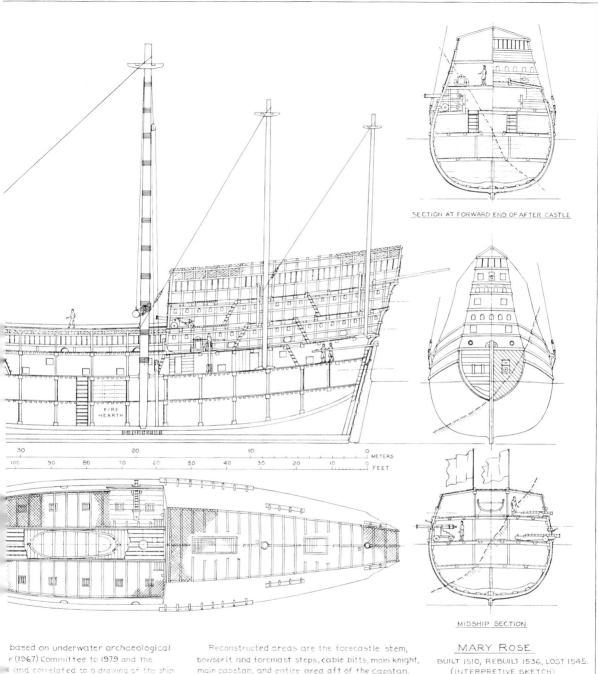

SECTION AT FORWARD END OF AFTER CASTLE

MIDSHIP SECTION

30   20   10   0   METERS
100 90 80 70 60 50 40 30 20 10 0   FEET

FIRE
HEARTH

based on underwater archaeological
e (1967) Committee to 1979 and the
and correlated to a drawing of the ship
Roll of King Henry VIII's ships, 1546.
rated or missing parts of the ship are
necessarily represent the views of the

Reconstructed areas are the forecastle, stem,
bowsprit and foremast steps, cable bitts, main knight,
main capstan, and entire area aft of the capstan,
including the upper part of the after castle and after
masts.

MARY ROSE
BUILT 1510, REBUILT 1536, LOST 1545.
(INTERPRETIVE SKETCH)

Raymond Aker, August 1981
RAYMOND AKER
PALO ALTO, CALIFORNIA

REVISED MARCH 23, 1982   SHEET 2

31

Southsea Castle in July, 1545, from the Cowdray Engraving. Bottom right: Henry VIII rides up to the castle to take command of his army which is encamped on Southsea Common, and of his fleet lying off Spithead. Offshore, the *Mary Rose* is depicted just after she went down. The brand new castle, only just completed, was designed to mount artillery. The guns are identical with those on board the *Mary Rose* but they are mounted on field carriages with large wheels. The soldiers are dressed in the same way as those on board the ships: Photo: Portsmouth City Museums.

Detail from the Cowdray Engraving, showing the two tallest masts of the sunken *Mary Rose* rearing out of the waves, heeled over at 40 to 45 degrees. Drowned men are floating in the water and one man is apparently swimming towards the rescue boats. Photo: Portsmouth City Museums.

Final defeat of the French. Three galleys acting as landing craft are retiring from the beaches of the Isle of Wight covered by stern fire from a small carrack. The English militia, carrying pikes and hand guns, are blazing away at the retreating French. Photo: John Owen.

the French attacked. Both leaders fell, wounded, and the assault failed.

On the left, a determined attempt to secure the Bonchurch heights was commanded by the Seigneur le Tais, Colonel-General of the infantry, and the Baron de la Garde, the flamboyant 'Captain Crossbreed', leader of all the galleys. The advance was ambushed by English archers and its leader wounded. But the main body of French scrambled uphill and drove the English back, the last shout of a stout Wiltshire militia officer, Captain Fischer, being 'A hundred pounds for a horse!' Soon Bonchurch was in flames, the smoke rising above the Isle of Wight to signal another French success.

But Henry welcomed these invasions: the more French soldiers who came ashore, the fewer who remained to defend their ships.

He was helped by the recklessness of some 2,000 French who landed without orders in Whitecliff Bay and tried to scale the top of Bembridge Down. On the crest they were ambushed by archers and a makeshift cavalry force composed of the horses from the English transport wagons. 'We killed many, took many

prisoners, and drove the rest as far as the ships, killing all the way,' recorded Sir John Oglander. Du Bellay told the same story, of 'a fierce attack by horse and foot soldiers' which drove the French survivors 'in disorder down to the foot of the mountain near the ships.'

D'Annebault and the other French leaders decided that the English fleet's anchoring position made it invulnerable to attack from any direction, and that they themselves were not strong enough to take and hold the Isle of Wight against the English reinforcements; there was no course left to them but evacuation.

The parties covering the withdrawal had to fight hard. On the right, at St. Helen's, Leone Strozzi's men broke the English attack and 'after putting more than thirty to the sword, routed the remainder.' On the left, at Bonchurch, the French lost a Knight of Malta, the Chevalier D'Aulps, as Du Bellay related:

> He climbed to the top of the hill and there he found the English soldiers in ambush. They attacked so fiercely that his men took flight and abandoned him. At that moment, he was hit in the knee by an arrow, which made him stumble. Then, as he was picking himself up, he was struck such a blow on the head with a bill, that his morion flew off, and he stumbled a second time. There he was dealt another blow with a bill, which spilled his brains on the ground.

At sunrise on 25 July the watchers over Seaford Bay in Sussex saw an intimidating, awesome sight: 'twelve score French sails . . . and above 20,000 men, if each ship carry his full freight.' The local commander, Edward Gawge, called for reinforcements, adding 'Hast, hast, post hast, for thy lyff, hast.'

Fifteen hundred Frenchmen burnt the village, stormed across a bridge and were ambushed by English archers, who drove them back into the river, drowning, shooting or cutting down a hundred of them, and forcing a hasty evacuation.

At the end of July, the French fleet landed 7,000 men—but not in England. D'Annebault put them ashore in France, to help retake Boulogne. Meanwhile, at Henry VIII's command post on Southsea Common, the Privy Council were busy cancelling the orders for men and guns to be sent to Portsmouth while at the same time trying to organise a major salvage operation at Spithead: the raising of the *Mary Rose*.

Chapter 4
'Some Wreck, Completely Buried in the Sand'

Salvage: 1545–1549; 1836–1840

THE *Mary Rose* had sunk on Sunday, 19 July and the long spells of hot, breathlessly calm weather which had so frustrated the fleet were extremely favourable for salvage. Even at high water, her tallest poles—the foremast and mainmast—rose from the waves, heeled at a crazy angle. At low water, part of the bow and stern castles must have broken the surface.

Sir William Paget, Secretary of State, co-ordinated the attempts to raise her. He had good hopes of recovering the ship, he told Lord John Russell, who replied on 23 July referring to the 'rechenes and great negligence' responsible for the disaster, and lamenting 'the great loss of the men and the shipp also'. The two executives under Paget were Sir Charles Brandon, Duke of Suffolk, the army commander for whose wife the *Mary Rose* had been named, and John Dudley, Viscount Lisle, the Lord Admiral. On 31 July, Suffolk wrote to Paget: 'Will with speed set men to the weighing of the Mary Rose.' Next day, having consulted Venetian salvage experts from Southampton, he was able to forward a schedule of ships and gear which would be required:

A remembraunce of thinges necessarye for the recovery, with the help of God, of the Mary Roose.

Fyrst, 2 of the greatest hulkes that may be gotten, more the hulkes that rydeth within the havyn.

Item, 4 of the greatest hoys within the havyn.

Item, 5 of the gretest cables that may be had.

Item, 10 greate hawsers.

Item, 10 new capteynes, with 20ti pulleys.

Item, 50 pulleys bound with irone.

Item, 5 doseyn balast baskettes.

Item, 20lb. of talowe.

Item, 30 Venyzians maryners, and one Veneziane carpenter.

Item, 60 Inglishe maryners to attend upon them.

Item, a greate quantitie of cordage of all sortes.

Item, Symond, patrone and master to the Foyst doth agree that all thynges must be had for the purpose aforesaid.

On this same Saturday, 1 August, Suffolk also wrote:

I trust by Monday or Twisday, at the furthest, the *Mary Rose* shall be wayed upp, and saved. There be twoo hulkes, cabulles, pulleces and other things made redy for the waying of her.

Next day, Sunday, 2 August, Suffolk could report: 'All is ready for the weighing of the Mary Rose tomorrow.'

The method recommended by the Venetian experts was the classic one, described by Olaus Magnus in a history published ten years later, in 1555:

Occasionally it happens that large ships are lost as a result of bad weather, or are wrecked, even whilst in the safety of a harbour and in good weather, as a result of carelessness. When this happens, it is customary to place two or four special ships above a wreck, fill them with water and let skilled divers pass strong ropes under the wreck and fasten them to the ships. The ships are then baled out with the result that they start rising, thus bringing the wreck to the surface. The possibilities for raising sunken warships, however, are small seeing that they are loaded with cannon of copper and iron and stone balls.

In the Baltic or Mediterranean this was very true because there is little or no tide; but off Portsmouth the tide can rise 16 feet or more twice a day, a free gift to any salvor. The two great 'hulkes' were 700-ton ships bought by the navy but not yet converted for war; they were the *Sampson*, master Thomas Bell, and the *Jesus of Lubeck*, master John Seintclier, a Hanseatic trader, later to feature in the careers of John Hawkins and Francis Drake. A third large vessel was earmarked as a lifting pontoon, and this was the *Great Venetian*, commanded by Sir Peter Carew, the dead admiral's younger brother. Lord Lisle was worried by the diversion at this time of three of the largest battleships in the fleet, but on Wednesday, 5 August he and Suffolk were able to report a success:

To the Illustrious and Aspiring Glory of the *British* . . . . . . *Nation* PRINCE WILLIAM HENRY *Kn?* of the Most ANTIENT ORDER of the THISTLE, *this* . . . . . Plate *being an Exact Representation of the approved* Plan *now in Execution, for the effectual raising His* . . . MAJESTY'S *Ship the Royal George, is most* . . . *submissively subscribed by His Royal Highness's* . . . . *most hble & obed? Serv?*
William Tracey.

William Tracey's abortive attempt to salvage the *Royal George* in 1783, the year after she sank, using the same method as proposed for the *Mary Rose* in 1545—a lift employing two big ships as pontoons. Photo: National Maritime Museum.

And as touching the Mary Rose, her sailes and saile yards be layd on land, and to her masts there is tyed three cables, with other ingens to wey her upp, and on every syde of her a hulk to sett her uppright, which is thought by the doers thereof, God willing, to be doon tomorrow, one tyme in the day; and that doon, they purpose to discharg her of water, ordenaunce, and a other thinges, with as moch diligence as is possible, and, by litell and litle, to bring her nerer to the shore. . . .

Lisle's worries were compounded next day, when three French galleys looked into Portsmouth and observed the salvage attempt before being 'canvassed away again' by some of Henry's new galleasses. On 7 August Lisle was optimistic, telling Suffolk that 'he had good hope of the waying upright of the Mary Rose this afternone or tomorrow.' Sunday, 9 August was the black day.

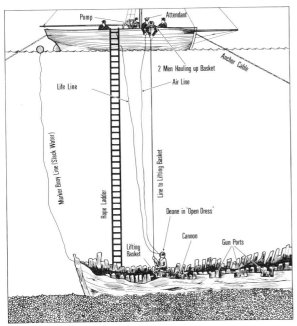

Labels on diagram: Pump, Attendant, 2 Men Hauling up Basket, Anchor Cable, Air Line, Life Line, Marker Buoy Line (Slack Water), Line to Lifting Basket, Rope Ladder, Deane in 'Open Dress', Cannon, Gun Ports, Lifting Basket

John Deane working on the *Royal George* 51 years after she sank—an explanatory diagram based on a contemporary sketch.

Master Secretary, Theis shalbe tadvertise you, that this daye thitalians which had the doyng of the wayeng of the Mary Roos haue been with my Lord Chamerlayn and me to signify vnto vs that after this sourt which they haue followed hetherto they can by no meanes recouer her, for they haue alredye broken her foremast. . . . And now they desyr to prove an other waye, which ys to dragg her as she lyeth vntill she come into shallow ground, and so to set her upright, and to this they axe vj days prouf.

Clearly, the ship was so deeply embedded already that the pull of the cables on her masts, intended to upright her, had merely broken a mast, without much moving the ship. The Italians now wanted to try to drag her bodily into the shallows, without correcting the heel. While they were still laying out anchors on 10 August, the English fleet sailed for battle—104 ships and 13,748 men. Lisle had had to leave his salvage operation and seek a decisive battle with the French who were still at large in the Channel. On 15 August the two fleets met, but once more the wind fell away and only the French galleys on the one hand and the oared galleasses of the English on the other, could engage. By 17 August, the French were back where they had started from, Le Havre. In both fleets there

were many sick. So hot had been this summer that the food may have spoiled in the holds.

After 9 August there is only one more reference in the surviving Tudor state papers to the raising of the *Mary Rose*, and as usual it concerns money. A warrant dated 8 December, 1545, was authority to

> pay Petre de Andreas and Symonde de Maryne, Venetians, 40 marks in regard for their pains about the weighing of the Mary Rose.

Although the hull was abandoned, the guns were not. There are some uninformative, single-line entries in the Rolls: in 1547 to pay Peter Paule, an Italian, £50 11s. 5d. for recovering ordnance from her; and in 1549 another £50 for the same. What methods were available then? Probably some sort of underwater apparatus, perhaps a diving bell, was used. There are some slender clues. A Piero Paolo Corsi appeared in court charged with stealing blocks of tin salvaged from an Italian ship which sank at Southampton in 1547. Was he the same Peter Paule who worked on the *Mary Rose*? And if so, is this the same man as the Pedro Paulo, who definitely was a diver, for in 1562 he was mentioned in the context of a large salvage operation elsewhere of guns and treasure 'which are recoverable by divers, amongst whom is one Pedro Paulo, who was entertained at Portsmouth about the *Marie Rose*.'

The last reference to the wreck as it appeared in Tudor times was not published until 1623, when Admiral Sir William Monson wrote:

> The *Mary Rose*, next to the *Regent* in bigness and goodness, after this was cast away betwixt Portsmouth and the Isle of Wight. Part of the ribs of this ship I have seen with my own eyes; there perished in her four hundred persons.

Monson was born in 1569, after the *Mary Rose* had been on the bottom for 25 years. Another 15 to 25 years may have passed before the young Monson saw some part of her hull, perhaps the shallowly submerged ruins of her upperworks on a day when the water was particularly clear. Certainly, the hull must have remained intact for a very long time, the currents swirling and boiling around the obstruction, scouring out deep pits and helping to dig the great oak structure deeper still into the mud.

So long as the *Mary Rose* remained a substantial obstruction above the seabed, oysters would grow on her timbers, lobsters and congers would live in the caverns of her hull, fish would surround the weed-

One of Deane's 1836 recoveries: a wrought-iron breech-loading gun on a slide carriage. Bore 8 ins, total length 13 feet. Found on the *Mary Rose*, lack of conservation has allowed the barrel to deteriorate, clearly showing the stave-and-hoop method of construction. It fired stone shot. Photo: Science Museum.

shrouded wreck in glittering shoals. And local fishermen would know the location of the site by 'marks' on land. But when the protruding parts of the hull collapsed or were eaten away and all that remained was swallowed by the mud, the fish would leave and so would the fishermen. Indeed, they would now avoid the site because the few timbers which still showed would only be a damaging trap to their nets and dredges. And after a time the very name of the ship which lay there would be forgotten, like the identity of the men who had died in her.

Nearly 291 years had passed since the *Mary Rose* had gone down. Now it was the 16th of June, 1836, and a diving craft was moored 90 feet above Portsmouth's most famous wreck—Admiral Kempenfelt's 108-gun first-rate *Royal George* which capsized at Spithead in 1782 and sank with 900 men, women and children aboard. Every English school child knew William Cowper's poem:

> 'Toll for the Brave!'
> The brave that are no more!
> All sunk beneath the wave
> Fast by their native shore.
>   Eight hundred of the brave,
>   Whose courage well was tried,
>   Had made the vessel heel
> And laid her on her side.

Salvage attempts on this great ship had failed and now she was merely an awkward obstruction in the battleship anchorage at Spithead. To John Deane, the diver who was now working on her, she appeared 'one huge, indescribable mass of old, decayed timbers and materials confusedly mixed and intermingled with mud, clay, sand, etc.' However, in this ruin lay many of her guns, valuable as scrap metal. John and

his brother Charles Anthony had since 1832 raised from the forbidding, weed-wreathed carcass of the great line-of-battle ship three bronze 18-pounders, 19 bronze 24-pounders and eight 32-pounders, for which, however, the government was paying them only half the value.

Near the diving boat that day lay the 74-gun two-decker H.M.S. *Pembroke*, and about half a cable's length ahead of her a Gosport fishing boat came to a dead stop in the water. It was manned by five men, John and Jasper Richard, Job Redman, and the two Burnetts, William senior and William junior. Buoying their snagged gear, they came across to Deane's boat, asking him to free it for a half-share in whatever it had caught in. They knew this 'fastener' well, but not what it was. It could be valuable, if it was a wreck. Clearing snagged nets or dredges is always a deadly but interesting proposition, and it was John Deane's life which was at stake, not those of the fishermen; but he accepted.

John and his brother wore diving gear which they themselves had invented, as the *Hampshire Telegraph* reported in 1840:

The merit of having first introduced the diving helmet into general use, and applied it to practical purposes of a most important nature, is due to Messrs. Charles and John Deane, and their apparatus is the simplest that has yet been suggested, and is very serviceable for general purposes as it never fails, excepting when the diver's head by any accident comes lower than his body, in which case the water must necessarily enter, and drive out the air, upon which his safety depends.

It was the simplicity and security of Deane's apparatus which made it a classic step in the development of diving gear. A helmet and attached breastplate was all it was, with an air hose attached to

Watercolour of some of Deane's recoveries from the *Mary Rose*: a grapnel for boarding an enemy ship, an oyster-encrusted bottle, an 8-inch iron shot partially concreted, and a 6 ft. longbow. Photo: Portsmouth City Museums.

a pump. In cold water, protective clothing had to be worn, but this was separate from the breathing gear; in warm water, it could be discarded. The idea had come to John while he was watching a fire in a barn that seemed as if it would burn alive the farmer's horses. No one could come close because of the smoke, and the old pump and hose-pipe the farmer had brought up threw only an ineffectual jet. There was an old suit of armour in the farmhouse and John's mind made a great leap: if he put the helmet over his head, and led the hose from the pump into the helmet, he could enter the choking smoke still breathing fresh air, for the pump could supply either air or water. He tried it, and saved the horses. In 1823, he and his older brother (John was then eighteen) secured the patent rights to an 'apparatus to be worn by Persons Entering Rooms filled with Smoke, &c.'

It was only a step from there to adapt the same apparatus for underwater breathing, but there were five dangerous years of experiment and cautious progress, from the simple task of retrieving lost anchors to salvaging treasure or guns from sunken

Teredo-tunnelled timbers raised from HMS *Venerable* by John Deane. The original water colour was intended to illustrate his book of underwater discoveries. Photo: Alexander McKee.

ships where, literally, one false move could be fatal. The concentration there of rich wrecks such as the *Royal George* (Spithead, 1782), the *Boyne* (Southsea Castle, 1795), and the *Carnbrea Castle* (Isle of Wight, 1829) brought the Deanes to the Portsmouth area in the Ramsgate smack *Mary*, owned by their partner, William Edwards, and fitted with a pump powerful enough to send down compressed air to depths in excess of 90 feet.

Now, as the smack *Mary* tied up to the fishermen's buoy, Deane dressed first in two layers of warm underclothing, then slipped on a watertight, india-rubber suit, and finally put on heavy outer working-wear of canvas trousers and jacket. Next, the actual breathing apparatus, a helmet with air hose and breast-and-back plates was slipped over his head; weights were tied to the plates with a safety-knot for quick release in emergency; and a light signalling line was led round his shoulder.

The weighted rope ladder was already over the side, hanging just clear of the seabed. As, step by step, he entered the water, the pressure pushed in the india-rubber suit, so that Deane could feel the creases and folds; the waves rose above his helmet, and the water rose inside, also, but not as far as his chin, as long as he kept his head upright. Halfway down, the water became very black, but lightened again as he neared that unseen and unknown seabed. Deane stepped carefully off the ladder, his feet raising a cloud of fine sediment which wreathed his legs, and gave one sharp tug on the signal line which was secured under his armpits and then led up vertically past the front glass. That pull told the signal man in the *Mary*, many fathoms of green water above him, that he was safely off the ladder and on the bottom. As Deane went forward, the man paid out more line, but keeping it taut all the time as a precaution in case the diver stumbled and fell, which would instantly flood his helmet. A continuous series of jerks on the line were Deane's signal that he was in danger and must be hauled up at once.

This seabed was a barren plain of clay and mud with a little fine sand here and there. No wreck loomed as a menacing shadow. All that had caught the fishermen's gear was a single, softened, blackened timber barely protruding from the plain. Casting around to see if it was only an isolated piece, Deane found several more—but so nearly flush with the bottom that they were hard to see. There *was* a wreck here, but it was almost completely buried. A trawl or dredge could go right over it and nine times out of ten, snag nothing.

Prospecting further, Deane noticed a dark shadow which rose about a foot above that dull, grey undersea desert. The vaguely cylindrical mass was unyielding and green in colour. Copper or bronze. A gun. But not like any from the *Royal George*.

Hauled aboard the *Mary*, it proved to be over 12 feet long, with a bore slightly over six inches, and it weighed 54 cwt. The shot, wad and powder were found still to be in place. Moulded behind the two trunnions, fashioned in the shape of lion's heads, was the Tudor Rose. Even the inscription could be read.

HENRICVS VIII
ANGLIE. FRAN
CIE. ET. HIBERN
IE. REX. FIDEI. DE
FENSOR. INVICT
ISSIMVS. F.F.
ARCANVS DE ARCANIS
CESENEN FECIT
MDXXXXII
HR. VIII

The gun was a bronze demi-cannon cast by an Italian founder in 1542 for Henry VIII, King of England, France and Ireland, Invincible Defender of the Faith.

When Deane's report of his find reached the Board of Ordnance at the Tower of London, its historical importance was realised instantly and a copy of his letter was made and sent to the King; and because

Deane was claiming full salvage on the grounds that the gun came from an unknown wreck which might be a private, and not a Royal ship, a committee was set up under a major-general to study the gun and establish the identity of the wreck.

On 15 August a whole batch of historic ordnance was landed at the Gunwharf in Portsmouth by Deane's team. One was a cast-iron 32-pounder of the reign of George III, raised from the *Royal George*. The others were all from the new site, which had still not been identified, the *Hampshire Telegraph* being able to report only that they had been discovered 'resting on some wreck, which was so completely buried in the sand that the diver could find nothing to which he could affix a rope.' Two were bronze with the Tudor Rose plain to see and two were of wrought-iron and of such antique construction that the general reaction was amazement.

One of the bronze guns, a cannon royal, was of heavier calibre than anything carried even by the great eighteenth-century three-decker flagship *Royal George*. It had a bore of just over 8 inches for a total length of 10 feet, and weighed more than 42 cwt. It was an exceedingly powerful short-range battering piece made by Robert and John Owen in 1535, the year before the *Mary Rose* was rebuilt and rearmed. The second of the bronze pieces, instead of being round, was a long cylinder with twelve flat faces. Almost the same length as the squat 68-pounder cannon royal, it had the much smaller bore of $4\frac{1}{2}$ inches for a weight of just over 23 cwt. and was clearly a long-range, high-velocity piece. It was inscribed 'HR' and 'THYS COLVERYN BASTARD WEYS ZZ99'. There was no date or maker's name.

19th century mortar firing an 13-inch 'bomb shell' (hollow, filled with gunpowder). Deane asked for six of these to dig down into the *Mary Rose*. Photo: Alexander McKee.

A 19th century 'bomb shell' recovered by Maurice Harknett and Alexander McKee at Spithead in 1965. A grapnel-fluke through the fuse hole was the means of lifting. Photo: Alexander McKee.

The iron guns caused a greater furore. One was intact, the other consisted only of a length of broken barrel. Like the bronze guns, both were loaded, but with stone-shot instead of cast-iron balls. Their barrels had not been 'cast' in one piece, but had been 'built-up' of many staves and hoops of wrought-iron. And they were breech-loaders. The intact gun had an 8-inch bore and was 9½ feet long; it was still mounted in a wooden bed, without wheels, giving a total length of 13 feet. The *Hampshire Telegraph* referred to them as 'objects of great curiosity', for the fact that such guns had ever existed had long been forgotten; and even those few who knew about them, knew little. The discovery offended a Mr. C. D. Archibald, who was writing a thesis to prove that although the first guns to be 'cast' (as opposed to 'built-up') in England were made by John Owen in 1521, on the continent the secret had long been known. In *Archaeologia*, Volume XXVIII, he wrote, of the large iron gun:

> It must at all times have been an unwieldy and inefficient engine, and I cannot imagine that it could have co-existed, for purposes of active service on shipboard, with those highly finished pieces (of bronze) just mentioned. . . . It seems to me, therefore, that these rude pieces of the olden time, if indeed they were ever on board the *Mary Rose*, must have been used for ballast or some other illegitimate purpose.

The urgent convolutions of scholars in danger of being proved wrong are always interesting to watch, and to be fair to Mr. Archibald, his quite desperate theory about the guns being 'illegitimate ballast' was to be restated as late as 1971, regarding a similar gun which I had just raised at Spithead, by an academic anxious to show that I was wasting my time on a wreck long since blown to pieces by John Deane and others.

In contrast, when I finally uncovered the document, it was a pleasure to read the crisp, accurate report of the committee set up by the Board of Ordnance. They had combed the early historians, and had avoided being misled by Holinshed's vague position indication—'drowned in the middest of the Haven'—which led many then and since to assume that he meant inside Portsmouth Harbour. They concluded:

> It appears quite certain that the *Mary Rose* was lost at Spithead, that the Ship never was weighed up, and from the description of the Guns lately discovered there is every reason to believe that they formed part of her Armament.'

More than that, the committee recommended that Deane be encouraged in his work, not as a matter of mere commercial salvage, but because of the historical value of what he was doing. Deane himself took the same enlightened view and had his recoveries recorded by means of beautiful watercolour drawings clearly made on the spot. He intended to publish them in a book to be titled *John Deane's Cabinet of Submarine recoveries, relics and antiquities.*

Deane did not have another successful season on the *Mary Rose* until 1840, suffering 'repeated attempts and failures of discovery.' The most spectacular find of 1840 was a great bronze culverin nearly 12 feet long, with a 5¼ inch bore. The inscription showed that, like the demi-cannon found in 1836, it had been made in 1542 by Arcanus de Arcanis of Cesenen in Italy, after the rebuilding of the *Mary Rose*, proving that rearmament was a continuous process in Henry VIII's navy. More of the wrought-iron 'built-up' guns were found, together with gunpowder chambers and swivel guns. Then the finds began to peter out.

On 13 October, with the diving season coming to an end, Deane decided to try small charges of gunpowder, and was allowed to draw six 'old condemned bomb shells (13 in.)' from the Gunwharf. To ignite them underwater, a long tube had to be fitted to the fuse hole, the open end remaining in the boat above so that a match could be dropped down. For maximum effect, Deane used a spade to dig out a hole for the bomb shells, the explosions producing 'a crater of large dimensions'.

The guns had to go to the owners, the Board of Ordnance, but the timber and miscellaneous items were for the finders to sell. On 12 November, 1840, Deane and Edwards held a public auction of *Mary*

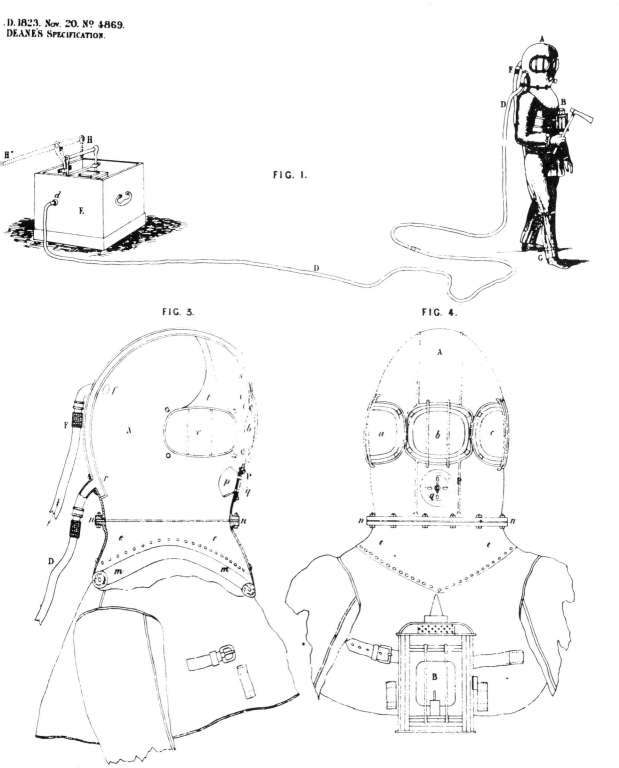

.D. 1823. Nov. 20. Nº 4869.
DEANE'S SPECIFICATION.

FIG. I.

FIG. 3.

FIG. 4.

Patent for the Deanes' fire-fighting helmet and dress which they developed into diving apparatus. Today's firemen also wear breathing apparatus, but based on the aqualung. Patent Office.

Rose recoveries at Portsmouth Point. Among them were 8 'warrior's bows' which sold for between 10s. and 15s., as did the 'common glass bottles'; 'iron and granite shot' reached 20s. to 30s.; while '15 ft. of the mainmast' brought in £30. There was also a grapnel

Alexander McKee going down for his first dive in helmet gear at a Royal Engineers training centre in Hamburg, 11 December, 1951.

and 'part of a pump'. Also for sale were 'a few lots of Oak Timber—the wood in a high state of preservation and calculated for converting into ladies' work tables and boxes, picture frames, and any fancy articles and models'. Some of these objects can still be seen in the Portsmouth area (I have one myself). It was this sale of 1840 which caused a contemporary nautical historian to write grandly of the *Mary Rose* that 'the hull has been recently broken up'. His conclusion, but not the remarkably slender basis for it, remained in print to mislead later scholars.

Also misleading were the inscriptions the buyers put on the objects, such as:

> This box made from the timber of H.M.S. *Mary Rose*. Sunk at Spithead 1545 recovered 1840

As late as 1970, the owner of such an item, reading of my hopes of raising the *Mary Rose*, wrote to a most superior publication that 'Mr. McKee is perhaps 125 years too late'. It was an understandable error, no less irritating for that. Hardly understood in 1840, however, was the curiosity that all the iron shot from the *Mary Rose* weighed much less than they should. For instance, a shot of about 32 lbs. weighed only 19 lbs. Some of them, on being raised to the surface, actually became hot and soon fell to pieces. Clearly, a chemical change had taken place, but what this was, or how to arrest it, let alone reverse the process so as to make the object chemically stable once more, was quite beyond nineteenth century science.

Deane himself was soon forgotten. His book was never published, the manuscript lost, the watercolour sketches scattered among his relatives. Even the fact of the invention of the diving helmet went into historical limbo, and became ascribed to a different man, Augustus Siebe, who had merely made the pumps and collaborated with Deane. Deane's discovery of the *Mary Rose* was likewise forgotten and then, again, attributed to someone else—to the divers of the Sappers and Miners unit employed by Colonel C. W. Pasley to blow up the wreck of the *Royal George* with giant barrels of gunpowder. From there it was but a short step to a general acceptance among historians and scholars that the *Mary Rose* too had been blown up with one-ton charges laid under Pasley's direction. And as nothing now protruded from the seabed to show the place where Henry VIII's great battleship had foundered, no wreck buoy was thought necessary and all knowledge of the site forgotten, for the second time since 1545.

PART THREE: 'SOLENT SHIPS'

Chapter 5

Return to the *Royal George*

Project 'Solent Ships', 1965–1966

IT WAS the 24th of April, 1965. 455 years had passed since the *Mary Rose* had been built, 420 years since she went down, 125 years since John Deane had last dived on her. A chill morning with the rain pouring down, but we had to undress and struggle into skin-tight neoprene-rubber suits on the beach at Portsmouth because our borrowed boat was so small, with little freeboard. There were five of us from Southsea Branch of the British Sub-Aqua Club: Alan Lee, John Baldry, Roger Hale, John Towse and myself. With only seven years of amateur diving behind me, I was the novice; but because I knew more about the ships we were going out to find, and about the early divers who had worked on them over a century ago, and because the whole project was my original idea anyway, in effect I was the director.

We had held a conference at my house on Hayling Island on 2 January, 1965. Towse and Baldry, Diving Officer and Scientific Officer respectively, represented Southsea Branch, and I had also invited Mr. R. W. Wells, a marine naturalist who in the 1930s had gone underwater with a cut-down dustbin on the Deane pattern.

In its early days, the British Sub-Aqua Club had stressed that underwater swimming was *not* a sport; it was an exploration. Earth was misnamed—it was a water planet. More than that—a saltwater planet. Nearly three-quarters of earth is ocean, and it is still largely unexplored. When I took up underwater swimming in 1958, even the shallows off the local beaches were in many cases unknown territory never seen by man. I was then 39 and the thought of this invisible, secret world lying at my feet was thrilling beyond words. It offered priceless opportunities which could never recur. I thought I had perhaps ten years in what a young French diver had called before he died, 'the Marvellous Kingdom'. After that, the masses would have moved in and all the vital discoveries would have been made. I had been extraordinarily lucky to come on the scene at just this time.

What one did with the opportunity was a matter for the individual. Some went to the Mediterranean in search of the wrecks of antiquity, believing that the cold, inhospitable and murky British waters offered little scope for the explorer. Others thought that nothing of historic interest could possibly remain in their prosaic local seas and concentrated on 'wreck diving'—that is, exploring the twisted ironwork of modern ships, torn open by bomb, mine or torpedo, with the prospect of valuable copper or brass to help pay their boat costs, and live lobsters and crabs to appease their wives or girl friends.

Against this background I was a freak. I knew perfectly well what I wanted to do. As a historian, I was certain that I had on my doorstep, only just offshore, two major underwater finds: a lost church said to have been submerged long ago in Hayling Bay, and the wreck of the *Mary Rose* lying somewhere in the much deeper and more dangerous area of Spithead. Although it was the *Mary Rose* that had absorbed my thoughts for years, the sunken church had to come first; one must gain experience and build up a team. I spent the five amateur diving years of 1960–1964 on the 'Church Rocks' project, designed to find out how much truth there was, not only in this particular case, but in all those other romantic tales of church bells tolling under the sea. For the first time in human history, there could be an end to speculation; given time, training and a little cash, one could actually go down and find out. There proved to be a basis of truth in the story which I published in my book *History Under the Sea* (Hutchinson, 1968), and I also included the results of my research into the work of the early divers at Spithead, the men who had blown up the *Royal George* and *Edgar*, and come across the wreck of the *Mary Rose*.

During this time I was learning, by actual exploration around my own shores, that

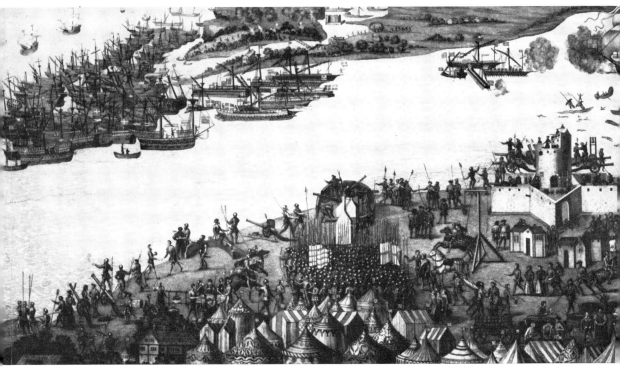

The Cowdray Engraving. The best clues to the course of the 1545 battle and the wreck site of the *Mary Rose* were in this panorama which shows the French fleet off Bembridge (left), French galleys firing at the *Great Harry* (centre) and the English fleet on

Mediterranean-based theories of how long timber, metal and other materials last underwater did not apply elsewhere, particularly here; that, in fact, there was no such thing as 'The Sea'. Every area was special and different and you could only find out how different by going underwater and systematically exploring it. This discovery was vitally important when assessing the likely preservation of historic wrecks, but sadly it evoked a sceptical reaction from many authorities in Britain and elsewhere; indeed most refused to accept it.

Even in the local sub-aqua club I was regarded as something of an impractical visionary. I was given to rhapsodising on the potential of the Solent area, stressing its importance as a focal point for shipping of some sort for at least 5,000 years. Many vessels, I argued, must have been wrecked and buried in the preserving mud to lie there forgotten, including the ship whose name had preoccupied me for so long. The proposition I put to Towse and Baldry in January, 1965, was that we should organise a search aimed specifically at the *Mary Rose*, the most important of the known, named wrecks in our area, but also, I explained, the most important known wreck in North-West Europe.

For nautical historians there was at that time a great gap in their knowledge, stretching from the end of the well-documented Viking period in about 1100 A.D. to the beginning of the eighteenth century. From that date to Nelson's time, the British National Maritime Museum alone boasted no less than 25,000 ship plans, plus many shipbuilders' models. Almost the only facts missing from the record were the colours of the carpets in the captains' cabins. Wrecks of this later period, although old, were not worth looking for.

The *Mary Rose*, however, was a different proposition. There were no plans of her or of any similar ship, nor were there shipbuilders' models. And yet she had been the first English battleship to have gunports and to mount complete batteries of heavy siege artillery—a really key ship in the development process at a time of rapid technological change. Virtually nothing was known about her; there was

Spit Sound (right). The original painting was contemporary, but this engraving, by James Basire, was done in 1778, shortly before the fire at Cowdray House. It looked almost like a chart, but could one rely on its accuracy? Photo: National Maritime Museum.

only a single authentic picture and that not very informative. The hull alone would be a priceless store of information, but there were also the guns, many of them of unknown type, again from a time of rapid technological change. And there was the crew—at least 400 men and possibly as many as 700—of whom I was certain several hundred must remain in and around the wreck. Many would be complete with their clothes, equipment, weapons, personal possessions and so on: a complete cross-section of Tudor military and naval society—aristocrats and commoners, bowmen and mariners, pikemen and gunners, officers and men—all cut down in the same place on the same day, in their prime. Unlike the contents of a cemetery, where the old and the sick are laid in their winding sheets, a thorough scientific examination could almost bring these men of the *Mary Rose* back to life, so great would be the detail and so representative the remains. No land site could offer such a vivid picture of Tudor society as it actually was.

The one great drawback to any search was the lack of certainty as to where the *Mary Rose* had gone down.

In *Sailing Ships*, a Science Museum publication, 1932–62, G. S. Laird Clowes stated that, 'The *Mary Rose* sank in the mouth of Portsmouth Harbour.' In *Administration of the Royal Navy*, published by the Navy Records Society, 1896, M. Oppenheim wrote that, 'The *Mary Rose* capsized off Brading when getting under way.' The *Catalogue* of H.M. Dockyard Museum, Portsmouth, 1919, referred to: 'The *Mary Rose*, sunk in action with the French Fleet off St. Helen's, Isle of Wight, with the loss of all hands.' And in *Deep Diving and Submarine Operations*, a classic manual written by the head of Siebe, Gorman, the firm founded by Augustus Siebe, Sir Robert Davis gave a more specific account:

> The wreck (of the *Mary Rose*) was abandoned and forgotten until, during the *Royal George* operations, divers came accidentally upon the remains of the ship sunk 237 years earlier, lying but a short distance away.

The distance between Portsmouth Harbour and Brading is some six sea miles, so the disagreement between the experts was measurable. The conflicting

"Wreck of the Royal George." Previous Sale

Diving operations at Spithead, 1839–1844: men of the Royal Sappers and Miners demolishing the *Royal George* and salvaging her guns under the direction of Colonel C. W. Pasley who took over where the Deanes had left off. In Pasley's biography it was stated that in addition to the *Royal George* and the *Edgar*, 'the wreck of the *Mary Rose* was also dealt with.' The author did not believe this.

testimony of three of them could not in any case be reconciled with the contemporary evidence, vague though it was—the Cowdray Engraving and Monson's statement that he had seen part of her ribs with his own eyes. Since 1962, I had made a number of enquiries and drawn blank each time. On this evidence the chances of finding the *Mary Rose* seemed very poor, and the possibility of the British Sub-Aqua Club accepting a search for her as a Southsea Branch project for 1965 quite out of the question. So what I put forward was a 'failsafe' project, certain to obtain some measure of success.

I called it 'Solent Ships'. I chose a baker's dozen of notable historic wrecks in the Solent area, which extends roughly from the Needles to Selsey Bill, and proposed that we find and examine as many as conveniently possible. They had all sunk on known

dates and would therefore provide a guide to the deterioration of wooden structures locally. At that time, British archaeologists accepted Mediterranean-based dogma, that wood in the sea lasted only about five years, ironwork some 30 to 40 years. Actual scientific tests on the Pacific coast of North America had shown remarkable deterioration of wood; in just over a year, sample panels deliberately put down had been riddled by timber-eating molluscs popularly called 'shipworms'.

My documentary research into the local wrecks investigated by the pioneer helmet divers in the 1830s and 1840s showed a startlingly different picture. The *Royal George* was still a solid obstruction after 57 years under the sea, while the much older *Edgar* was standing two gundecks high after 133 years' submersion at Spithead, admittedly in an extremely fragile state. And it was precisely because their timbers had lasted so long that they remained as obstructions to anchoring, and why the early divers of Colonel Pasley's Sappers and Miners unit (now the Royal Engineers) had been asked to blow them up. These old records suggested that heavily-built battleships sunk in our waters might not open flat in the well reconstructed sequence demonstrated by the work of the American diver, Peter Throckmorton, on brigs and other small vessels at Methone in Greece.

On suitably soft seabeds, they might sink in deeply, the scour of the tides helping to bury them. Over a long period of years the parts exposed to the sea would be rendered fragile by fungi and bacilli, by gribble and teredo; and then collapse. As soon as these remains fell into the wreck or into the surrounding scourpit, they would be covered by a light film of sediment which would serve to preserve them at that stage of their decay. Those parts of the hull which had sunk in and been covered quickly might not only be in good condition but still structurally sound. Indeed, I did not exclude the preservation of some organic human remains.

How valuable such a wreck would be historically would depend also on its angle of heel. Fortunately, few ships sink upright. An upright ship ship sunk 15 feet into the seabed would only have the lower part of the hull left—the hold. But a vessel lying on one side might have many decks preserved on that side—and not much on the other. The *Mary Rose*—and this was a primary factor in deciding me to press for a search—had been shown lying heeled over at something like 40 to 45 degrees, if the Cowdray Engraving could be believed. That was most encouraging.

But so far, all this was theory. It had to be proved. And not least among the difficulties would be the problem of identification, when an ancient wreck was found. This was difficult enough where modern wrecks were concerned, standing proud of the bottom; for a very old, buried wreck, the process of identification could be a long business, made lively by frequent disputes. What, for instance, would infallibly identify the *Mary Rose*? She was a virtually unknown ship from an almost unknown era.

At the back of my mind there was a small surge of hope that we might find her quickly. Sir Robert Davis's statement that she had been found *accidentally* by divers working on the *Royal George* implied that she might be only a hundred feet or so away. While serving with the British Army of the Rhine I had taken a short course in helmet (or 'hard hat') diving with the Royal Engineers. This helped me to understand the technical problems encountered by the pioneer helmet divers and showed how difficult it was to move around. 'Walking' is not the right word to describe one's slow progression, leaning forward at an angle impossible on land and pushing at the seabed with one's steel-clad toes. If one took Davis literally, the *Mary Rose* must indeed be close to the *Royal George*.

And so I proposed to Southsea Branch that we begin by finding the *Royal George*. This should be a simple matter, because her position was accurately shown on many old charts, and we were all of us getting very good at finding pinpoints in the sea. The remains would be interesting in themselves, as examples of dated underwater items; but above all, they would give us a true-so-far-as-it-went cover

Underwater operations at Spithead, 1965: the *Dreadnought*, Britain's first nuclear submarine, passes over aqualung divers searching for the *Royal George* as a first step to finding the *Mary Rose*. Photo: Alexander McKee.

Typical diving boat of the 1960s: Maurice Harknett's 26-ft. cabin cruiser *Gina-Annè* picking up divers. Photo: Alexander McKee.

story—that we were working on the *Royal George*—to camouflage a discovery of the *Mary Rose*, should we be lucky enough to find her. This was an exceedingly serious matter, because there was then no law to protect historic wrecks. The only existing one, the Merchant Shipping Act of 1894, would actually encourage any salvage firm to blow the *Mary Rose* to pieces in order to get at the valuable bronze guns which they could then legally sell for scrap metal.

So on 24 April we got into Alan Lee's open bass-boat, 15 feet long and with only 18 inches freeboard once it had been loaded with the five of us and our diving gear. I felt terribly vulnerable, perched on top of some bottles, and cold even under an oilskin which was over an anorak worn on top of a neoprene suit. The first day of the project, as I had always imagined it, would be carried out from a large, roomy, covered boat with a chart table, working space and protection from the wind and rain. As it was, I couldn't unroll a chart for fear of getting it soaked and possibly lost overboard, and the rain and spray smearing my glasses would make it difficult to watch the shore for the 'marks' or 'transits' which I had worked out for

placing the boat just south of the *Royal George* wreck mound, and comparing them with the 'marks' which John Towse had worked out independently, so that in effect we would check each other's calculations. Furthermore, I was afraid.

I had been ill, this was my first dive of the year, and the idea of Spithead as a dive site was intimidating. It always had been, and was now, a focal point for shipping heading into or out of Portsmouth and Southampton, for ferries between the Isle of Wight and the mainland, for anchoring, and for naval exercises of all sorts. In addition, there were supposed to be obstructions down there which in bad visibility could be hazardous or lethal to a diver. Most certainly, these must include explosive devices of both British and German origin. The place had been a battlefield in 1940, as it had been in 1545. I had myself seen a Heinkel minelayer flying low overhead at night, being fired at by a machine-gun mounted on Henry VIII's Southsea Castle, and at high noon seen the stukas come screaming down out of the sun onto the dockyard and the ships, watched the fires gouting smoke 5,000 feet into the sky and the sides of the

French battleship *Courbet* rippling with the yellow flashes of gunfire; much as the sides of the French battleships must have done in 1545.

On the other hand, we were much better equipped than John Deane had been. A neoprene suit, a weightbelt to counteract its buoyancy and ours, mask and flippers to give vision and mobility, and, in my case, twin 'tads'—ex-Air Ministry oxygen bottles bought for a few pounds as war surplus and now filled with compressed air. This was better than my first aqualung dive on Church Rocks in 1960, when I had worn only three heavy jerseys underwater in lieu of a suit. For a deep dive such as Spithead, we wore a depth gauge and a watch as well as a compass. As some protection against shipping the first pair down, Baldry and Hale, towed a large surface buoy attached to an artefact bag, and carried out a square search to the north of our anchored boat.

I noted at the time that I felt both 'tension and exhilaration', although the prospects for a quick *Mary Rose* discovery had faded a little. In the hope of finding position clues, I had carried out further research on the early divers, and had recently discovered that the story told by Sir Robert Davis, which was repeated in almost every underwater book in the world, was false. The *Mary Rose* had not been accidentally discovered by Colonel Pasley's army divers while working on the *Royal George* using diving dress invented by Siebe. She had been found by John Deane using diving gear he and his brother had devised, when called away from their work on the *Royal George* to clear some fishermen's lines. I did not then have the full story of their work, which lay hidden in the Public Record office and many other places, so it was still possible to hope that the *Mary Rose* might be very close and that the first step to

Typical diving boat of the 1970s: Tony Glover's trawler *Julie-Anne* (a converted lifeboat from the *Queen Mary*), which could carry a small fire pump or compressor, and up to eight divers. Photo: Tom Hale.

finding her might be the location of the *Royal George* this very day. Intently, I watched the surface buoy towed by Baldry and Hale come to a stop, and a few minutes later the two divers rose to the surface, obviously carrying something heavy.

Their haul included one 32-pounder iron shot heavily concreted, a length of standing rigging, a carving which was possibly scrimshaw work, two tibia from two different sheep which had not been butchered (i.e., they may have entered the water alive), and a floppy, repulsive slab of modern anti-fouling paint. All except the paint could very well be from the *Royal George*, which did have a manger. Equally, they could be from almost any one of thousands of warships which had anchored here over the centuries. There is a traditional naval jingle which is all too true:

'Tinkle, tinkle, little spoon,
Knife and fork will follow soon.'

And for all we knew the whole of the Spithead anchorage might be littered with items from old 'wooden walls'.

Therefore, although the artefacts found to the north looked 'right' for the *Royal George*, when Alan Lee and I went in as a pair, I led off away from their area, going southwest. The visibility, encouragingly good on the top, went almost completely black at 70 feet down, before the bottom came into view at 80 feet or so, greyish with reflected light in a kind of shadowless gloom. After waiting a minute or two, one could see clearly for five or six feet, dimly for perhaps eight feet. I finned slowly, inspecting each artefact. There was one to the square yard! All of it was just lying there, proud of the bottom. There was a motor car tyre (which did not, to me, indicate a sunken motor car but a boat which had lost a fender), a used tube of toothpaste, innumerable fragments of broken pottery, a perfectly undamaged bottle (of ginger beer, circa 1900?), a spoon with a date stamped on it (1957), and many, many similar items on:

> a layer of small shingle and dead slipper-limpet shells on grey clay-mud-ooze, and under that, hard clay. Hermit crabs and dahlia anenomes. No fish. No weed. Very dead. And as near no tide as made no matter. Like an old forgotten museum half a century after the last atom bomb has fallen. Nobody been here for 122 years, as far as we know.

So I noted in my log. Actually, it was more than likely that ours were the first human eyes to see that place.

Recovery from the *Royal George*, 1965: John Baldry with concreted 32-pounder iron shot. In the background, the open boat used for diving that day. Photo. Alexander McKee.

The *Royal George* wreck-dispersal area was certainly to the north, where Baldry and Hale had made their finds. We were not looking for a ship. My research made clear that Pasley had blown the *Royal George* with thoroughness, leaving a great mound, and had then raked over the wreckage, spreading it still further.

Having satisfied myself that there were no 'wooden wall' items to the south, I navigated back to our boat along the seabed, being most unwilling to surface anywhere except alongside it, because I had left our buoy behind marking a large, heavily concreted piece of ironwork. From the boat, the others saw four NATO warships in line ahead drive right over our bubbles—the American destroyer-escort *Hammerberg*, the British frigate *Leander*, the Canadian frigate *Columbia*, and the Dutch destroyer *Overijssel*. Lee thought he heard them, I didn't. The reason why the tide was not a menace was that we had chosen slack water; ordinarily, it runs very fast. We could do no more that day, because we had used all our air; being comparatively poor men, we could not afford to buy a collection of cylinders.

Not many people were keen to do this sort of diving as a regular thing, or to loan their boats. One of those who could very often be helpful was Maurice Harknett, a lecturer in electronics who owned a neat 26-ft. cabin cruiser *Gina-Anne*. But it was another month before he could take us out. On that occasion I chose to use the slack water period for a recce of the *Boyne*, sunk at the side of the main navigation channel off Southsea Castle, where at times the currents could run at five or six knots. Here there was hardly any 'anchorage gash', but a lot of small wood splinters around a great mound of shingle some 10 feet high from which weeded, concreted pieces of ironwork protruded.

By the time we reached the *Royal George* area, the fast tide run had begun, making free swimming impossibly dangerous. So Harknett dived with Jim Dipnell, and when they reached the anchor, they lifted it out of the ground, so that the boat drifted, giving them a free ride across the seabed. If they saw anything interesting, they simply dug in the anchor. They passed over an undulating seabed covered with scattered debris. While they were doing this, and I was in the boat above them, I heard a booming noise, and was astonished to see the great whaleback and high 'sail' of an underwater monster sliding past on the surface a hundred or so feet away—HMS *Dreadnought*, 3,000 tons of nuclear submarine.

Then it was my turn and I found that on my own, I could not lift the anchor and was compelled to swim up-tide, unconnected to *Gina-Anne*. I ignored the clay plains and searched the mounds, interrupted now and then by drifting objects which wrapped themselves around my mask—mostly dead weed, but on one occasion a newspaper; there was a positive hail of moving flotsam coming at me. The bottom was littered with slightly heavier debris, mostly pottery sherds, simply lying on the surface like leaves in a park in autumn, and I ignored them. After nearly exhausting my air, I saw something different, the rim only of what proved to be a small, intact pot largely buried in one of the small mounds; and this I collected for examination. I had to come up free, surfacing close to the protection of the boat.

On this occasion we had with us in the boat for the first time at Spithead a land archaeologist, Margaret Rule, who was also the conservation expert on the current excavation of the Roman Palace at Fishbourne. Some materials require immediate treatment and for this reason I had invited her to come out with us; in addition, however, she was knowledgable on bones and pottery. Two days later she showed the bowl to a meeting of archaeologists, without saying where it came from; Barry Cunliffe, the director of the Fishbourne dig, dated it as late eighteenth century; that is, to the time of the *Royal George*. It did look as though the area of small mounds might represent the outlying dispersal by Pasley's huge rakes of *Royal George* debris from the main shipmound which, on his closing down of operations in 1843 (having begun in 1839), he had mapped as some three feet high. I had found a copy of this map.

I could not afford to waste people's valuable time or scarce air in doubtful conditions, but only when tide and weather promised an effective search, so the next operation was not for two weeks, on the following neap tide. This time there were four divers—Maurice Harknett, Jim Dipnell, Tony Bye and myself, with Pete Cope as cover. I went first with Dipnell, towing a buoy. Visibility was a good 15 feet and the light was so bright on the bottom that you could read the dates on the anchorage gash even at a depth of 75 feet. Jim and I therefore spaced ourselves well apart on the bottom of the buoyline and swam east side by side, in contact both by line and eye. I wrote in my log:

> Obviously still on *George*. Small mounds at first, then a large, significant one, Dipnell thought 5–6 feet high, and it was certainly substantial and continued at slight angle to current as far as the eye could see in both directions (i.e., at least 30 feet).

This great mound seemed identical in size and alignment with that shown on Colonel Pasley's plan, but several feet higher. Clearly the main mound of

Baldry's iron shot, after conservation, with the broken-open concretion stuck together again, to show the corrosion process. Photo: Alexander McKee.

the *Royal George*, I thought. We dug experimentally at various points along it and found that it was studded with wood and ironwork like a cake with raisins. Now, we could have dug happily in it all day, searching for 'goodies'. But we didn't. Certain that it represented the bulk of the remains of the compost heap to which I knew the *Royal George* had been reduced, I decided to use it as a secure starting point for a further search to see whether Davis was right, that the *Mary Rose* indeed lay 'but a short distance away'.

With the aid of borrowed cylinders and making two dives each, we obtained repeated, definitive negatives: the *Royal George* main mound was surrounded by smaller mounds and likely debris, but beyond that was just a featureless plain of clay, mud and ooze littered with modern artefacts only, lying proud and unburied. There was no other wreck mound; no indication either that a ship would sink in very deeply here. That finished the *Royal George* area as far as I was concerned, and Sir Robert Davis, too.

I reconsidered the Cowdray Engraving in the light of this knowledge—that all stated positions for the *Mary Rose* were without exception not merely wrong but baseless—since we now had more practical experience of the battlefield, its contours, currents and seabed soil. The original painting had been commissioned by Anthony Browne, Viscount Montagu, a vain little man disliked by other members of Henry VIII's court. The panorama showed him riding onto Southsea Common behind the King on the day of battle. In 1778 the much-maligned Society of Antiquaries had commissioned James Basire to make an engraved copy and a member, Sir Joseph Ayloffe, had written a detailed description of the painting, and the colours used, to go with the black-and-white copy. From this we know that Henry VIII was wearing a black bonnet with a white feather, a jacket of cloth-of-gold and a surcoat of brown velvet; and that Suffolk's beard was white. Then the painting had been destroyed by the burning of Cowdray House, leaving only copies of the engraving.

The evidence, it seemed to me, was like looking down a telescope from the wrong end. I knew from experience that engraved copies sometimes bore very little relation to the original—so how accurately had Basire copied that contemporary picture? Some of the ships, and part of Southsea Castle, seemed very doubtful. Perhaps the original had deteriorated and

Typical items of 'anchorage gash' found in the *Royal George* area, 1965: these include ginger pop bottles and animal bones, but the length of standing rigging on left is almost certainly from the *Royal George*. Photo: Alexander McKee.

Basire had had to use his imagination here and there? I was also aware that the original sixteenth century picture must have been drawn in accordance with sixteenth century artistic conventions, virtually without perspective. The opportunities for errors on my part were endless, but I nevertheless had a feeling that Tudor regard for literal accuracy in representation, as opposed to modern naturalistic convention, might work in my favour. The original might very well be virtually a chart (although these too contain specific errors resulting from the method of projection employed). On 8 June, 1965, I reduced a great deal of reading, study and hard thought to a note that a line drawn from Southsea Castle, through the half-drowned main and foremast of the *Mary Rose*, to the Isle of Wight near Ryde, also passed very close to the place where the *Royal George* now lay, but that the Tudor wreck was 'nearer to Southsea Castle, quite definitely'. And that agreed with the contemporary evidence of Admiral Monson, who also seemed to suggest shallower water.

Consequently, I decided to search the arc northeast of the *Royal George*, starting in the shallows three-quarters of a mile away and steadily working closer. Modern charts showed some odd contours plus one definite 'obstruction', which had to be something. These were checked as economically as ever, only two half-days being spent on them. Purely by 'marks' taken from a chart, I got the anchor down 40 yards from the 'obstruction', which proved to be a real pinpoint in the sea—a metal dustbin-shaped object six feet high, set on three metal legs. We took samples from the area for the biological survey and I made trial digs; using a knife only, one could dig down two feet in a few minutes; very soft soil indeed. For the preservation of any wreck this was good news, she would go in deep and be well preserved; but that made visual search difficult. I wrote in my log: 'But with this composition, may be no mound. *Most unsatisfactory.*'

I decided to halt direct search for the *Mary Rose*, as a waste of people's time, until I could get the loan of scientific search instruments which were then being perfected but had not been used for archaeology. In the meantime, the general survey of wrecks and local marine life would continue. This was on 7 August, three and half months after we had begun.

Mediterranean divers thought little of the instruments I believed essential. 'Let the reader have no illusions about electronic detectors, supersonic sounders, Asdic and so on,' wrote Frederic Dumas, co-author of Cousteau's classic *Silent World*, in his book *Deep Water Archaeology*, published in 1962 (the very year in which I had begun to ask questions about the position of the *Mary Rose*).

I had other disagreements with accepted doctrine, some much nearer home. In March, 1965, while I was preparing the 'Solent Ships' programme, a body called the Committee for Nautical Archaeology was formed at the University of London, with Joan du Plat Taylor

The wreck in the Hamble River that proved to be a direct ancestor of the *Mary Rose*, the giant carrack *Grace Dieu*, built at Southampton in 1416–1418 and burnt on her mud berth in 1439, so that only the lower part of the hull is left. In the 1960s the author's team investigated it by diving, by walking (on the few days a year when it was visible above water) and from the air. Note how the presence of the wreck has altered the mud contours of the river bank, an example of 'scour'. Photo: Alexander McKee.

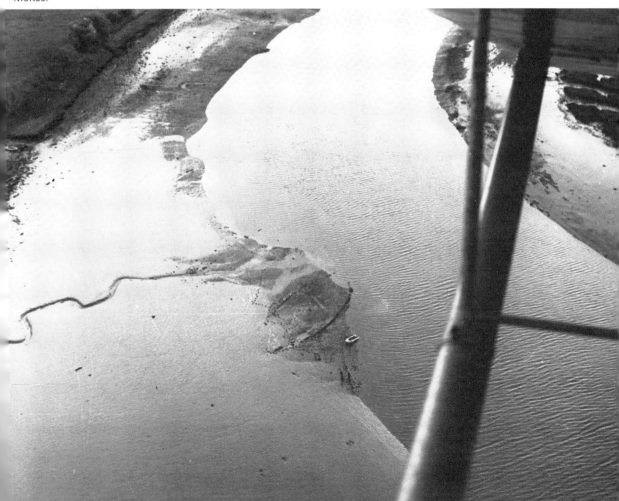

at its leading light. She had taken part as conservationist in the classic excavation by George Bass and Peter Throckmorton of a Bronze Age wreck off Cape Gelidonya in Turkey, in which Frederic Dumas had also taken part; this had been in 1960, following two years search work by Throckmorton. It was the first scientific excavation of an underwater site and I was not alone in my admiration. I ranked it almost with Anders Franzén's *Wasa* project, which predated it, Franzén having prepared his wreck programme in 1950, carried out searches part-time during 1953–1956, which resulted in the salvage of this Swedish galleon in an operation lasting from 1957 to 1959, the year after I took up amateur diving. What he had done was to recover a hitherto unknown type of battleship, a galleon, to fill a gap in history; a feat which I hoped to emulate with the carrack *Mary Rose*, the type which immediately preceded the galleon—provided that there was enough of it left and that I could solve all the formidable problems of search, excavation and finance.

Now it seemed that there was a nautical expert on this new body, the CNA, who wanted to use it as a vehicle for finding the *Mary Rose* himself. His team of divers had begun searches at Spithead at the same time as we had and, like us, had aimed first for the *Royal George*. Alas, their *Royal George* and my *Royal George* were not the same. They had found several pieces of 'old-looking' timber some 600 feet away, according to their chart, from where we had discovered a great shipmound. It was impossible to co-operate because they were doing sextant-searches, the big ship Navy method, while we were using 'marks', the traditional method used by fishermen in small boats which are not a stable platform. We had been 'finding' a particular rock two miles out to sea with this simple procedure, which they proclaimed was possible only with a sextant.

In February, 1966, Miss Taylor brought us together for a conference from which it was hoped a compromise might result. It was a vain hope. I found myself in a minority of one, arguing that Davis was wrong in implying that Pasley's divers had found the *Mary Rose* near the *Royal George* and that she must in fact lie in shallower water to the north-east. The others would have none of it. They thought my *Royal George* must be some other wreck, and that their position must be right, despite the fact that their evidence was minimal and their depth range inaccurate (14 fathoms as opposed to the 12 fathoms

which all my old charts gave as the low water depth). But if I was wrong, if I had found the wrong wreck, then my delimitation would be meaningless. As for Monson and the Cowdray Engraving, they brushed them aside. I was mistaken. The *Mary Rose* was deep, next to the *Royal George*, their *Royal George*. As I would not budge either, it was obvious that our two teams would have to continue to work separately, and therefore we divided Spithead between us, according to our rival theories, they to take the 10-fathom line (60 feet) and everything deeper, we to stay inside the 10-fathom line nearer to Southsea.

However, we did decide to compare charts, to find out where the discrepancy lay between their 14 fathoms for the *Royal George* and my 12 fathoms. John Towse and I arranged to meet their dive leader at the Navy's Hydrographic Department, then in London, to inspect the original chart he had used for the search sponsored by the nautical expert on CNA. On the agreed date, 10 May, he was too busy to get away, so Towse and I went to the Hydrographer's on our own and found a pile of old charts waiting for us. These included the original of my main chart, Mackenzie's survey of 1784 (made two years after the sinking of the *Royal George*), and also the main chart the CNA representative had employed, Commander Sheringham's survey of 1841 (the year after the Deanes finished work on the *Mary Rose*, as I subsequently discovered).

The charts were large and stiff and had to be held down at the corners by heavy weights. Sheringham's chart was unrolled and Towse and I leaned forward over the table, taking in the red cross and name *Royal George* (in 12 fathoms, not 14 after all), then sliding down to the right to where we saw the red cross and the name *Edgar* in 12-13 fathoms as we expected; and finally, almost automatically, going back to the *Royal George* and then looking up in the north-east arc towards the shallows of Spit Sand into our own search area. And there it was. A red inked cross and the name *Mary Rose*, in six fathoms. Towse gave an audible gasp.

The distance between the two red crosses denoting the two wrecks on the actual chart was $3\frac{3}{4}$ inches (half a mile on the sea). No one, I thought, studying that chart for a search aimed at the *Mary Rose*, could fail to see that the words '*Mary Rose*', in red, were written on it. But they apparently had.

It had taken us 15 seconds.

Chapter 6

Echoes from the Sea

Searching by Sonar, 1966–1968

I COULD SEE clearly for at least eighteen inches and dimly perhaps five feet ahead. My depth gauge was steady at 40 feet most of the time, although once my ears registered deeper. On this tide, an actual depth of 40–45 feet was correct for the charted six fathoms of the *Mary Rose*. Going round in my head was a description of the site as the Deanes had found it, printed by the *Hampshire Telegraph* on Monday, 15 August, 1836, announcing the discovery of two more brass guns:

> These pieces, with the iron-hooped one, were discovered on the same spot, resting on some wreck, which was so completely buried in the sand that the diver could find nothing to which he could affix a rope.

There had been yet another mention of sand in a little booklet, bound in wood from the *Mary Rose*, published by S. Horsey in 1849:

> Mr. Deane, with spade, shovel, etc., then excavated a portion of the sand, etc., and fired a charge of gunpowder, and found on descending again that he had got into the hold of the unfortunate ship, having made a crater of large dimensions by this explosion.

That had been in 1840. Now it was 14 May, 1966

and I was down there myself with John Towse, four days after finding Sheringham's chart of 1841. We found the most complicated seabed we had yet seen, consisting of juicy harbour mud, occasional eroded lumps of clay upstanding from it, beds of slipper limpet shells in layer-lines as if sorted by wave-action, and now and then, 'quite wide pools of sand'. This was the first sand we had seen either at Spithead or in the shallows of Spit Sand, and the flanking mud was the softest and deepest yet. To demonstrate, 'Towse just thrust his hand down into it anywhere he liked, and his arm promptly disappeared as far up as the shoulder.' Unlike the plain around the *Royal George* this area was not flat, 'there were odd little configurations all over.' Another significant feature was the rarity of the 'anchorage gash' so familiar from the deep water areas and the nature of the few items which we found. I noted a large tin can, a scrubbing brush, a light carrier bag in blue, a piece of coal, a portion of clinker. It was almost all light stuff, or had a large area in relation to its weight. Even the slipper limpet shells were feather-light. They would not have been there in John Deane's time, because they had entered British waters only in the last part of the

Left: Testing a Wardle & Davenport magnetometer in rough seas at Spithead, 1966. The rest of the equipment (little more than a stick and two bottles) is being towed astern in a dinghy. Photo: Alexander McKee.

Right: Testing the magnetometer on the wreck of the *Boyne*, 1966. *Left*: George Cooke, operating the instrument; *right*: Margaret Rule. Photo: Alexander McKee.

Using an EG&G sub-mud sonar at Spithead, January 1967. Rough seas flooded the generator and ruined the experiments. Photo: Alexander McKee.

nineteenth century along with imported North American oysters. If, by some remote chance, anything at all of the *Mary Rose* protruded even slightly from the mud, it was likely to be obscured by the masses of limpet shells. Otherwise, there was very little sign of life. We saw a few spiny starfish (which feed on slipper limpet), Towse spotted a 1-lb plaice and I saw one baby plaice take off under my nose and do the usual port-turn evasive manoeuvre practised by the adults.

There never was a more depressing or hopeless seabed. The thought of a visual search and probing made the heart sink. I scribbled in my log:

> After one look at that lot, neither of us thought we were going to find the *Mary Rose*. She'll be deep in it, perfectly preserved with probably nothing showing (the Deanes having thoughtfully removed the heavy guns which were on top of the old heap and the only things even partially showing in 1836). The gunpowder charges they used cannot have damaged her much. Even if a little bit did show here and there, the odds are it would be camouflaged by slipper limpet beds.

But for a search using new types of instruments, such as the 'pinger' (sub-mud sonar) or a magnetometer (to detect metallic anomalies), the *Mary Rose* must represent 'a big target—as large as Spit Fort,' I wrote. And in the long term I was optimistic:

> With the firm conviction that the remains of the ship will be in a good state of preservation, I would suggest the ultimate possibility of lifting her intact on a flexible cradle; raise the complete ship rather than to pick it to bits.

I sent these findings to Joan du Plat Taylor, the secretary of the Committee for Nautical Archaeology, hoping that she might be able to help with the instruments and perhaps also with legal protection. The thought that the site, if we exposed it, could be pillaged legally and the vandals rewarded by the law as it stood, was a brake on any impulsive action.

Independently as usual, Towse and I had looked at our own charts and come to the same conclusion. Before our dive on 14 May, 1966, John, who is an Admiralty scientist by profession, had explained that all wrecks in the Solent area were surrounded by scour-pits, of which the 'Norman Castle' wreck he had helped discover in 1964 was an excellent example, still being studied. On 8 August, 1965, in excellent visibility of 35 feet, he had made notes:

> The wreck lies in a hollow or 'dish' created by tide scour and resembles a Norman Castle surrounded by a moat. The depths are as follows: on the hull of the wreck—32 feet; in the bottom of the scour pit around the wreck—40 ft; while the average level of the surrounding seabed is 35 ft. That is, the top of the wreck is nearly flush with the surrounding seabed, separated from it by a deep 'moat' dug by tide scour on a clay bottom. The tides are notoriously fast at this site (the Princessa Shoal, south of the Isle of Wight).

They subsequently identified this wreck as the freighter *France Aimée* (ex-*Laura*) sunk by collision in 1918. (See echo sounder profiles, figs. 1 and 2, opposite).

Now, said Towse, on a cohesive clay seabed, these scour-pits may remain long after the wreck has dug itself by this means downwards and out of sight, as may soon happen with the *France Aimée*. Therefore, what we are really looking for at Spithead is a scour-trace such as a big ship might leave behind, and, he went on, there are two such marked on the chart near the *Mary Rose* position. To this rabbit from his hat I silently produced my counter-rabbit—my chart, with just those two features already boldly outlined in yellow crayon. Because of its shape, alignment and position, I preferred the northern one; as did Towse.

I had first noted scour pits on Church Rocks, but it was not until 26 May, 1964—the same year as the *France Aimée* was discovered—that I found out how these pits were produced. I was snorkel-diving (without an aqualung) on the boom defences built in two world wars to protect the Spithead anchorage against U-boats and torpedo-boats. The current was running very fast, so while I got my breath back between dives, I tucked into the eddies behind the concrete blocks and steel piles. All four corners of the blocks were eroded away at the bottom, but it was the thinner piling which visually demonstrated the principles. At surface level, the current was causing bubbles to swirl around the pile, while at the bottom was a 'regular sandstorm, revolving left to right like a tornado, which had dug out a deep hole around the base of each pile: a circular, revolving, upward-evolving eddy.' (Fig. 3 below).

Clearly a rock, a wreck or any other similar object is an obstruction to the tidal stream, and as water is almost incompressible, it is forced to speed up at that point, the energy so created triggering off these whirling eddies, which are natural eroding and excavating machines.

In 1966 a Southampton shipwright called Maurice Young, who was soon to join our team, made a series of observations which tied all this together and, in addition, despatched to the dustbin a notion, beloved of many classical archaeologists to this day, that a wreck is a 'time capsule'—everything in and around it must date from the same time. Their theory did not explain why a post-World War II plastic toy was found in the First World War *France Aimée*, but Morrie Young's observations most certainly did.

At Netley on the eastern shore of Southampton water a large wooden-hulled cabin cruiser sank during the hours of darkness for reasons that were never ascertained.

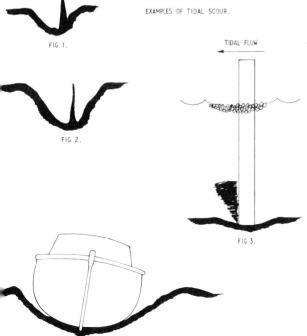

EXAMPLES OF TIDAL SCOUR.

FIG 1.

FIG 2.

TIDAL FLOW

FIG 3.

FIG 4.

M.G.YOUNG.

Approximately eleven weeks after the sinking I was asked to dive on the vessel to carry out an examination and to assess the possibility of rigging lifting slings with a view to her eventual salvage. I located the structurally undamaged cruiser under conditions of unusually good visibility in a little over 20 feet of water. She was in an upright position but had settled into the very soft muddy seabed almost to her original waterline.

What appeared to me to be unusual at that time was that the mud into which the hull had eased itself did not touch the side planking or the stem or stern, and did not in fact make contact with the vessel at the sides until slightly below the turn of the bilge. The cruiser was sitting in a self-made pit considerably wider and longer than herself, which made the task of passing slings under the forward and after ends of the keel much less of a task than I had imagined.

It was also noticeable that this natural moat—I cannot think of a more apt description—had a prominent 'lip' on the edge of it and was rapidly being filled with a variety of seabed debris that had been transported there by the tide. There were bottles, beer and lemonade cans, numerous plastic cartons and cups, and even a large fire-extinguisher still showing its bright red paint. None of these items came from within the hull and were in no way related to it other than by having fallen into its unintended trap. It was much later that it dawned on me, that what I had witnessed was the little-known burial process of a wreck while it was actually taking place. Furthermore, it was clear that much of the accumulated debris that had been washed under the bilge would have been carried down into the mud along with the vessel.

It would be reasonable to assume that given a few more years for the structure to decay and collapse, the whole craft would have disappeared into the seabed and been covered leaving, I suspect, little more than a slight depression flanked by low mounds to mark the spot. The more I thought about this phenomenon and its possible parallels in marine archaeology, the more obvious became the problem of the trapped debris. In this particular case I feel sure that the burial would have been so rapid that the contents of the 'grave' would almost certainly have spanned only a few years. Given a much sturdier-built hull, however, the moat—which seems to last for as long as the hull remains reasonably intact—may well exist for a century or more, and that means the ship and its attendant artefacts could vary in date by the same figure.

What Towse and I were hoping for, was that some trace of the giant scour-pit left by the *Mary Rose* would still be visible after more than four centuries. On our first dive the visibility had been too poor to recognise any such feature, but some magnetic anomaly had affected my compass, and this gave me an idea which had my children falling about in fits and rushing off to tell their mother that poor Daddy was using a compass to find his way about the house. In fact, I was marching up and down outside the cupboard where I kept my aqualung cylinders and weightbelts and noting what the underwater compass had to say about it. The answer was nothing. It reacted only to the car, when I was two feet away. So it should not respond to anchorage 'gash' but only to a large amount of metal. Therefore it might act as a *Mary Rose* detector, provided I did not have to use it to steer by.

The plan I devised was to find two prominent 'marks' on the Portsmouth shore which, when in line with each other, led across the odd-shaped feature on my chart. A dinghy, steered by a bearing compass, would be rowed along that line at slack water, towing myself and a young girl archaeologist, Margot Varese, who had learned to dive. We would start off the site, positioning ourselves by two other 'marks' on the Gosport shore, and would be approaching the feature on its long side. Going towards Portsmouth there, the general trend of the seabed is up, so if we saw the bottom drop away from us, that might indicate a scoured depression. We would not dare to leave the anchor line to examine it, however, because it was low water slack when the Isle of Wight passenger ships use this route.

One was bearing down on us at 15 knots as we prepared to leave the protection of Maurice Harknett's cabin cruiser. Pete Cope got into the dinghy and took up the oars, Margaret Rule, who was not to learn to dive for another five years, got in with a land compass; Margot and I jumped into the water and finned down the dinghy's anchor rope in good visibility which reduced to eight feet on the bottom. I picked up the anchor and tugged the rope sharply to show Pete Cope that we were ready, Margot took station on my right, holding a probe rod, and off we went, finning slowly to help the rower.

Twice in the first 20 minutes, my compass showed a wild swing; but it was not detecting buried metal, for the anchor rope was twitching violently in my hand, and Margot was making rapid signals. Simultaneously, on both occasions, our 'silent world' was filled by a high-pitched whining noise (the sound of ship's screws revolving rapidly) against a background roar rather like an express train in a tunnel (the ship's engines plus water disturbance). The ships' keels were probably passing about 20 feet above our heads, for it

was low water and we were swimming off the bottom. We would not dare surface anywhere but up the anchor line direct to the dinghy.

After 20 minutes of slow travel the seabed changed. Basically it had been mud and clay with narrow bands of slipper limpet beds aligned roughly north-south. This gave way to sand and wide, irregular blobs of limpets. Then the anchor I was holding appeared to lift some three or four feet clear of the seabed—which meant that we were passing over a depression. I would like to have let go the anchor and made a close search, but that would have meant surfacing, when our air ran out, directly in the path of a procession of Isle of Wight steamers.

On the next occasion, which was not for two months—Spithead was an unpopular diving site with most boat-owners and we had no money with which to hire a boat—Margot Varese and I crossed the scour-feature from the opposite direction, riding with the tide, towing a buoy and closely followed by Harknett's cabin cruiser. Margot noted that we passed over 'a low, broken bank' which led into 'a continuous and deeper depression with a higher and more irregular bank on its right.' I recorded 'a real rise of seabed to a marked crest, coupled with a depth reduction of an indicated 5 to 6 feet within a short distance; the crest curved round and then led away to South or South-East.' This was highly unnatural. Without the need for signals, we both turned left and swam south along the crested mound, probing. Then Margot's air supply stopped. It did not run out gradually, the air just stopped coming; she breathed in—and got nothing. She had to fin up fast forty feet to the surface to get her next breath, a hazardous proceeding, because the air still in the lungs expands rapidly with the lessening pressure of the water outside and can cause a fatal embolism. To keep in touch, I had to streak up to the surface with her, breathing out hard all the way to the top; but our training worked and we both surfaced without damage—and with no Isle of Wight steamer bearing down on us! Such an incident may not seem as dramatic as an encounter with sharks, but it is a lot more dangerous.

Necessarily, a scour-pit covers a much larger area than the wreck which has caused it. And not all wrecks scour equally all round; sometimes the scour is on one side only. So what we needed now was an instrument capable of telling us whereabouts the hidden ship lay in relation to the widespread pattern above it. In the first week of September, 1966, we were twice able to get the loan of a Wardle & Davenport proton magnetometer operated by George Cooke; but we had to accept what came in the way of tide and weather.

The first time, when we rendezvoused with Maurice Harknett in Langstone Harbour, it was already Force 6, gusting 7, with Force 8 (full gale) 'imminent'. Sonar gear does not work in these conditions, but magnetometers do, provided you can keep them dry. This proved difficult, because sheets of rain were sweeping along the wavetops of a violently agitated sea, as Harknett's 26-ft. motor boat plough-ed into it. This type of instrument detects anomalies in the earth's magnetic field and had been used on land to find kilns, fireplaces and sites of that sort now lying invisible under the soil. In case it detected the iron keel of Harknett's boat, or the pile of chain in the forepeak, we put the instrument into the dinghy (first removing the metal rowlocks).

After two brief tests, off Spit Fort and over the wreck of the *Boyne*, we made a run from Southsea towards the *Mary Rose* site. Just before we reached it, the needle became agitated and remained so for a surprisingly long distance. We made a second run and dropped a buoy on the area of maximum agitation. Then it was up to me alone. I swam down Harknett's anchor rope, unreeling the line of my own marker buoy, for the waves were very steep by then and would hide a diver's head most of the time. The anchor rope kept pulling and plucking violently in my hand, with the force of wind and wave on the boat; the green pea soup around me turned to black, giving the impression of forcing one's head into a black velvet cushion inside a darkened room; then I felt chain in my hand and saw a tinge of grey in the dark. I was actually lying on the bottom and could see part of one fluke of the anchor, which was ploughing a furrow across the seabed. I nosed down into that furrow and breathing hard from the physical effort of swimming against a strong tidal stream, bored on up-current.

The anchor's track led me over a marked ridge and past several likely-looking lumps which, however, dissolved when I prodded them; and then I found one which did not dissolve. Thankfully, I hung on to it in that pouring tide; and began to dig. There was no doubt about it—a buried cable about 4 inches in diameter, which had no right to be there. For obvious reasons, undersea cables have to be marked on charts, and this was not on any chart; not unnaturally, as the *Mary Rose* site was in No. 3 Berth of the Spithead anchorage. When I surfaced, the waves were so steep that all I could see was sky; but Harknett had kept track of my buoy and moved in for the pick-up. On the return, his boat was literally surfing in the waves, rudder useless.

A week later we went out again, this time with two Mediterranean archaeologists—Joan du Plat Taylor and Peter Throckmorton—who must have believed that we exaggerated English Channel conditions, for the day was warm and sunny and the sea flat calm. We ran the same line, but more accurately, and obtained slight positive readings over a fairly large area. I dived with Throckmorton and found the mound again, but it was Cooke who located the cable once more. So what had the magnetometer detected: just the cable? Or the cable lying above the *Mary Rose*? I suspected the latter, and noted a very good 'mark' which would help bring me back there on demand. Later, I solved the problem posed by the cable being where no cable should be—it wasn't a cable, it was a length of old hawser (but you needed good visibility to see that).

Peter Throckmorton was one of the very few people who had dug underwater at all, let alone with care and method; he knew what results could be obtained, that the sea could be potentially a good place for the preservation of man's handiwork—the recovery of a wicker basket from a 3,000-years' old Bronze Age wreck which he had discovered off Cape Gelidonya in Turkey was a striking example. So his verdict on the possibilities of the *Mary Rose* site were

John Mills and Robert Henderson studying the unrolling graph paper from the 'pinger' (foreground) and the 'sidescanner (background) at Spithead, October 1967. Photo: Alexander McKee.

Left: The hydrophone hose of the 'pinger' after it had been nearly cut in two by the propellor and recovered by the author, October, 1967. This damage made the graph hard to interpret. Photo: Alexander Mckee.

Right: Sidescan graph of a half-mile of seabed at Spithead. *Top left*: a distinct anomaly is shown among the natural ripple patterns. It proved to be two long mounds with a depression in between, which the author interpreted as the scour mark left by the *Mary Rose* before all trace of the hull vanished from the seabed surface.

heartening—likely to be well buried to some height up the hull, well preserved, with the artefacts in good condition, and possibly even documents surviving. Digging with an airlift here should be cheap and simple, and the existence of a great naval dockyard only two miles away made a strong contrast with the barren Turkish shore off which the Pennsylvania expedition had worked.

But we were not yet excavators, we were merely the reconnaissance party without money or resources. The latest sonar instruments, which I thought were the real answer to our search problems, were then rare, expensive and with their archaeological potential virtually unknown. For the next eighteen months the few who thought them worth testing in this context— George Bass off Turkey, Robert Marx off Jamaica, Peter Throckmorton off Greece and myself at Spithead—were to be in friendly competition to obtain what in many cases was to be the same instrument, with the same operator. Ours was to be a very small and special world.

Probably its leading figure was Professor Harold E. Edgerton, of the Massachusetts Institute of Technology, an inventor and explorer of the world underwater, first by deep sea photography and then by sonar. An American, he thought little of space exploration because, as he was to tell me, 'there's nothing there'. In 1981, looking back to the years 1966–1968, 'Doc' Edgerton was to write:

As technical orchestrators of the adventure of its discovery, MIT alumnus John Mills and the author shared an exciting chapter of *Mary Rose*'s rich history. . . . As technical representative for EG & G's line of survey instrumentation, John Mills was given a demonstration model of one of the company's early sidescan sonars, type 259. While marketing the product in England he met McKee, then anxious to end his literal groping in the dark for the *Mary Rose*. McKee was quick to enlist Mills' services for an electronic survey effort.

That was in March, 1966, after a lecture by Mills at the University of London, where he showed a number of 'pinger' slides. There were technical problems still to be overcome, said Mills. Low frequencies gave good penetration of the sub-bottom sediments but did not show detail of small objects, whereas high frequencies gave good detail of unburied objects on the bottom but would not penetrate the sediments below. And where the sediments had a high organic content, this served as a reflector to the sound waves sent out by the instrument—and nothing below them was shown. Still the slides were intriguing and although I could have no idea how the *Mary Rose* would look on sonar, I was sure it would give some indication, and might provide a pattern of rapidly created, invisible, non-destructive trenches across the site.

To anyone who had seen that dismal, depressing mud plain and had calculated the man-hours and the machinery and the money that would be needed to dig trial trenches in a conventional manner, as in land archaeology, those slides with their, at first sight, unreadable complexities, were a comparative promise of paradise.

But it was not until January, 1967, that a seabed-penetrating instrument could first be freed for one day from the bread-and-butter business of North Sea oil and gas exploration. Five days of mirror-calm seas had preceded that day, but overnight snow fell and next morning an unforecast wind got up from the south-east, the deadly direction for Spithead. And there were small unavoidable delays, including a flat tyre on the vehicle bringing the instrument from Hull. Had we got underway just one hour earlier, all might have been well; but now the tide was running strongly out of Langstone Harbour, with the wind driving the seas against it at an angle. John Mills and Dr. Paul Marke rigged the instrument, a 'boomer', in the cabin of Bert Knight's hired boat, but that did not save it. As we neared Langstone Harbour bar, a monstrous freak wave rose up to overwhelm us, and Bert spun the wheel violently to meet it head on.

As the owner of an underwater camera impervious to rain or spray, I welcome such moments; but not this time. I had to use both hands just to hang on. The wave burst clean over the cabin top and swept the stern where the generator supplying the 'boomer' had been mounted. It died in a cloud of steam. Mills and Dr. Marke got it working again, and it was still working when we picked up the Southsea 'marks', turned, and lined up for the first run. But as the Gosport 'marks' began to move towards the closed position, the generator died once more. Our small boat would not lie head to sea, but hung along the crest of the waves as we tried to anchor, and nearly rolled its gunwales under. It was impossible to dive or to repair the generator. From this direction, the wind had a grip on hundreds of miles of surface water and was driving it up onto the banks and shallows of the Solent area, where the waves fought with the outgoing tidal stream.

Back at Hayling Island, my family were very worried when they learned what conditions were like outside and knew we were overdue. They walked out along the drying Winner sandbank as far as they could, and from there caught sight of the unmistakable mast and derrick of our boat, between one wave and the next. Donald Campbell had been killed in a speedboat a few days before, and a friend had been up there taking underwater pictures for television. It was this which prompted my eldest daughter to say, 'At least let's hope it's not like Campbell, and they've found him.' They were waiting at the pontoon as our boat slid alongside, very wet, decks in chaos from fallen gear, everybody very cold, very bitter, very blue, but all undeniably present, with dusk about to bring the next snowstorm. 'What fun you must have with your underwater archaeology!' people tend to remark.

We had to wait nine months, until October, 1967, before another opportunity occurred. John Mills, as British representative of 'Doc' Edgerton's company EG&G, planned a technically spectacular demonstration of private trials (the set-up was *that* new), followed by two days of customer-evaluation. He chose Southampton as his base, so that if the weather was favourable, there would be a chance to explore Spithead, while if it was bad, the almost enclosed arm of the Solent which is called Southampton Water could still be used. The weather *was* bad, Force 5 to 8 for the first three days, with gusts blowing at 70 m.p.h. on top of a big spring tide. John invited me to be present on all four days if I wished and, eager to learn the new techniques, I accepted with alacrity.

Two EG&G instruments had been combined in what was then a novel way to investigate simultaneously the seabed and the soil below it. Both worked by sending out sound pulses and then recording them on graph paper when they returned as echoes. Parts of both systems were towed astern underwater, the 'pinger' in an oil-filled length of hose, the side-scanner in a torpedo-shaped 'fish'. The controls and the graph paper were housed in flat metal boxes about the size of a large record player.

The side-scanner was dual-channel—that is, it

looked sideways to port and starboard of the boat simultaneously. It could be set for three ranges—250 feet, 500 feet, 1,000 feet—but the longer the range the larger the object had to be before it would show on the graph paper. In effect, it instantaneously mapped the seabed in paths up to 2,000 feet wide. As underwater visibility in our area at this time was two feet or less, the advantages it gave over visual search by divers or, for that matter, underwater television, were obvious; I could not understand the aversion to it shown in English academic circles. Two months earlier, in August, 1967, Dr. George Bass had secured the first-ever archaeological success with such an instrument, finding in two mornings' work a visible Roman wreck which had previously escaped even a month-long search with an underwater television camera and a towed observation chamber. These had failed to

locate so much as a single amphora lying on the bottom.

For our 'invisible' wreck we needed more than this, and so John Mills had also brought along a 'pinger'. This works like a very high-grade echo sounder and then, in addition, penetrates the sediments lying below the seafloor in a narrow band below the keel of the boat, showing the shapes and patterns of the underlying layers, rather like a knife slicing through a cake or a sandwich. But it does not tell you what the layers are composed of. These have to be interpreted on the basis of previous experience, and although a number of people had acquired skills in using the graphs for geological surveys, in October, 1967, there existed virtually no comparative information of what archaeological objects might look like if recorded by these machines, or indeed whether the machines

Example of a scour caused by a wreck. The entire beach pattern has been disturbed by the presence of such a huge 'foreign body'—the schooner *Blanche*, wrecked in Bracklesham Bay, 1910, and studied by the author as part of his 1960s project, 'Solent Ships'. Photo: Alexander McKee.

Professor Harold Edgerton operating one of his special 'pingers' at Spithead in July, 1968. Photo: Alexander McKee.

would record them at all. As far as I know, the sum total of human knowledge at that time was represented by Professor Edgerton's inconclusive experiments with a pinger on the 'Tobermory Galleon' and Doctor Bass's not then fully evaluated work on a Roman wreck off Turkey.

For the first three days, the weather was too bad to attempt Spithead; the second day also saw damage to the pinger. EG&G had hired a small steamer, the *Solent Queen*, which while turning in a sea kicked up by a Force 7 to 8 gale, entangled the pinger's hydrophone hose in the screw. Moving slowly and clanking ominously at the stern, the steamer moored to a buoy. Now all it needed was a diver—and my set was the only one on board. The current was really racing by, the turbulence around the screw and rudder buffeted me around and tried to tear my mask off; but clear visibility was at least $2\frac{1}{2}$ feet. To my surprise, we had not lost the hydrophone hose; it was wrapped round the shaft and screw together with its towline. It took me 25 minutes to cut the towline in

two strategic places and without losing the hose in the rushing torrent which was banging my cylinder against the steel hull of the steamer all the time. Next day, the hydrophone was working again, after a fashion; and the same might be said of me. At 49, such hard, high-speed work was fatiguing.

For the fourth and final day we had perfect weather and a score of potential customers aboard— oil men, a geological team from the Netherlands, people from the Home Office and the Police. At the end of the day, passing Spithead, John Mills said there was just sufficient time, perhaps ten minutes, to make a quick run or two over the *Mary Rose* site. Because the helmsman did not know our 'marks' and I was used to conning a motorboat and not a steamer, the first run passed just south of the site. As we came abeam, so the sidescanner picked up a large anomaly several hundred feet to port: a depression 200 feet long flanked by mounds 75 feet apart at the widest end pointing roughly south or south-east.

I made the next run dead along the Southsea

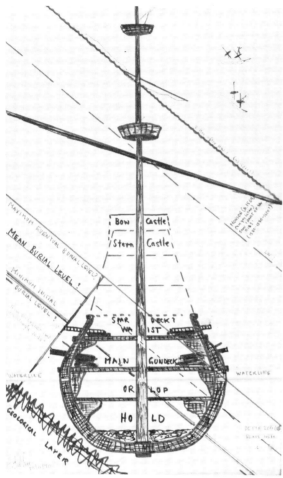

The author's interpretation of the 'pinger' graphs obtained by Professor Edgerton in 1968: a ship heeled over, with one side largely preserved, the other missing. He expected the ship to be cut off on the line marked 'Mean Burial Level', all timbers above this line being eaten and eroded. This rough drawing, made in 1970, was for the benefit of divers on the boat at Spithead. It proved to be basically correct.

'transits' and just as the Gosport 'marks' closed, so both sidescan and pinger recorded an anomaly—the one instrument on the seabed, the other below it. I made a third run and the instruments repeated once more. What the scanner had done was to pick up the pattern of mounds and depression seen by Margot and myself the previous year; what the pinger had done was to show an object possibly several feet thick 20 feet below one of the mounds, and a geological

layer at 35–40 feet. John Mills and his American colleague, Bob Henderson, were in little doubt that an anomaly unique to the area, recorded by both instruments, must mean an artificial disturbance of the seabed at that point, rather than, say, a rock formation. I could say that the alignment of the scourpit fitted that shown for the *Mary Rose* in the Cowdray Engraving and its size—200 feet by 75 feet—was what one might expect from a ship which I thought would be in the region of 150 feet long with a maximum beam of perhaps 45 feet; and it was also at the charted position of the *Mary Rose*. Optimistically, I thought we had 85 per cent proof already.

It was at this point that I formed a small committee to try to obtain legal protection in advance of any excavation, and to raise money to support a more extensive sonar survey and to build an airlift for a trial excavation. The sum in question was £250. This was turned down by one body to whom we applied on the grounds that sonar search was useless, an airlift excavation would fill-in, and to prove that there was a wreck there, we must take hundreds of core samples. Eventually, a Sunday newspaper agreed to pay the boat costs for a full pinger survey which Professor Edgerton personally was prepared to carry out for us free of charge.

Before coming to England in July, 1968, 'Doc' Edgerton had just searched a barren seabed off Jamaica where the two scuttled caravels of Columbus were supposed to lie; and had found two distinct anomalies in a simple sub-bottom strata, which when dug later by Robert Marx proved to be wooden ship remains. Arriving in Britain, the Professor went to Tobermory in Scotland for another attempt at the 'Spanish galleon', which again gave inconclusive results because in the known area of the wreck—and there only—the pinger was baffled for reasons not understood, whereas nearer to shore it had recorded at 20 feet below the seabed what proved to be large boulders. The 'Doc' and John Mills then came down to Portsmouth with two pingers, a 12 K/c instrument which did not penetrate deeply but gave fine detail and a 5 K/c instrument which gave deeper penetration with some loss of detail. They were with us for the generous period of five days in July, but on only two days did the weather allow work to be done.

It was a fascinating exercise, watching the shapes of former plains and buried hill-tops and one-time lakes appear deep below the present seabed, as traced by sonar. There was no trouble in identifying these,

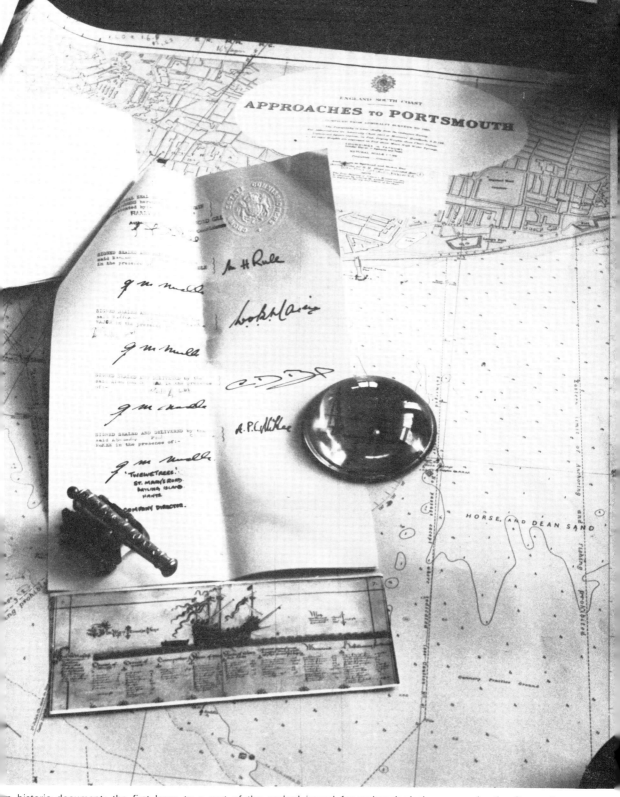

An historic document: the first lease to a part of the seabed issued for archaeological purposes by the Crown Estate Commissioners to the four members of the Mary Rose (1967) Committee in 1968. Photo: Alexander McKee.

Margot Varese at Spithead, 1966. Photo: Alexander McKee.

because Professor Edgerton had so much experience with geological interpretation. It took me three weeks to compute the results of the survey, but on 17 August I was able to write to Professor Edgerton.

To recap, we found four of what I shall call 'suspect features'. At the time, this rather threw me, as I was expecting one only. The feature which Pierce (the EG&G diver) probed and which he thought was clay showed up on every run and must therefore be more than half-a-mile in length. As it has been possible to build ships of this length only in recent years, we may dismiss the possibility of wreck and assume clay. The small feature which you told me had 20 feet of sediment on top of it showed up on only one 'track' and therefore is too small. Probably, as was suggested at the time, it is a glacial boulder, and the deep and undisturbed sediment on top would appear to indicate that it is geology rather than a 'foreign body.' The 'far out' feature with a possible 'scour' mark proved, on plotting, to be 900 feet SW of the charted position of the *Mary Rose*. You stated that this feature appeared to reach almost to the surface of the seabed, and therefore I decided to dive it when conditions were suitable. We did this on 7 August in excellent visibility of 15–20 feet, and to cut a long story short, I found myself on a hillside which may be a submerged beach, as the presence of sand and shingle at Spithead is distinctly unusual. On probing, I found a stiff clay layer underlying the apparent beach material at distances as little as 6 inches down. . . . these clay interfaces are perfectly explicable in the geological history of the Drowned Solent River Valley, which has been subjected to emergence and submergence many times. Further, the line of the 'scour' was NW/SE, which

is the line of the drowned river. Geologically, therefore, your operations were in effect an exploration of the history of this drowned valley, the tops of which are in places only 6 feet below water at low tide while the river bed lies as deep as 115 feet at low tide . . .

All these factors were important in considering the last 'suspect feature.' This is the one which is at the exact charted position of the *Mary Rose*. It is also the same feature as that picked up by the sidescanner and pinger operated by Messrs. Henderson and Mills last October; i.e., this one is a surface disturbance, as well as being sub-mud, with all its implications of an inserted 'foreign body' which I believe to be extremely relevant . . . Looking at the plotted results what we have is:

(a) an oval-shaped feature about 200 feet long headed towards No Mans Land area.
(b) the interfaces give the impression of a flattened letter 'W'. i.e., they are exceedingly angular and nothing like the rounded shapes of the clay interfaces. They are smaller at the ends than in the middle. Oh, ho!
(c) the feature appears to form some sort of discontinuity or 'break' in the geological strata, and as this cannot be the results of an earthquake the hypothesis that it results from the insertion into the seabed of 700 tons of battleship seems likely, particularly when we consider that the findings at (a) are consistent entirely with the wreck of the *Mary Rose*.

If the suspect feature proves to be the *Mary Rose*, then I expect we shall be able to claim the carrying out of the first electronic trenching survey of a sub-mud historic wreck.

A really fascinating time was over. Now came the long hard haul to get the support needed to begin the next interesting period, to dig down to the 'W' feature. To carry out even a trial excavation on a wreck completely buried in a seabed which is itself 50 feet or so under water requires heavy, costly machinery which in turn needs large, expensive boats which in their turn require substantial moorings which require permission to lay from the Harbour Master; plus a great deal of money. We had no money, no boats, no machinery, no permission. We had nothing. Except a small enthusiastic team of true volunteers, willing not merely to work without pay at weekends, but prepared to pay out of their own pockets to do so. Without them, nothing further could have been done and the *Mary Rose* would today lie silent and forgotten in her four-and-a-half centuries old grave under the seabed.

Chapter 7

'Mad Mac's Marauders'

Digging on a Shoestring, 1968–1970

OUR PRIORITY now was to excavate for proof—irrefutable evidence that the 'W' feature was indeed the remains of the *Mary Rose*. After that would come the time to ask how much remained and in what condition. Towards that proof, timber dating by the tree-ring method would be acceptable, provided that we could recover sufficiently large samples. Of course, an antique gun would establish both Tudor and warship in one, but the chances of making such a spectacular find so quickly were several hundred to one against.

We were able to dig—and thus reveal the real location of the *Mary Rose* site—because I had been successful in obtaining legal protection in spite of the fact that there was then no law to protect historic wrecks from either pillage or commercial salvage. In November, 1967, immediately following the first sonar success by Mills and Henderson, I formed a Mary Rose (1967) Committee consisting of three other people besides myself—Margaret Rule representing the Joint Archaeological Committee for Hampshire and Sussex, Mr. W. O. B. Majer representing the Society for Nautical Research, and Lt-Cdr. Alan Bax representing the Royal Navy. My chief aim with this Committee was not to change the existing laws of salvage but to use another old law in a new way.

During research for my book *Farming the Sea* (Souvenir Press, 1967) I had become aware that quite large areas of foreshore and seabed have owners, with the same rights as the owners of an ordinary land holding. The old laws had been used to protect the rights of oyster-cultivators and there were new ones to take account of exploration for gas and oil in deeper waters. The owner of the seabed at Spithead was Her Majesty Queen Elizabeth II and it was administered for her by a body called the Crown Estate Commissioners. They advised me that we might apply for a lease to an area containing the *Mary Rose*. I drafted the letter of application, stating that the purpose of the lease was archaeological prospection, attached a diagram of the *Mary Rose* heeled over on one side to show the possibilities of the site, and sent it off on 3 January, 1968. On 11 March, I received a favourable reply and the lease, at an annual rent of £1, came into effect on 1 April. I have never said a harsh word about Whitehall since!

The Board of Trade were similarly swift in agreeing to an arrangement I suggested, based on the divorce laws, that the Receiver of Wrecks should retain 'legal custody' of the sample artefacts we raised (so as to comply with the salvage laws), but that their physical control should lie with the conservation laboratory to which they were sent. Apart from stone and gold, most materials deteriorate if the equilibrium in which they have been preserved under the soil is broken by exposing them to the gas mixture breathed by human beings. So from April, 1968, we were free to excavate, but not to mark up any site on the bottom because fishermen were still allowed

One of the two 'stormboats' we were glad to borrow once a fortnight in 1969. Photo: Alexander McKee.

Barbara Andrews, diving officer of Southsea BS-AC, in telephone communication with a worker on the seabed. Note the three tiny boats which have brought out more divers. July, 1969. Photo: Alexander McKee.

to trawl and dredge there, frigates and oil tankers to anchor there. But anything we raised need not go to the Receiver of Wreck, to be kept for a year without conservation and then sold, as the existing salvage laws laid down.

The day when the four of us signed the lease was a great moment: the nightmare of pillage was lifted. Meanwhile, I had also gained immense encouragement from a succession of documentary discoveries, which had unravelled the tangled story of the work done by the early divers at Spithead, overturned completely an old falsehood, and produced new evidence concerning the *Mary Rose*. The trails I followed began in the Portsmouth Public Library, led to the Royal Engineers' Historical Society at Chatham, and from there both to the Science Museum in London and the Public Record Office. As

I leafed through the red-taped old files of the Board of Ordnance, searching for information on early diving gear, I found a thick sheaf of letters boldly headed 'MARY ROSE'. At last I had before me the full story of John Deane's discovery of the wreck in 1836, and a detailed description of the guns he raised from her and delivered to the Board. The long-accepted tale of Colonel Pasley's alleged discovery in the 1840s was totally and officially disproved. Further, the file gave exact details of the explosives which Deane had used to blow that crater. I had his actual indent before me. Not the fabulous one-ton charges, merely six 'old condemned bomb-shells'. That is, hollow 13-inch diameter cannon balls filled with gunpowder, a 'low' explosive.

I made this eye-opening discovery in November, 1966, and in July, 1967, had an equally great stroke of

...ry Tudor, sister of Henry VIII, after whom the *Mary Rose* was named, painted by an unknown artist with her second husband, ...arles Brandon, Duke of Suffolk. Photo: by kind permission of the Marquess of Tavistock, and the Trustees of the Bedford ...ates.

...less otherwise credited, the colour photographs reproduced here were taken by Alexander McKee.

From John Deane's portfolio. Deane diving at Spithead during his operations of 1832 to 1840.

From John Deane's portfolio. Two watercolours of the Tudor guns raised by Deane from the *Mary Rose* site. *Left:* Three bronze guns; *right:* Two views of an iron gun and part of another.

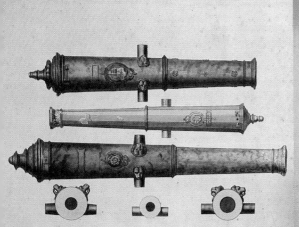

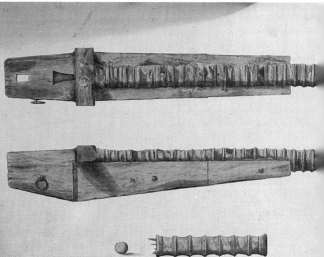

One of our early diving boats, Tony Glover's *Julie-Anne*, pitching in a heavy swell.

The results of the sonar survey at Spithead. The *Mary Rose* appears as a definite disturbance in the substrata below two mounds.

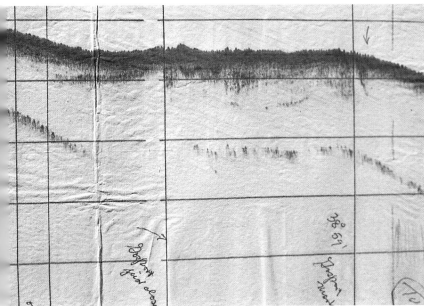

A view of Spithead, with the burning oil tanker *Pacific Glory* in the distance.

A pollack disappears into the gloom of the seabed. This was the typical murky visibility we encountered underwater.

Our inflatable boat, loaned to the Mary Rose Committee, picks up surfacing divers.

Julie-Anne as she appeared to surfacing divers.

The first timbers are exposed and measured.

On the deck of a bigger diving boat, a catamaran. Divers prepare to descend the ladder.

Airlifting the mud in the South Trench, with the diver's bubbles all around.

The surface eddy caused by the airlifting, seen from the catamaran.

Our diving platform capsizes and sinks in heavy seas. It was soon buried in the mud of the seabed.

Our logkeeper and look-out, a vital part of the operation . . .

. . . with such hazards to divers as this yacht race going on all around us.

HRH The Prince of Wales makes his first visit to the site in 1975. The author briefs him before his dive.

Photo Eric Sivyer.

During the time we were digging with spades, this notice mysteriously appeared above the trench, 50 feet under water. Photo: Alexander McKee.

luck. The Science Museum was planning an exhibition of early diving gear; I contacted them for evidence of the Royal Engineers' work on the *Royal George* and *Edgar*, and at the same time a descendant of John Deane, a Miss Muriel Pettman Pout, got in touch with them, as she possessed an actual diving manual written by him—*Method of Using Deane's Patent Diving Apparatus*. I then wrote to Miss Pettman Pout, asking about a book which I knew (from my Public Record Office file) John Deane had been planning to publish. She did not have this, but she did have what turned out to be some of the original illustrations intended for it—remarkably good watercolours of guns and other artefacts that Deane had recovered from the *Mary Rose* and other wrecks.

When I put all this evidence together I was able to produce a documented 'biography' of all the guns and many of the other artefacts that Deane had raised from the *Mary Rose*; in most cases I was also able to establish where the items were now. It meant that when, in due course, we raised the *Mary Rose*, the recoveries of the 19th century divers could be added

Pierhead briefing in Langstone Harbour, 1969. The author and George Clark (*far right*) explain how they intend to start digging with jets powered by a Portsmouth Fire Brigade pump. Photo: Portsmouth *News*.

The pump mounted on a flimsy pontoon boat. Fireman Ted Pearn is at the pump, while Sub-Officer Tom Smith holds the surface-demand air line to Station Officer George Clark, 50 feet down on the seabed. Tom is wearing overalls on top of a wet suit for work diving, which is hard on neoprene. Photo: Alexander McKee.

to our 20th century ones, making the picture complete except for unknown salvage work carried out in the 16th century by such divers as Peter Paule. With all this work behind me, the results lining the shelves of my office, I was able to turn in a happier frame of mind to the apparently impossible task of probing down to the long-buried wreck.

In fiction, 'Doc' Edgerton's pinger survey would have rallied immediate support and we would have dived happily ever after; in fact our financial sponsors went off on a world trip for three months, so we lost the summer (with visibility up to 20 feet) and the autumn, too, and were three weeks into the doubtful month of October, when an elaborate operation was misted out. 'Seven days' organisation wasted,' I noted bitterly, for it was my time and money which was going down the drain as well, and I had foreseen (and had warned of) the dangers of that season with its tendency to gales or fog. There was only one bonus from it, the test of a water-jet—a small, cheap digging tool which seemed to me to have possibilities. I was desperate to achieve some sort of success in time to fight 'the battle of the winter', so that we might gain sufficient finance to plan an orderly programme for next summer.

Hutchinson, who had published my book on underwater archaeology, *History under the Sea*, paid the boat costs for an operation late in the year, on 28 November. At first, it seemed that this would be

fogged up too, but we had a quietly determined team who sat it out for hours without question or complaint, until, briefly, the sun came out, lighting up a couple of 'marks' on shore; with that and the help of a recording echo-sounder, I was able to anchor on an outlying part of the *Mary Rose* site. The divers had been very well briefed, and even if they didn't believe in what they were doing, they nevertheless did exactly as they were told.

The third probe team that day consisted of two members of Portsmouth Fire Brigade, George Clark and Tom Smith, plus Don Bullivant, who were used to working together as a team on harbour jobs all the year round. Fourteen years later, Don recollected:

I must admit that in 1965 when I joined the Southsea Branch of the BS-AC, I had no intention of diving with Mac; in fact, members of Southsea thought his project 'Solent Ships' a little far-fetched and impossible.

But my only way of qualifying as 3rd class diver was to become one of 'Mad Mac's Marauders' with George Clark and Tom Smith. Diving on the site in those days was not very exciting. It was just after Prof. Edgerton had done his survey that dives started to change. The Prof. had indicated a position, Mac had all the cross bearings. Mac managed to get those 10-ft. long iron rods from somewhere, and gave us our instructions. Down the anchor chain, set compass, walk NE 30 yards and start pushing the rods into the mud. The rods would disappear under the mud, so pull them out, move a foot or two, probe again. This went on for approximately 15 minutes, then it happened. The rods pushed into the mud stopped after only probing four or five feet down. But move the rod back slightly, and it would disappear.

Our excitement at hitting something solid was one of our most memorable occasions. Leaving the rods sticking out of the mud I swam back and found Mac digging near the anchor. Grabbing his hand, we swam back, almost out of breath, to the rod sticking out of the mud, and demonstrating that the probing had once again discovered the *Mary Rose*. In our excitement we

George Clark talking to Tom Smith 50 feet down. The yachtsmen seem uninterested. Photo: Alexander McKee.

Left: 'Dry Jacket'! The Fire Brigade hose, rigid with the water being pumped through it at high pressure, extends below the sea surface to the seabed 50 feet below. Photo: Alexander McKee.
Right: George Clark, with the hose over his left shoulder, digging a 6 ft. deep trench 50 feet underwater. Photo: Alexander McKee.

Left: Business end: the nozzle of a fire hose blowing away the mud with a gentle stream of water. Photo: Alexander McKee.
Right: With one hand holding the hose, the other keeping direction along the guiderail, the diver works amid clouds of smoke-like sediment and bursts of bubbles from his own aqualung. Photo: Alexander McKee.

had forgotten all the rules of diving, and I believe Mac nearly lost his mask and mouthpiece during our speed tour to our probe.

I was none too keen to go with them anyway, for I had found a contact of my own, only three feet down, and was trying to dig to it. Using a four-ft. long steel hand spear painted alternately red and white in 12-inch bands, I had methodically probed the crest of the mound, pushing in at intervals of nine inches; at the third push, the hand spear came to a silent stop. That meant that it was not rock, shingle or metal. It took me three minutes to work it free—and that, too, indicated timber. In my log I wrote:

With spear free at last, I followed them along the tape to see what it was they wanted me to look at. About 30 feet

away along the crest of the mound, they had two probes in; the eight ft. iron one was sticking well out; the 12 ft. light one was bent into a 'V', having folded in the middle, such was the resistance underneath. I probed both these spots with my four ft. hand spear and met the same solid resistance about three feet down. That is to say, three points in all of a solid object were located under the crest of the mound along a 30 ft. marked line aligned along the mound.

Morrie Young and I put up the money for one last operation on 8 December. Air visibility was poor, so I used the echo sounder as well as 'marks' to make a bombing run with a heavily-weighted buoy, aiming to hit a particular mound indicated by the sounder. The drill worked beautifully, the buoy going over at exactly the right moment—but then it vanished!

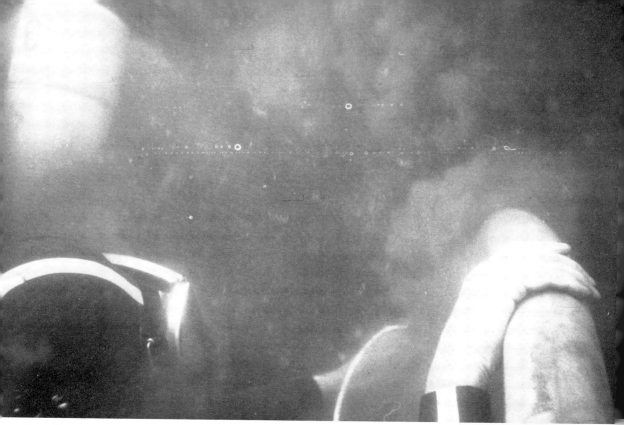

Two divers excavating with a fire hose. Photo: Alexander McKee.

Thinking that the line had tangled, I came round and repeated the procedure, this time dropping the anchor from amidships. No sooner had we done that, than up popped the buoy, six feet from our port side! I made a mock bow and apologised for careless navigation. The rest of the day went less well. George Clark, then a Station Officer of Portsmouth Fire Brigade, recollected:

In my team of professional Firemen were some members of the Southsea Branch of the BS-AC of which I had been a member for a few years. I was asked if we as a team would like to assist Alexander McKee in moving mud and silt covering a visual feature which McKee felt was the wreck of the Tudor warship *Mary Rose*.

We were patrolling an area south of Spit Sand Fort and McKee was watching some landmarks on the Gosport shore and also taking some transits on Southsea seafront. We had in the boat a buoyed weight and Mac was taking a stance and giving a preliminary order to try to bomb aim with the words 'Steady, steady—Bomb!' and one of the lads dropped the weighted buoy

Left: The seabed before excavation: a 2½-foot skate lying on heaps of slipper limpet 'chains' which cover the mud above the *Mary Rose*. No wreck is visible. Photo: Alexander Mckee.
Right: Clouds of sediment pour out of the trench after digging has stopped, creating the visual impression that the seabed is on fire. Photo: Alexander McKee.

Percy Ackland probing for contacts in the newly-dug trench which is hazy with disturbed sediments. Photo: Alexander McKee.

over the side. I thought this was all highly amusing and that this man McKee must surely be mad!

We eventually donned our diving gear and went over the side down the shot line. There was absolutely no sign of any wreck! All I could see was mounds and mounds of mud. Mac had issued us with small garden-type trowels and asked us to start digging. After a heavy and abortive dig I was convinced Mac was a crank and the idea of a Tudor warship was just a figment of his vivid imagination. He persuaded us to make further dives and we slowly added to the digging implements making the task that much easier.

My log shows that it was on this day that,

The fire-pump was run and tested for more than half an hour and proved adequate only for boring holes. It would not trench. Data regarding pressures, weights and nozzle-design effectiveness were noted and the requirements for an effective underwater trenching machine theoretically devised for next year.

It was George Clark who actually carried out this exercise:

I managed to get permission from George Brunner, the Chief Fire Officer of Portsmouth City Fire Brigade, to use the 350-gallon-a-minute Coventry Climax fire pump. My intention was to use a high-powered water jet to wash away the silt. This proved to be successful and after a few experiments in Langstone Harbour in one of the old prison hulks which was buried in sand, we proceeded out to Spithead and started the long task of blowing away sand and silt. Although still doubting Mac's theory, we had built up quite a team of volunteers and we were now going fairly regularly to the site where I was able to train our non-Fire Brigade colleagues to use the high pressure water jet.

Our amazing armada first sailed out to Spithead on 5 July, 1969, and took about two hours to get there, on top of an hour or so's loading; and, of course, a couple of hours back, and an hour's unloading. And when out there, it took time to anchor up so that the boats rode above the point on the seabed where I wanted to dig. At least the boats cost nothing. They were frail pontoons about 18 feet long, propelled by low-powered outboard motors; one was loaned by Southsea BS-AC, the other by the College of Technology in Portsmouth, on a regular basis—once a week on a Saturday. As some Saturdays were spring tides, and others blew a gale, we managed about two days per month, with six hours of each working day perforce spent unproductively, coming and going at about three knots, loading and unloading. It didn't need a gale to stop us, for the Fire Brigade pump had to to be mounted precariously, high up on one of the frail pontoons, and often our hearts were in our mouths when a sudden breeze blew up. But as our total finances had now reached a peak of £4—from the proceeds of a lecture and the contribution of one well-wisher—there was nothing to be done but get on with it.

I dived first that day, to mark up the mound, and then two 50-lb weights had to be lowered to the digging position in order to anchor the water jets, which otherwise would whip about the seabed like demented serpents, dragging the divers with them. Then, as team succeeded team, they reported progress to the surface by a telephone line which was combined with the airline of the leader's surface-demand set. They dug a six ft. by six ft. trench along the mound for 15 feet and, once they had dug themselves six feet into the seabed there was no visibility at all. I noted in my log:

While trenching, Clark found an object six feet down

The first contact, 7 feet down, proved to be an eroded ship's plank. Morrie Young explains the fastenings to Andy Gallagher, a diver-Fireman from Chichester. Photo: Alexander McKee.

which he gave to Parr to hold. It slipped out of Parr's grasp and fell into the trench and was lost. Parr said it was wood, and this was reported to us on the surface, so we had high hopes for a moment. On intercom, George said there were wonderful photographs to be obtained of the mud welling up; so I put on the tads and joined him.

George appeared to be swimming forward with a heaving motion through the seabed, immersed to the shoulders in the trench, and towing intercom line (orange), surface-demand line (black) and the hose (white-grey canvas). No difficulty in seeing these, because the bulk of the mud did not rise high at once, but welled from around his shoulders. It was like looking down from an aeroplane on a man walking jerkily through the clouds, with only his head and shoulders visible. A kind of off-grey, slow-swirling pattern of convoluted circles, evolving in slow motion from around George's head and shoulders as he dug the trench forward. He had a peculiar kind of bounding motion, half-swimming, half-walking, with this immense, intricately entwined mud pattern unrolling around him. It was extraordinarily beautiful, particularly when the silver bubbles burst up through the slow-motion patterns of the welling mud.

At the end of the day, Morrie Young noted that in the very deepest part of the trench a layer of stratification had been exposed, consisting of light shell and grit. This suggested an old seabed, possibly the Tudor one. In conjunction with the timber found at that depth, it looked as if we might have hit the

Mr. S. J. Utley, a Portsmouth Dockyard diver, about to go down to the *Mary Rose* in 1969, the first 'hard hat' man to do so since 1840. Talking to him at the top of the ladder are the author (*left*) and George Clark (*right*). Photo: Alexander McKee.

disturbance area around the *Mary Rose*, for probing revealed no structure. But what sort of structure were we likely to find? There were two theoretical alternatives, based on depth of burial initially. Either it could have collapsed by stages as the upper parts were eaten and eroded away, leaving a partly flattened-out hull, or a deeply-buried hull might have been strong enough to retain its original shape, the unburied part only being eaten and eroded away to leave, in a steeply-heeled ship, a virtually one-sided wreck open on that side like a doll's house. Because his knowledge of ship structure and its weaknesses was so much greater than mine, Morrie undertook to work out a theoretical collapse sequence, while I explored the optimistic alternative of the 'W' feature being a sonar reflection of the slanted decks and supports of a hull heeled at 45 degrees, cut off at a point I still had to determine. I also produced a site plan based on the many 'pinger' runs along known transits, as a guide to deciding where it might be best to dig trial trenches. These would not be where the 'W' came closest to the surface, at the south end of the site, because a shallow excavation would expose the remains to the destructive action of anchors, trawls and oyster dredges.

The summer of 1969 proved to be the best for ten years with underwater visibility up to 25 feet at Spithead, 40 feet at more favoured places off the Isle of Wight. In July we made three more sorties, having to turn back only once. George Clark and the other firemen began to instruct the rest of the team in the use of the water jets. A trained fireman using a branch and hose was one thing, but there had to be modifications for those lacking experience. One of those who took most readily to the method was Dick Millerchip, an aircraft engineer:

I vividly recall one memorable dive. It was in the earliest days of the fire pump, which was lashed to the deck of our dive boat with twin hoses dangling over the side. I was down on the seabed, holding the nozzle, when the signal was given to switch on. I was immediately propelled to the surface by the force of the water, still clutching the nozzle. Never before or since, have I arrived at the surface from 50 feet in such a short time. It was hilariously unsatisfactory.

The next step was to attach heavy weights to the nozzle by means of short lines, as a basic anchorage to prevent me losing control. My recollection is of one half-hundredweight sinker on about three feet of line. We then prepared for another trial! The signal was again given and the pump restarted. This time, although straining at its tether, it was crudely controllable.

The results were quite dramatic. As the jet of water cut into the clay, visibility was immediately reduced to zero and one could only hang on and hopefully direct the jet at the clearance area. After ten or fifteen minutes the pump was stopped and the tide permitted to clear away the clouds of mud: one could then see the incredible results of this primitive but highly effective method of seabed excavation.

This early dive was mainly experimental, to arrive at the most manageable weight and length of line required to effect a satisfactory anchorage.

Later, I introduced a weighted guide rail which both tethered the jet and indicated direction. The trenches tended to 'smoke' for some time after digging had ceased and even after a week or more were very sensitive to water movement, belching up sediment if ships went overhead or a diver finned hard. They also tended to fill up with dense accumulations of the loose weed which circulates in masses at certain times of the year. After a short time they collected a permanent population of fish—the pretty, black-and-silver-striped whiting pout to begin with, then the big, green pollack as well—species which previously we saw only around wrecks and in rock areas. These were the most prominent colonisers of the trench, but there were many others.

I was ready to try anything once, but when first offered the use of a crane-grab dredger turned it down as probably too brutal for archaeology. But what we were doing was only the first stage—stripping off the overburden. At the second time of offering, I accepted, by then knowing much more of the composition and depth of the soil laid down since Tudor times. The dredger was 180 feet long and the depth of dig could be pre-set by the crane operator. By using a gravity-powered mud grab, a surprising amount of sensitivity could be obtained; so much so, that I feared this grab might not penetrate the consolidated layer of grit and shell which, we now knew, could be found some six feet down. The dig revealed an interesting, if expected, pattern. From the top layer came slipper limpets, indignant hermit crabs and unspeakable sponges. There were few artefacts in the first five feet, but under that was a distinct layer of anchorage 'gash', mainly modern, similar to that which lay unburied on the harder *Royal George* site: a strip of lead, a concreted staunchion, clay pipes, pottery, animal bones, and an enormous glass jug. In two days we removed 480 cubic yards of overburden and only once did I ask the crane driver to penetrate the shell and grit layer. The immediate result was a very old elm plank, holed by gribble, and found loose; exactly what one would expect to lie on and around the wreck of the *Mary Rose*.

A team of helmet divers from Portsmouth Dockyard, led by Mr. S. J. Utley, offered their services; and I gladly accepted. With aqualungs we had to change over shifts of two men every twenty minutes, and in near zero visibility, whereas only one helmet diver was required on a jet, and he could stay one or two hours at a time, if necessary. He could also make himself heavy at will, was in telephone communication with the surface and would almost certainly survive a cave-in of a trench, whereas an aqualung diver almost certainly would not. Moreover, this team possessed a waterjet of their own which had been designed for the job and was automatically balanced by a reaction device.

Any connection with the organisation of land archaeology was purely fortuitous. The helmet divers and their compressor were in one boat, which must be positioned exactly and could not drag its anchor without endangering the diver; while the pump for the water jet was in another boat which had to lie close by; the helmet men had to be guided directly from their boat to the particular part of the seabed where the guide rail was. The closest analogy would be to imagine oneself above a bank of cloud, trying to drop plumb lines on exact spots on the earth below from a couple of barrage balloons kiting about in a gusty wind, while attached to insecurely fixed winches. You cannot, alas, apply the brakes and park on a wave.

However, it all worked perfectly, and I saw Mr. Utley's helmet disappear into the green water, the first helmet diver to visit the *Mary Rose* since John Deane in October, 1840, almost 130 years before. A continuous stream of air boiled to the surface above him, supplied by the big dockyard compressor roaring away at my ear; in contrast to the bursts of bubbles which mark the breathing rhythm of an aqualung diver. The weather was perfect, with only a slight swell. Then there was a tremendous bang and I saw rubber rings fly out of the compressor before it died. And Utley was fifty feet down, without air. I was immensely relieved to see him rise slowly to the surface and be rapidly hauled in to the side of the boat by his safety line. The irony of the accident was that he had been careful to obtain a newly-overhauled

compressor instead of the old one his team normally used.

The aqualungers, many of them new recruits and inexperienced with jets, had to carry on the job alone; but briefed by George Clark, they succeeded. On my last dive of the day, at sunset, I found myself four feet below the seabed with the side of the excavation above me, like a moonscape without shadow, until the striped pout moved in so close-packed that I couldn't even see water, let alone seabed or trench. Outside my mask was simply a wall of living fish. We had all suffered from the insidious 'clay psychosis', the deep conviction that nothing would shift enough of the seabed this side of Christmas. But now we had a continuous trench for the full 38 feet of the guide rail, five feet wide, three feet deep at one end, six feet deep at the other. We could probe for contacts along it.

As a further boost to our morale, the Royal Engineers Diving School at Marchwood, near Southampton, had offered to run their next advanced course for diving supervisors at Spithead, using a massive one-ton airlift with an eight-inch diameter tube powered by a gigantic compressor. Through no fault of theirs, or ours, this excellent plan became less promising. They had to alter their dates, and most of our divers who had arranged to take unpaid time off work could not alter at short notice. Instead of a low-profile 'Z' craft mounting a mobile Coles crane to suspend the airlift and move it about, they had to use a high-sided RPL without a crane; with bow doors down, this 74 ft.-long landing craft made an excellent diving platform, but it caught the wind and kept veering about; and when we asked for moorings from another authority, we were refused. On the first day, fog delayed everything, followed by mechanical troubles. But the next day was the 21st of October, when Portsmouth celebrates Trafalgar Day: a good omen, we hoped.

For an hour or two the RPL held position. First, I tried a delimitation hole on the Isle of Wight side of the 'W' feature; the airlift went in 17 feet in a few minutes, when the air was turned off to avoid a blockage—a firm negative. Then I had the RPL dropped back towards Southsea so that it lay over the outskirts of the disturbance area. Sergeant Ferguson, the R.E. diver, dug a funnel-shaped cavity to eight feet and then came up to report trouble. Pete Powell, from Southampton BS-AC, guessed that the airlift had been stopped by something solid and went down with a manual corer made by Morrie Young. Lying head

Unless otherwise credited, the colour photographs reproduced here were taken by Alexander McKee.

A diver with the survey gear beside the water pump for backfill.

Using the airlift, a diver excavates at the stern of the *Mary Rose*.

Fourteen feet down into the mud at the stern, and the keel is exposed.

The fantastic colours of the stern post.

A pout above the eroded top timbers of the port quarter. Lower down they were still intact.

Pout at the stern on the port side. Not normally found in a muddy environment, they became our permanent companions.

The carriage and breech of a bronze gun as we uncovered it.

A dramatic and pathetic find: the bones of a drowned pikeman, at the stern of the ship.

Our floodlight illuminates a bronze gun, rope and basket lying well preserved among the timbers.

Torchlight reveals the muzzle of an iron gun in our more usual bad visibility.

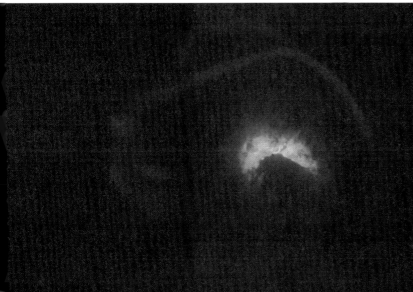

The bronze gun shown on the opposite page, raised to the deck of our diving ship.

Excavating the gun deck: a bronze gun with shot piled around it.

Another bronze gun amid a confusion of shot and fallen timber.

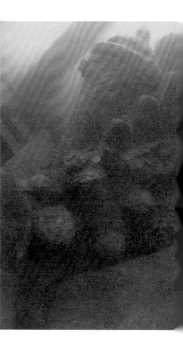

The exposed gunport in the stern castle.

Pollack swimming among the
deplanked timbers of the carling.

A shoal of pollack around a main
deck beam, with the team's grid
in the foreground.

A skull unearthed beside a
swivelgun.

The diving ship *Sleipner,* our final headquarters for diving operations.

The author suited up for a dive from *Sleipner.* Photo: Reg Vallentine.

The Royal Engineers arrive in 1969, the successors to Colonel Pasley's Sappers and Miners who worked at Spithead from 1839 to 1844. Photo: Alexander McKee.

down in the cavity, he put the corer into the solid and brought up a sample of it—splinters of dark wood mixed with tiny shellfish. Lance-Corporal Flannigan was next; after digging a bit, he probed in a circle: 'I got solid—solid—solid every time. Not a plank, but definitely solid timber.' Then the RPL veered with the wind and tide and dragged the airlift out of the hole.

Next day, the RPL hung perfectly positioned for three hours during which the airlift broke down three

Aboard the 74-ft. landing craft used by the Royal Engineers. Note the size of the compressor required to power an 8-inch airlift. Photo: Alexander McKee.

times and was three times repaired. Only one useful cavity was dug, in which Percy Ackland of Southampton BS-AC used a hammer to drive home a probe into some soft solid, perhaps an iron concretion, he thought. The last two days of 'R.E. Week' were ruined by high winds.

The last chance of the year was on 2 November, exhausting in further boat fees the last pennies of the £50 which had financed the season's work. I planned to use aqualungers *en masse* to probe for shallow contacts less than six feet down, and helmet divers with a waterjet to expose anything they found. I led off myself, followed by Ackland and Powell.

> The buoy was bucking and smashing and throwing up white water, the chain was shaking and jerking all the way down. Visibility on bottom a very clear 12 feet. Water warm for November.

South of our main trench I found a subsidiary excavation made by the dredger, some three or four feet deep—and in the bottom of it my hand spear went

On the deck of a dredger, 1969. Maurice Young with Pete Powell and Reg Cloudsdale inspecting a shoe and a piece of rope recovered from the upper layers. Smeared with mud, their dating is not at first obvious. In fact they are modern. Photo: Alexander McKee.

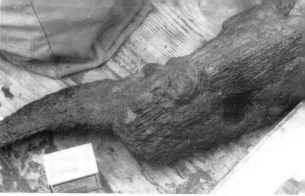

When the grab of the dredger was set to go deep, it produced (undamaged) scattered timbers from the *Mary Rose*, such as this eroded cleat. 1970. Photo: Alexander Mckee.

in full-length the first time, and stopped two or three feet down the second time. Exactly the easy depth required, which could be cleared during a short winter's day! Around it, Peter Powell got no contacts even eight feet down. This did not mean that it was not structure, because a wreck rarely presents a flat surface upwards. We then marked it up so that a water jet and weight could be lowered to it—an action I was bitterly to regret. I should have ordered an immediate hand-dig, less thorough but much simpler.

It was blowing Force 6 with high waves and white horses, but the two boats were riding easily together at their anchors—one boat carrying the helmet divers and their compressor, the other holding the aqualung divers and the fire pump. The contact was securely buoyed, the weight was down, and a Chichester fireman, Andy Gallagher, was swimming out the hose to the buoy. Perhaps the extra drag caused it, perhaps the veering breeze; or both together. With shocking suddenness, the pump boat went out of control, dragging her anchor to port. Tony Glover, our skipper, started his engine and put the wheel hard over, but there was no observable effect. It seemed that the pump boat must collide with the helmet divers' boat. That was the least of it, for Andy Gallagher was down on the seabed in what must now be a tangle of swinging, dragging lines; and the pump would probably be pulled bodily out of the boat on top of him.

Instantly, George Clark uncoupled the hose from the pump. With equal speed, some of the divers snatched the yellow line leading to the 56-lb weight beside the contact, and threw it out over the sea to the

men in the helmet divers' pinnace, who caught it. We still had a line to the contact from a boat, plus a bottom line from a marker buoy. What we did not know was that the anchor of the pump boat had dragged across in a crazy tangle, with Andy Gallagher in the middle of it. By quick thinking, 45 feet down, he escaped and reached the white-capped sea. We roared out to him to swim down tide to a marker buoy and hold on to it. Then Dick Millerchip went racing by in his inflatable and with Leslie Lemin leaning right over the side they picked Andy out of the water, very flushed, excited and pleased with himself.

Mr. Utley sent a helmet diver down at once and I jumped from the pump boat to the pinnace to listen to the crackling telephone as his diver reported: all lines carried away, my contact no longer marked. Back to square one. I put in Percy Ackland to make another search and against all odds, by following the drag marks through the mud, he found the contact; but he was out of air, so he gave the distance line to his companion to secure. But here the drawbacks to the aqualung showed: divers cannot talk to each other and they are blinkered like horses. His friend had not even seen the drag marks and did not understand that the contact crater had been relocated. So he just carried on swimming.

And that really was that, for 1969. But no one wanted to pack up yet, so I suggested a general survey of the excavated area to take note of any changes that might occur during the winter. For George Clark and myself, this meant the luxury of a dive instead of controlling events from the surface. George went first.

There was a great swell running, and although I had carried out one dive, I felt the last place for me was down on the seabed. However, by this stage of the project we had a fairly long trench several feet deep running in the

Above: The crew of the dredger did not believe that this weirdly concreted object could be a gun. But it was, and it positively identified the *Mary Rose*. September, 1970. Photo: Alexander McKee.

Below: Part of the concretion broke away to reveal a blue-grey metal gun-ring, exactly the colour shown in Tudor paintings. Photo: Alexander McKee.

direction which Mac felt would lie across the wreck. I was swimming along this trench, glad to be off the rolling boat, when I saw through the murky water what I thought was a large piece of newspaper lying against the trench. I slowly swam over to it and much to my surprise it was an enormous flatfish. I almost burst with excitement. I stopped breathing and was frightened to move for fear of spooking this fish. If I told my pals above about this monster of the deep, no doubt they would think it a fishy tale!

I slowly passed the tube of Morrie Young's auger through my hands, hoping I could impale the fish with it, only to find that I had the wrong end of the pipe. By sheer luck the fish remained motionless as I laboriously handled the pipe to get the other end. I aimed at the bit beneath the head and then placed it into the fish, screwing it into the mud. The creature went berserk and the slightly clouded water erupted into a big violent cloud of black ink. Visibility had completely gone and I was plunged into darkness. I managed to get my hands on the fish which was now well and truly impaled and flapping about like a Vulcan bomber. Slowly I made my way to the surface where the boat was prancing up and down like a wild horse at a rodeo.

When they saw me wrestling with a 10-lb turbot, one of the divers managed to come down the boarding ladder and take the fish inboard.

I missed this spectacle, because I was already absorbed in my last inspection dive of the year. When I surfaced, Force 8 was almost upon us; we would never get back to Langstone Harbour by sea, so our

The 1970 gun, roughly splinted with timber to spread the load, is lifted by Dockyard crane into a lorry waiting to take it to the conservation laboratory at Southsea Castle.
Photo: Alexander McKee.

Left: Peter Aitcheson explains his firm's compressor to Pete Powell, Reg Cloudsdale and Percy Ackland, who became early veterans of airlifting. 1970. Photo: Alexander McKee.

Right: Snagged! Learning by experience, we soon learned how to rig the airlift without (as here) getting the airhose through a buoyline. Photo: Alexander Mckee.

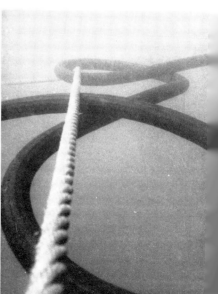

boats fled for the shelter of Portsmouth Harbour. George Clark was good enough to write later that, 'There was no doubt whatever that had it not been for Mac's enthusiasm and drive the whole project would have been dropped long ago; his perseverance has kept it alive.' Actually it worked both ways: the team spirit and determination shown on days like this encouraged me to continue when, as happened now and then, everything seemed hopeless.

It seemed that 1970 might be such a year. We lost George Clark, the Fire Brigade chief, sent off on a three-months course; we lost Mr. Utley, the leader of the helmet divers, drafted for three years to Gibraltar; we seemed likely to lose Lieutenant Bob Lusty, drafted to HMS *Reclaim* as diving officer to replace a casualty; and I learned in April that the person who was supposed to be making our application in March to Portsmouth City Council for a £100 grant, had failed to do so at all, let alone in time.

These setbacks only made us the more determined. A baker's dozen of us decided to band together as the Mary Rose Association, paying all costs out of our own pockets. We were able to do this because of an offer from Tony Glover for the use, one day a week at cost, of his boat *Julie-Anne*, which amounted to £7 10s. 0d. (compared to the £20-£25 a day such a boat would normally cost). As it was licensed for 12 people only, we all agreed to pay a minimum of 10/- per trip, the difference if any to be made up by myself. *Julie-Anne* was a converted *Queen Mary* lifeboat with plenty of open space at the back for mounting heavy machinery, stowing cylinders and kitting up, while the forward end gave semi-covered protection out of the wind for half-frozen, damp divers. Also, it was based at Flathouse Quay in Portsmouth Harbour, about four miles from the site, thus avoiding the long, slow haul round from Langstone Harbour which had in the past cost us so much precious working time. Tony, however, did not get quite what he expected.

I saw an article in the Portsmouth *Evening News* by Alexander McKee about this old wreck, saying he could not get a boat to take them out; so I phoned him. He then told me they never had a lot of funds available. Anyway, I thought I would make lots of money with all the 'pieces of eight' that might come up. I quickly realised what I was into: lifting compressors and water pumps onto my boat; other boats tied alongside; the compressor shaking my boat to pieces; and the biggest headache—anchors that would not hold in the soft mud.

This was a problem every time; then I laid some moorings on site and this helped.

We still had no permission to lay buoys as surface moorings or mark the site in any way; it had to be laboriously rediscovered every time. As a temporary expedient, I now laid 'drowned' moorings. Morrie Young made the concrete blocks, someone else supplied the wire hawsers to connect them in a line, another source supplied the manila which, when picked up, we would take to the surface for Tony to tie on. No more problems with anchors dragging, but the ropes had to be visually located by diver search; in visibilities often of only two or three feet, this also could be time-wasting. On 16 May the new moorings were laid and the trench inspected after the winter. It had filled in only slightly with soil. On 30 May I had the trench staked out with numbered rods at measured intervals, and further probing produced more contacts in it, which were marked up with lettered rods.

Andy Gallagher's contact was the shallowest, only two feet below the bottom of the trench which was five feet deep at that point. I sent down a succession of divers to expose it by hand-digging. Several took samples in case by some dreadful mischance—to which we had become accustomed—we lost it again. One diver reported: 'We are not going to get any more off today—best to open up a bit more. It's a deck beam, I think. I should say it's part of the ship.'

I dived at six in the evening. In the floor of the trench was a further excavation four feet deep, and dark in the dim light. As I sank down into the hole I did not expect to see much, so it was quite a feeling when for the first time my eyes focused on wood. Some five feet of timber about a foot wide was exposed there, both ends continuing in to the faces of the excavation, and part of it already lightly dusted over with sediment. The last diver had dug down beside the timber and then excavated underneath, so that I could see plainly that it was a plank, not a beam, a number of trenail holes showing where it had been pegged to a ship's frames. I wrote in my log:

My impression was that this was not part of the ship's structure in situ, but a piece broken off or collected.

This turned out to be the case. Morrie Young thought the stagger of the fastenings indicated frames of approximately 12-inch siding; about right for the *Mary Rose*; and so it proved, in due course.

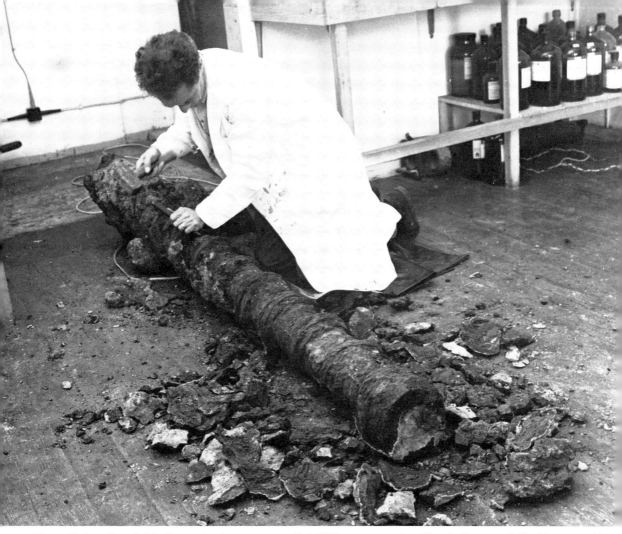

The multi-ringed barrel of the first gun begins to appear as Chris O'Shea, conservation officer for Portsmouth City Museums, chips off the concretion. Photo: Bertram Lemmon.

We spent three days carefully excavating around the plank before we lifted it, to determine its context; there was some evidence for a scourpit having existed at that point. To dig out the ends meant working into walls of clay and mud some eight feet high, mostly with our hands and a spade. Once, a partial collapse lightly buried my legs, but this was more alarming than dangerous; nevertheless, the utter silence in which the underwater wall collapsed on me was intimidating. There was no warning at all. After the plank had been raised I made a last inspection and found that the lads, assisted by my daughters, had played a joke on me. There, standing on the edge of the trench, was one of those well-known road signs depicting a man with a spade. A minute inspection of

the bed where the plank had lain produced only a single artefact—a car key belonging to the diving officer of Southsea BS-AC. He was relieved to get it back.

The plank, which was badly eroded and showing marks of gribble and massive teredo attack, was drawn, photographed and expended scientifically. The better preserved end was to go to Margaret Rule's laboratory at Fishbourne for conservation tests with polyethylene glycol, the end most massively infested by teredo was to go to Patrick Board of the Central Electricity Research Laboratories who had developed extraordinarily fine techniques for X-raying teredo tunnels so that the habits of what is in fact a mollusc, not a worm, could be studied accurately. The sawing in two of the plank, which had the look and feel of soft, black, flaky cheese, produced the first surprise, for as the blade bit deep, there came an unexpectedly harsh noise—and sawdust! The second surprise was when the X-rays revealed not merely the species of mollusc—*Nototeredo norvavica*—but the remains of an actual specimen in one of the tunnels, probably the oldest teredo in existence. Lying underneath the plank we had found part of a ship's lantern dated to around 1700, suggesting that the scourpits were active even then. As teredo is very rare in the Solent area today, the evidence pointed to a change in the local underwater environment.

The next contact I decided to investigate was nearer to Southsea and the 'W' feature in what was now a 100 ft. long trench overlapping it on both sides; this contact was also deeper, but as we had the Fire Brigade with us again, it seemed worth a try. We also had, for one day only, the loan of a miniature airlift for test purposes. This consisted of a $2\frac{1}{2}$-inch diameter plastic tube 10 feet long, powered by a small compressor which fed air down through a rubber hose to the bottom of the tube. The compressed air should rise up the tube, expanding it as it went, creating a suction effect at the bottom; and, with this size of tube, all our troubles would be little ones. While the jetting went on 50 feet down, I put the airlift over my shoulder like a rifle at the slope, and swam with it down the fire hose leading to the waterjet.

On removing the concretion round the breech, Chris O'Shea discovered this shiny, almost mint-condition iron shot and rope wadding. The last hand before his to touch it was a Tudor seaman in the *Mary Rose*, probably on the day of battle. Photo: Portsmouth City Museums.

The first sign of the jet work was a white cloud of murk ('whiteout'), which meant trailing one finger along the seabed to try to feel when you came to the trench. Then there was a colour change of the murk from white to black ('blackout'). Occasionally, the whirling cloud broke up and one could look along a kind of tunnel some six feet below the seabed. I stopped for a test. I turned the tap on and compressed air gushed in and began to roar up the tube. I sucked at various distances from the seabed and found that, although the miniature machine could not clear the massive murk being stirred up ahead, it did improve my local visibility, in contrast to the jet, which made the worker blind. When we ceased to deal with mere overburden, the airlift was clearly the tool to use. At this size it was controllable and selective, capable of really delicate work. My logbook notes read:

> I spotted a small crab among the slipper limpets and moved the end of the tube over his back. ZING! BLAM! SWOOSH! and he had gone, taking a fast ride up the tube, and presumably being released in something of a state eight feet up and down tide. Then I started on the slipper limpets, and a stream of them followed the crab heavenwards. WHOOSH! ZING! BLAM! OOUCH!

The power was controllable in no less than two ways. Basically, by turning the tap a little or a lot, but also by varying the height of the tube above the seabed. One could use merely a touch of power, so that the effect on the sediments was minute. The trick was not to let the airlift dig itself into the ground, where it was liable to blockage, but to hold it always above the seabed at the appropriate sucking distance, so that it kept visibility clear while one dug manually. Easy at this size, we should have to learn how to perform the feat with a much larger and more powerful machine.

The contact being dug by the jets at this time was where the main trench was only about $3\frac{1}{2}$ feet deep. By 8 August the shaft being driven towards the contact was at least $3\frac{1}{2}$ feet deeper still, for a width of six feet—a classic cave-in situation. So my next order must be to widen, not deepen. While I was considering this,

> I inspected the walls for stratification. Near the top and some four feet from the original seabed level, there was a marked black discoloration. I took a sample, which felt fibrous to the touch. It proved to be the remains of an old weed bed, and consisted of: weed holdfasts only (no fronds) and some part of their attachments—small fragments of glass mixed with tiny pebbles and molluscs.

The Tudor gun conserved and on display in Southsea Castle. Photo: Alexander McKee.

This evidence of past organic activity and the presence of some major collection area was 'locked in' under at least four feet of mud and clay.

On my second inspection dive, after further digging had taken place, I noticed little puffs of sediment bursting up through the clay, and actually managed to photograph one of these as it erupted. I thought this might be caused by the decaying organic matter building up gas which had been trapped by the clay layer above, until our jets removed most of it and the compressed gas was able to burst through. Suggesting how the weed got there in the first place was easy — all our trenches filled with weed in short order. And a scourpit is only a kind of trench dug by the tides. But wrecks also tend to fill up with this loose weed which drifts across the bottom or just off the seabed. Only a few days before I had been looking down an open hatch in the deck of a First World War German submarine, UB-21, and the boat seemed to be filled entirely by masses of dead weed.

It was entirely possible, I now thought, that the 'W' feature shown by Professor Edgerton's pingers might not, strictly speaking, be the *Mary Rose*, but rather a layer of dense, dead weed which had collected in and around her. The ship itself would of course become an attachment surface not only for weed but for many other organisms, particularly oysters, so there would be a growth-and-death sequence lasting perhaps a century or more on the wreck itself.

A week later we had our first full-size airlift built

for us by William Selwood Ltd, a plant-hire firm near Southampton. Of six-inch diameter, it was powered by a moderate-sized compressor which was capable of being manhandled into Tony Glover's *Julie-Anne*. The tube was light and semi-flexible and would require a weight to anchor it; it would not of its own weight sit on the seabed and damage artefacts or structure. The first time, it worked like a dream, swiftly cutting trenches with vertical faces. The second time, it seemed to have hardly any effect (being partially blocked); and by now we were down to our last few pounds and the good August weather was almost over. I decided to play last year's two major cards again — two days' work with the crane dredger followed by five days with the Royal Engineers.

Now, with more experience of the use of the mud-grab on the dredger and of the actual soil layers we would be excavating, I first cleared overburden on both sides of the trench, so that it could be widened easily; and then, with caution, began to enter the clay layer. Without damaging them, the grab raised two pieces of ship's timber from this level — part of a teredo-infested 'fashion piece' and a large 'staghorn', or cleat, which had not been attacked by teredo at all.

On the last of the two days, I decided to excavate deeply into the mound in the area where the concreted iron contact had been located eight feet down by the Royal Engineers the previous year. I had Morrie Young and Percy Ackland with me, to dive if necessary.

At 12.20 a very large concreted object appeared, so big that it was held between the jaws of the grab. Morrie commented later that I went into 'a state of shock'.

It was many years now since I had dreamed of finding clear, dramatic proof that the site held the wreck of the *Mary Rose*—some single object, such as a built-up gun or a dead archer, which by itself, on top of the circumstantial evidence, would be conclusive. This object was like a long, thin sausage with knobs on it at intervals. I began to shout to the crane driver to be careful, I thought it was a built-up gun—and immediately found myself trying to explain the difference between 'built-up' and 'cast'. We managed to get ropes round and so lowered it to the deck (instead of dumping it in the hold). There was a slight bump as it touched the deck and about three inches of the concretion broke off, exposing a triple ring of grey metal. The crew looked totally disbelieving: 'You don't mean to tell us that's a gun!' they said. But by God it was!

They hosed down the concretion, which was studded with oyster valves, some stained yellow. This was exactly as John Deane had shown in his watercolours. But what did surprise me was the grey-blue, sharp-edged metal exposed where the concretion had broken off. This was exactly the colour of built-up guns shown in Tudor paintings, but from long study of such pieces recovered from the sea, I had come to think of them always in their rusted, degenerate state. What I was looking at now, for about ten minutes before it too rusted over, was the barrel of a built-up gun as it had appeared before the ship sank. However, within five minutes, we became aware of an insistent hissing noise coming from inside the concretion. The gun was not really in mint condition. It had gone through the classic process of deterioration and chemical change set up by immersion in salt water, had been buried and eventually become stable in an oxygen-free environment below the seabed; but now that I had lifted it back into its original environment, the gun was changing again and deteriorating further.

On shore at Southsea Castle, little more than a mile away, was a conservation laboratory used to dealing with guns. I got the dredger's master to radio a message for either Ken Barton or Bill Corney of Portsmouth City Museums:

> Have what appears to be built-up iron gun from *Mary Rose*, same size as yours or larger. Collect today at RCY 5 p.m. Bubbling already.

After so many years of being denigrated behind my back as a mad chaser after wild geese, it was with great satisfaction that I saw that message go off.

Left: A gamma-ray picture taken through the breech-end of the 1970 gun. The thin line shows that the barrel had been welded rather than 'built-up' of many staves, as most wrought-iron guns were.

Right: Another 'see-through' picture from 1970: X-ray through the first plank to be dug and raised shows not merely tunnels made by teredo, but part of an actual specimen of *Nototeredo norvatica*, preserved probably from Tudor times. Photo: Central Electricity Research Laboratories.

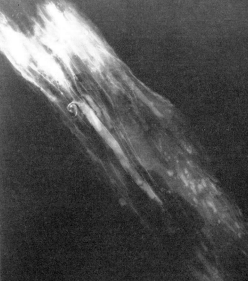

Chapter 8

'Unremitting Toil'

FOR THE last dig of 1970 we were without our firemen. We could see where they were working that day from the 20-miles long banner of smoke stretching from Bonchurch Down to Selsey Bill, marking the 42,000-ton oil tanker *Pacific Glory* burning south of the Wight. Even without their help, we were able to establish that the gun had been a single find; there was no solid structure near the hole from which it had come. Perhaps a castle had carried away, or either the Tudor salvors or John Deane had had an accident. Analysis pointed to the latter. But there were two surprises in store.

When the concretion was knocked off by the conservationist, Chris O'Shea, he found that the bed and chamber were missing; we had only a barrel some $7\frac{1}{2}$ feet long with a bore of $3\frac{3}{4}$ inches. At the breech end he uncovered primed gunpowder—and then gleaming metal! In the breech, wadded in hemp, was a shiny $3\frac{1}{2}$-inch diameter iron shot. The last human hand to touch it before him had been a Tudor gunner in 1545. The thought awed him.

These comparatively weak built-up guns normally fired the lighter stone shot, not cast iron; but that too was to be explained. The first stage of conservation was a long immersion in an electrolytic bath. This removed the salt but substituted hydrogen, which had to be burnt out by placing the gun in an industrial oven for four hours at a temperature of exactly 220° Centigrade. After this had been done, the barrel was unsuccessfully X-rayed to find details of construction. Then the gamma ray or 'cobalt bomb' method was tried, giving through wrought-iron a negative image similar to those obtained by Patrick Board's X-rays of teredoes through timber. The results gave me a shock. It was not a built-up gun! The rings were there all right, shrunk onto the barrel to hold it together. But there were no staves. Instead, the negatives showed a single white line—a weld! The barrel had been made from a single sheet

of wrought-iron, instead of many thin strips, rolled round a core, and then rough-welded. This method would produce a stronger gun, explaining why it fired iron shot and enabling me to identify it among the strange names on the gun lists: a sling, known to cost much more than an ordinary iron piece. The gun was evidence of that bounding Tudor technology of which the *Mary Rose* herself was a part, but which the documents could only hint at.

The gun proved a potent weapon in the battle for support that winter of 1970–1971. Lord Mountbatten, who had done a great deal of aqualung diving in the Mediterranean, heard about our project and mentioned it to HRH The Duke of Edinburgh (who had been trained in the aqualung by the BS-AC) and to the Commander-in-Chief, Portsmouth. One direct result was that the Navy declared our site a 'prohibited area' for surface vessels and allowed us to mark it off with full-size mooring buoys, ending for good the menace of anchors and trawls, and eliminating the old, time-wasting routines. Lord Mountbatten wrote to me in December, 1970:

> May I end by expressing my great admiration for the marvellous job you are doing in the hopes that one day the *Mary Rose* will rival and indeed outshine the *Wasa*, being such a much older ship.

Lord Mountbatten was interested in the *Wasa* because his brother-in-law, the King of Sweden, had helped finance that successful pioneer project. An additional factor to our advantage was that one of our divers, Reg Cloudsdale, was able to keep him up to date.

> While modernising a cottage on the Broadlands Estate for a fellow diver and his wife who were riding companions and friends of Lord Mountbatten, I was introduced to his Lordship as one of the divers on the *Mary Rose* site. His Lordship took a great deal of interest and asked on many occasions during the following

The 1971 gun at Southsea Castle, emerging from its concretion. The bore was 8 inches and the breech held a 6½-inch stone shot. The gunpowder chamber (left of the hammer) was 22½ inches long. Photo: Alexander McKee.

months about the progress of the diving, which I later found was passed on to Prince Charles.

I was introduced to Lord Mountbatten in June, 1971, a meeting that led to luncheon with the Queen and Duke of Edinburgh the following year and the start of the Royal Family's interest in the *Mary Rose* project. This connection with royalty was to prove a very important factor in our success. Another early supporter from 1970 onwards was Sir Alec Rose, the Southsea grocer who had sailed round the world in his little yacht *Lively Lady*.

There was also growing support from commerce and industry. Atlas Copco loaned a giant Silensair compressor for the air-lifts; a Sussex businessman, John Barber, bought a 40 ft. catamaran for us as a basic work barge for mounting the compressor; British Petroleum donated two large buoys for mooring our boats; Avon loaned an inflatable sportsboat as a pick-up and rescue craft; United Services Garages, of Portsmouth, loaned us a van to

carry all the extra heavy equipment we were now using; Rank Xerox contributed an underwater camera, while Kodak supplied film; Chesterfield Tubes provided aqualung cylinders. We even had a little money to pay for a boat to tow the catamaran which was engineless until Volvo gave us two diesels a year or so later.

Even now, there were sceptics. In April, 1971, the University of Bristol held a four-day symposium at which I lectured on the results of the sonar surveys and preliminary digs. A leading London nautical expert, the late George Naish, dismissed the gun as mere ballast, from the bottom of the ship, proving that there was virtually nothing left of the *Mary Rose* except her bottom timbers.

> Deane got right down to the bottom of the ship and brought up cannon-balls, bows and a lot of other objects; he might have destroyed far more than you realise. The Royal Engineers blew up three ships with tons of explosives: the *Royal George*, the *Boyne* and one other. I suspect they blew up the *Mary Rose* too.

Two sizes of stone shot. Being lighter than iron, stone would go further; but making stone shot must have been labour-intensive. Photo: BP Chemicals International Ltd.

There was a rather angry exchange. But I did overhear some perfectly reasonable people saying, 'He hasn't got very much, has he?' Physically, that was perfectly true. We had found no structure, only bits and pieces which I maintained came from the disturbance around the wreck. But what if they *were* the wreck—all that was left of the *Mary Rose*?

Percy Ackland was our 'gun dog'. A bricklayer by trade, his underwater navigation was more than accurate—it was uncanny. Quiet, willing, determined, he would have worked himself to death if we hadn't stopped him. On 5 May, 1971, he nearly did. That day we got away to a late start because all our latest sponsors were at the quayside with the new equipment on display. Percy in particular was delighted with it all.

> The Atlas Copco compressor will stay permanently on the catamaran bought for us by John Barber. Life should be easier in future—no loading and unloading a compressor on every trip. However, for today it was back to the old routine of humping the hired compressor down the quayside steps to enable Tony Glover to hoist it aboard *Julie-Anne*, using his boom. With the compressor safely stowed, we loaded on our personal equipment and just a short airlift, as gale force winds were forecast for later and we might not have time to retrieve a large one.

> 'Ready, Mac?' said Tony. After a cursory look around Alexander McKee nodded, Tony cast off and steered *Julie-Anne* out into Portsmouth Harbour. It was a fairly sunny May morning. We hoped to pick up the marks quite easily.

Once out of the harbour the sea got quite bumpy, and as *Julie-Anne* plodded on steadily past Spit Sand Fort, I started to get kitted up as I am usually the first man down.

Mac said he would like the end of the excavation dug last season buoyed, as that was where we aimed for today. I attached a length of line to a buoy and coiled it up so it would release without snags. By this time we were on site and Tony had anchored up. I finished kitting up and Mrs. Rule, who was doubling up as log-keeper, acknowledged my departure.

I gave an involuntary shiver as I hit the water and then made my way to the bow of the boat and down the anchor line, paying out the buoyline as I went. My descent came to an abrupt halt—the buoyline had caught around the anchor warp. Cursing profusely, I retraced my steps and started to free it. *Julie-Anne* was slapping around in the swell; the motion did not agree with my stomach which heaved a couple of times, but I managed not to vomit. Happily the line was soon free and I continued to the bottom.

Once there I paused and looked around. Visibility was a gloomy three to four feet. I didn't recognise anything. Never mind, the trench should be about 20 feet west-south-west. So I headed in that direction for 30 feet and found nothing, just virgin seabed—a light, semi-fluid silt that covers this area. So I returned on the reciprocal, tied the buoyline to Tony's anchor and executed an unrewarding first search.

Not wishing to waste time, I surfaced to check with Mac. 'Yes,' he said, scrutinising the marks. 'Anchor is not spot-on, go south.' After taking my reel out of my kitbag, I descended again.

At the anchor I took a short pause, feeling the current, and set out on a southerly course over the bottom. After 15 feet I started to vomit, but fought it back. However, I had barely covered another 15 feet before up came my breakfast. The natural reaction is to breathe in, which I did, and got some water as well. I gripped the mouthpiece with my teeth—up came another lot. I managed to control my breathing enough to take the mouthpiece out and give it a good purge.

Feeling a little better, I thought of surfacing but decided against it. I might be in trouble with the choppy seas topside.

In command of my stomach again, I pressed on. I had drifted eastwards whilst 'out of control', so I headed S.W. for about 80 feet, when I noticed a change in the bottom. I swam back and found a ledge. I swam along the ledge and found a fragment of timber. I felt around it. It was not attached to anything.

I looked ahead and saw an indistinct dark object. I moved towards it. It looked like a frame. IT WAS A FRAME! Eroded at the top like a pyramid about two inches by ten inches. Six inches away was another one,

Moulds for making lead shot, found by Reg Cloudsdale in the stern trench, 1972. Photo: Alexander McKee.

and beyond that yet another. I moved along, noticing they ran north to south; I found more frames—only this time with some planking attached. I touched it, half to reassure myself it was real and half to check the width of the planking which was about four inches. I swam along all the frames visible above the seabed. This *must* be the *Mary Rose*. If it was not, it needed investigating, so I thought I should mark it up. I attached the end of my reel line to one of the frames I had first seen. Now, where was Tony's boat?

A little uncertain, I headed north west, pausing every 40 feet to see if I had recognised anything. After four pauses I ran into Tony's big old CQR anchor.

Phew! that was a fluke. FLUKE! I laughed to myself deliriously, then pulled a bit of slack off my reel, attached the line to Tony's warp and buried the reel in the clay, as the current was moving. Then I surfaced to report.

On surfacing, a row of faces peered at me. Not wishing to cause too much of a stir I said to Mac, 'Can you dive, Mac?'

'As bad as that?' Mac said, not catching on.

'Yes', I replied. 'I have found something, but not what we expected.'

Andy Gallagher was chomping at the bit, waiting to dive, so Mac sent Andy along with me to buoy it.

Afterwards I dived three times to inspect Percy's find and explore its context. Part of a ship's side, consisting of three frames planked on the East side only, had been exposed in a deep gulley running East-West completely across them. On the East side were some loose timbers, including a 'Y'-shaped piece and the end of a fragile wooden box. Later I wrote in my log:

> Without the gulley, nothing whatever would have been visible of the wreck, which might well have been four ft. down at its highest parts and in between, very much deeper. A distinct anchor drag mark, large, ran across the gulley at right-angles.

The gulley ended in a high bank and beyond that, in a tangled heap, were piled some of our old ground moorings—concrete blocks connected by a wire hawser. I thought there might have been a shift of seabed, not unusual during the winter, possibly touched off by someone catching his anchor, trawl or dredge in our old mooring blocks and dragging them across the wreck to produce this wide gulley. To the north of the frames boldly exposed in the gulley, a line of similar frames could be seen if you looked very closely. They were eroded on top and virtually flush with the seabed. Deane's phrase sprang to mind:

> Some old wreck, so completely buried in the sand, that the diver could find nothing to which to attach a rope.

After so many setbacks and disappointments, we had an extraordinary stroke of luck, for I had swum across this southern part of the site late in 1970 and found nothing at all except a very disturbed seabed. Now, with the Elizabethan Admiral Monson, I could say, 'Part of the ribs of this ship I have seen with my own eyes.'

Of the two stone moulds found, the one on the left had been used for casting shot (note the burn marks). Photo: BP Chemicals International Ltd.

I'd done more than that, I'd photographed them too!

But I did not know at the time that Percy had been sick, let alone nearly died. When your sole means of breathing is through your mouth, being forced to vomit means that you go without air, a potentially deadly situation. Percy survived because he had not panicked. Instead of telling us about it, he just went into the cabin to write his report.

This made me queasy again and I decided not to dive again today. But the rest of the team could and a survey was started. On surfacing after his inspection dive Mac really belted out a report; he was clearly very happy.

Mrs. Rule wagged a finger at him, saying: 'Now, now, Mac! an excited archaeologist is a bad one.'

That day we surveyed 66 feet of framing belonging to one side of a ship perhaps 150 feet long. The bulk was still invisible under the mud, the upper parts buried by up to five feet of sediments. We organised two different types of excavation: long, comparatively shallow trenches following the lines of frames (or ribs) in order to 'outline' the structure and map it; and a few much deeper excavations at selected points of the hull designed to discover basic facts: which side of the ship was which, which end was which, what angle of heel it had, and how high up the hull it was preserved on this side or that. A heeled ship was bound to present an odd-looking map when seen in plan from above, because the structure preserved on one side would be very different from that preserved on the other. In terms of a house, on one side you might have the basement remaining, on the other parts of the attic. And this ship was of unknown design and build; we must treat it as if it were a Martian Flying Saucer.

I thought we would find the bow at the south end, because the Cowdray Engraving showed two masts, the most northerly one being the taller and therefore, presumably, the mainmast; further, the *Great Harry* was shown on that southerly heading as well, almost parallel to the sunken *Mary Rose*. It was all quite logical, but logic can lead you astray if you don't have all the facts. Gradually, the finds from the South Trench began to contradict my assumption. Under the layers of modern 'gash', and mixed with 17th century fishermen's rejects, there were some undeniably Tudor artefacts. Some, such as the stone-moulds for casting lead shot, found by Reg Cloudsdale, merely said 'warship'. But others said 'living accommodation' (as opposed to 'fighting area'); and

finally, one splendid item hinted at the class of people who had lived there. Again, it was Percy Ackland who made the key discovery.

I was making a tidying-up dive at the end of the day's work. My job was to excavate for a short spell and then switch off the airlift, which would signal the lads topsides to haul it up.

On peering into the gloom and precipitation of the excavation where the last team had been working, I saw sticking out of the side near the bottom what appeared to be an extremely friable saucer-shaped object. It did not look as though it would remain there till next week, so something had to be done about it. I measured it in from the nearest frames and jotted the figures down on my arm pad. Picking up the airlift, I opened the valve a little and got a gentle current blowing through it to suck away the debris as I carefully fanned away the silt around the object with my hand.

Percy Ackland making notes underwater. Photo: Alexander McKee.

Exposed frame tops before the start of the deep excavation outboard. The metal rods have been laid as indication of the area to be dug. Photo: Alexander McKee.

My plan of action was to clear around it and then fan under it until it was free. However, when fanning under it, it seemed to go on and on. First it appeared vase-like, then a handle appeared, and finally what might be a lid. My heart skipped a beat when I visualised it the right way up. A flagon! Dare I touch it? How should I transport it to the surface?

The airlift cut out and picked up again—the signal from the surface that I was running out of bottom time. I peered at the flagon and gave it a gentle prod. It fell over, so I switched off and untethered the airlift.

Very gently, I picked up the flagon and tucked it under my right arm. My breathing was becoming restricted and the current was now strong, so I switched on my reserve air supply and made my way over to the buoy line. On the surface I saw *Julie-Anne* quite a distance away, but a rope had been tied to the buoy to help me pull myself back to the boat. I signalled I was OK and set out strongly for the boat.

Cold and fatigue were setting in as I put my free hand over *Julie-Anne*'s gunwhale.

'Here, Margaret, grab this!' I shouted.

Mrs. Rule knelt on my hand and snatched the flagon to safety, the pressure on my fingers increasing as she straightened up. I lost my grip and drifted away in the current, before I could do anything. I swam frantically for the boat, thinking: Oh, no! not another long swim! But luckily the anchor was already up and Tony was very quick to fetch me.

On board, I asked Mrs. Rule what the flagon was made of. 'I think it's pewter,' she enthused. 'Just think, Henry VIII might have held this the night before *Mary Rose* sailed.'

'Didn't you realise you crushed my knuckles just now?' I asked .

Before she could answer, somebody interjected with a grin, 'Of course not, she was excited and an excited archaeologist is a bad one.'

As the Director of Excavations for the Mary Rose (1967) Committee, I decided, in conjunction with Morrie Young whose professional knowledge of ships was far greater than mine, to make the main excavation effort in 1971 a deep dig on both sides of the frames and planking exposed around an offset frame we had numbered '48'.

Two quite distinctly different pictures began to emerge. East of the frames and planking the soil was very soft and held much delicate material—so delicate that, not wishing to expose such areas to the pouring torrent of spring tides, I stopped and backfilled. On the other side, the West, the soft overburden gave way to layers of grit and shell and hard clay; in it were a few loose timbers, mostly planking. On this side the frames were unplanked, giving the

Up Top: the water heaves between the compressor barge and the Naval pinnace from the working of a 4-inch airlift. In the foreground, the next pair of divers prepare to take over the shift from the two divers down below. Photo: Alexander McKee.

false initial impression that the East side was the outboard side. But by the time we had gone down six feet we came on planking in position, trenailed to the frames. Clearly, the hull was planked on both sides, inside and out, and one could assume that the side where the upper strakes of planking were displaced and found lying loose, was outboard. What was puzzling, however, was that probing rods put down to 9 feet on the inboard side failed to locate a deck, while the outboard side began to curve outwards, giving a profile very like the 'tumblehome'* found high up on ships like HMS *Victory*. On the other hand, this stretch was entirely featureless—no gunports, no wales, no anchors—nothing to indicate our position on the hull, let alone the angle of heel.

Unlike houses, ships' hulls are a series of curves; therefore only a deck or the centre line would give us an angle of heel. Inboard, even when we probed down to more than 10 feet, we found no deck; and outboard we got a continuing curve. Digging was slowed by the dead weed which collected in this deep excavation—if bad weather kept us away for a few weeks, it became compacted and took hours to remove with an airlift, a process we called 'hoovering'. Once, a great, stinking mass of untreated sewage came up from the excavation with the weed, plus a disturbed conger eel; on another occasion, an enormous pool of crude oil, inches thick, came floating down to us from a tanker anchored off Cowes. I organised sessions of three or four days at a time, and by the winter the 'deep dig outboard' was 22 feet long, 18 feet wide, and nearly 12 feet deep. We had measured profiles at three separate points, all done with so much caution and care that a few divers complained at the 'painful slowness' of the work.

At the top were unplanked, badly eroded, partially eaten frames. About 5 feet down was the first plank, thin and distorted, but from 6 feet down one had what I described in my log as a 'beautiful brown ship'—not a wreck at all. Inspection by our two diving shipwrights, Morrie Young from Southampton and Hilton Matthews from the Isle of Wight, confirmed that the planks were perfectly tight and still caulked. But the only features on the hull were small chafing pieces over some of the seams, placed there to protect them against rubbing.

I remember going down at the end of a winter's day

* The term used to describe the narrowing of a ship's hull as it rises, designed to prevent it becoming top-heavy.

Down Below: careful excavation with the 6-inch airlift. While one diver (background) holds the tube in position, the excavator (foreground) uses his left hand to move soil towards the mouth of the tube which will take it away. This was an early model; later airlifts were rigged so that one man could handle them on his own. Photo: Alexander McKee.

The result of airlifting: frame heads and side-planking exposed in the excavation outboard, which reached 12 feet. Photo: Alexander McKee.

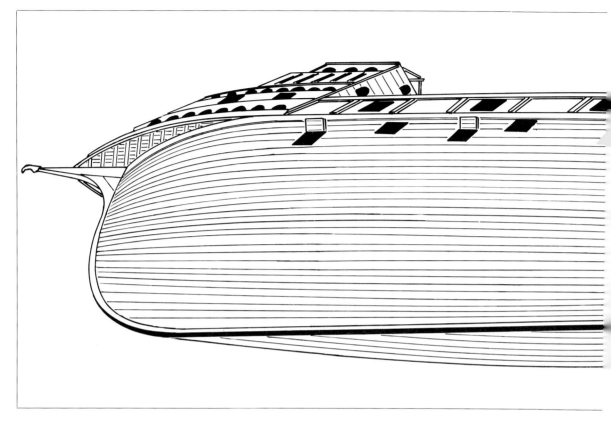

A ship is not a building site. Morrie Young's impression of the great hulk before erosion and collapse of the port side.

into this enormous dark pit with its neatly cut sides and corners inside a grid of scaffolding. Lying on my stomach at the foot of the wall of clay towering a dozen feet above me, I slid my hand as far as it would go down the smooth planks under the mud, fearful that the wall would collapse soundlessly upon me, and yet anxious to find, if only with my blind fingers, some feature of the hull that would indicate what part of the structure it was. My fingers felt a curve of the wood, and I assumed that this was yet another of those chafing pieces which we had uncovered. If we could have dug down another foot now, we should have had the answer to the mystery. But to dig further with safety, would have meant cutting back the 12-ft. high face of the excavation for at least four feet. Besides, I did not suspect we were so close to a solution. On 27 November, I had the gigantic pit 'backfilled' by blowing loose topsoil into it, thus reburying the timbers and protecting them from the ravages of marine creatures.

The finding of the gun in 1970 had brought in a large number of most useful recruits for this season, some living more than 100 miles away. Starting in mid-May, Margaret Rule had made her first few dives on the site, having been taught in a swimming pool by Morrie Young and his men. We admired her bravery. Most of us had taken up diving because we actually liked being underwater and were interested in it for its own sake, as a new environment, an unknown world. Margaret, however, had learnt to dive simply in order to see the *Mary Rose* for herself, after so many years of just sitting in the boat, listening.

The pattern of the years was now established, influenced only by the weather (which varied much), the base-boat set-up (which we were always trying to improve), and the immediate objectives (which changed as we learnt more). 1972 was a bad year—I had to abort or cancel 59 out of the 97 operations I had planned—but a little cash came in, and we were able to take on a one-man staff—Percy Ackland—to

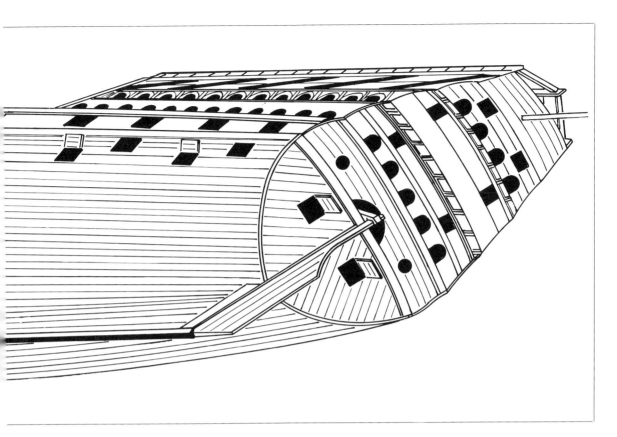

look after the boats, engines, and other equipment we were acquiring. These duties were in addition to diving, drawing the finds and helping conserve them. All the rest of us were unpaid volunteers, giving up in many cases, not just free-time, but working-time, to keep the project going. As boatman, Tony Glover had a key role, because for a few years the boats which held the big compressor had no engines and Tony had to tow them with his trawler.

There was the lifeboat for the compressor to go in—what a thing that was to tow! And when they were given the catamaran I nearly had heart failure trying to tow that about with no rudders and no engines, and manoeuvre it onto the site and get into position—that was hard work. And there were arguments on the quay with an official about taking the team out. He used to say they had no lifejackets and he wanted me to pay to pick up there. He came close to having a swim some mornings.

On site, I was amazed at the dedication of the people involved. Week after week probing the mud to find the hull of the ship. I thought, they have all got to be mad—until the day when, after a week of storms and big tides,

Percy Ackland went down and came up saying all these timbers were showing. The excitement was great. All the hard work was worth it.

Things started to happen. People became interested who previously thought we were a bunch of cranks.

What I liked most of all about my part in the

Stern castle excavation: a jumble of fallen timbers mixed with planks which may still be in their original position. The answer to the confusion may well lie 6 feet down. Photo: Alexander McKee.

This pewter flagon excavated by Percy Ackland in the stern trench proved to be the earliest known example of English pewter. Photo: BP Chemicals International Ltd.

operation was meeting, talking and working with some of the nicest people I have ever met—commanders, majors, doctors, solicitors, vicars, businessmen, policemen, firemen, plumbers, bricklayers, shipwrights—and the friendship I built with them and the laughs we had. I really enjoyed it.

People journeyed to work from the Isle of Wight, from mid-Sussex, from Romsey, and from north of London. Geoffrey Morgan, who worked in the Law, lived near St. Albans in Hertfordshire.

My memory is of monotony and unremitting toil. Money was extremely short and each expedition had to be carefully calculated. There was some outside financial support but it was far from lavish. Most participants paid for their own support, often contributing to running expenses themselves.

However, I do remember some of the hardships, though mine mainly arose from the fact that I lived over 100 miles from Portsmouth, so that on top of a day's toil I had quite a long journey. Often I had to rise at 5 a.m. and brave the early morning traffic, or what was often worse, the weary journey back to Hertfordshire, nearly falling asleep at the wheel on a couple of occasions. Few of us were commuters; most divers at least had the comfort of a hot bath and home to return to at the end of a hard day. For me, it was usually my tent at the top of Portsdown Hill.

Underwater archaeology is rarely exciting, rather in my experience, consistently tedious. Sheer painstaking, meticulous toil. We carefully dug our trenches, measuring, drawing, noting important features, reporting every man-made find, including broken British Rail crockery from the many ferries which passed overhead. On returning the following day the tide would have filled up our trenches with weed, so the process would begin again. The labour was not unlike weeding a very large, untidy garden, without the pleasure of the flowers or produce to show for one's efforts. In this way, many large volumes of logbooks and other journals were filled.

It was difficult to imagine that we were working on the most significant underwater archaeological site in British history. No one gave any sign of being particularly conscious of the importance of the *Mary Rose*, but seemed to take it in their stride. They were all very experienced divers, most of them much more experienced than I, and maritime matters seemed to come to them much more naturally than it did to me. The winds, the tides and the movement of the boat itself seemed so easy to them. The sea and its environment were as natural to them as ploughed fields were to my neighbours in Hertfordshire. I knew how to tie knots, but could not do so with the same facility that they could. Between them they had a variety of skills, but the knack of improvisation was impressive; we were

Some of the objects recovered from a Tudor 'housewife' in 1972: lying beside the base of the box that contained them, there is a rough comb, a thimble, an awl handle and two spinning bobbins. Photo: BP Chemicals International Ltd.

working in a sphere where there were at that time no professional rules, no professional underwater archaeologists. There were no guidelines. They themselves had made the tools that we used. What we were doing simply had not been done before. One had to cope with new and unusual problems as they arose.

The conversation was of Portsmouth and Southampton, of the Solent and its dockyards, naval matters and a great deal of maritime lore. They knew when an important ship like the *Queen Elizabeth* was due in Southampton, and of any other significant Solent happening, but rarely was the conversation of the historical significance of the *Mary Rose*. They could easily have been remote descendants of the men who sailed and sank in her; it was unnecessary to ask why they worked with such enthusiasm, sacrificing their time and in many cases their money, for these were truly sea people.

Since most of our volunteer divers came from coastal diving clubs, a number were professionally involved with ships. Among these was Morrie Young, who worked for Vosper-Thornycroft of Southampton, renowned builders of modern warships for many of the world's navies.

Part of my job as Shipwright Advisor to the *Mary Rose* (1967) Committee was the on-site identification of items of timberwork from the wreck. Loose pieces were first carefully plotted on the site plan before being raised to the surface and placed on the deck of the diving boat,

where I could examine them in relative comfort. It was during the course of one such operation (in October, 1971) that I discovered how much there was to learn about my Tudor predecessors—the shipwrights who built the *Mary Rose* so many years ago.

I had started measuring a large deck carling from the port side of the wreck, when I noticed something odd about it. Closer examination revealed that one of the dozen or so 'housings' that position and support the ends of four-inch wide half-beams had been incorrectly cut at five inches, and a one-inch graving piece inserted to reduce it to the right size. This, of course, was in no way damaging to the strength of the hull and I must admit to having corrected my own errors in a similar manner when working on wooden ships. Until that moment, however, it had never occurred to me that a shipwright working in one of Henry VIII's dockyards could have had the same human failings as I.

Who, I wondered, was this nameless, faceless man who, apart from his workmanship, had left no evidence of his existence? Alas, his name we shall never know, but a mental picture of him measuring, sawing and generally preparing this same piece of timber that I was now touching began to form.

It was obvious, for instance, that he had used an adze on the upper and lower surfaces, as the marks made by the now rarely used tool were there for all to see. The adze is certainly not the easiest of wood-working tools to handle correctly and requires many years of practice before one becomes fully proficient in its use. This man, however, had obviously been using one for a long time and that might well indicate that he was of advanced years.

A further inspection of the carling showed that a one-and-a-half-inch wood chisel had been used to 'pare' out the sides and bottoms of the 'housings'. This would have been quite a common tool to use on ship constructions such as the *Mary Rose* and once again, one in which this Tudor wood-worker was quite adept.

There was more to be learnt. Merely by studying the fixing arrangements of this nine foot long piece of oak I was able to determine that the recesses allowing the heads of iron spikes to be driven home flush had been cut with a half-inch wood gouge. I could also see that the holes to take the spikes were of half-inch diameter, drilled, I suspect, with a tool known as a pod auger.

From the way in which the various tools had been used it was obvious they they had been used in the hands of a skilled craftsman. True, he had made an error, but he had overcome it in such a way that his repair was still in position well over four centuries later. Even with all the vast array of wood-working machinery at my

disposal today it is doubtful if I could match his skill. Neither, I suspect, would I be competent to compete with his knowledge of ship construction. If, however, corrective work carried out by me in the future survives half as long as his, I shall be more than satisfied.

Most of us drove to Portsmouth from our various homes, although none were quite so far away as Geoffrey Morgan's; others joined us on-site in their own boats. Those who set out from the Isle of Wight, with the prevailing wind usually at their backs, could have a difficult return. One team came from Plessy Radar, but another consisted of two men only—John Cleaver, a farmer, and Chris Brownings, a hovercraft pilot (later to be killed in the Middle East by hijackers). They at first attempted to rendezvous by coming over on the Ryde-to-Southsea hovercraft service, arranging for our USG-donated van to pick them up there before transferring to our boat in the harbour.

Left: Base and staves of a wooden keg. The pitch inside is clearly visible. Photo: BP Chemicals International Ltd.

Right: Wooden handle of a kidney dagger, found in the stern trench, 1972. The iron blade was rusted away. On land, the revers happens; so while the blades were well known, the wooden handles were not. Photo: BP Chemicals International Ltd.

However, heavy and bulky diving equipment did not lend itself to quick stowage in the luggage panniers of an S.R.N. 6, and at the end of the first day we realised that an alternative means of transport would have to be found.

We decided to use our 10 ft. Avon Redshank rubber dinghy with a borrowed Seagull outboard. This outfit was always launched at Seaview, which gave us the shortest possible crossing—four miles—and approximately 45 minutes to reach the site. The dinghy was a buoyant little craft, but owing to its small size it gave us a rough time in a fresh breeze. On one occasion, following a fairly smooth outward trip, Chris and I were nearing the end of a shift with the airlift when one of the other divers appeared through the murk with a small blackboard on which Mac had written: *Surface immediately, weather worsening*. On obeying this instruction we found that Mac was not an alarmist. The wind was now much stronger and against the tide, which raised the well-known Solent short chop. We had a long rough run home that day; our progress was so slow that we were obliged to refuel halfway across, an exasperating exercise whilst bobbing about like a rubber duck.

Enough fuel reached the tank to get us back to Seaview, where we were annoyed to find that the tide was now right out, leaving us with $\frac{1}{4}$-mile haul across the sand.

After two seasons of 'bungying' our way to and fro we obtained the use of a 24 ft. cabin cruiser, powered, or rather underpowered, by a twin cylinder diesel. I can only think this craft was originally built for summer use on the upper Thames, because as a sea boat she was a non-starter. Anything over a ripple on the water, and she would pitch and roll in an extraordinary fashion.

Maximum speed was approximately 5 knots. On one memorable day, a fellow farmer and friend, Howard Johnson, came along to act as crew and see how much work on site was progressing. By the time we had finished diving, the wind had risen to Force 6 or more from the South-West, dead against us. We set off, but must have been making only 2 knots or so over the ground, pitching violently whilst trying to avoid a large container-ship that appeared to want the same patch of Solent as us. At one point in mid-channel, our bows plunged so far under a steep sea that a large plank that normally lay under the 60 lb. anchor to protect the deck, was washed out and smashed against the wheelhouse window.

After what seemed a very long time we reached the shelter of Wooton Creek and moored up. Howard, looking as pale as I felt, spoke for the first time in an hour. 'It's not always like that, is it?' he said.

Diving on the *Mary Rose* was sometimes very uncomfortable work and no doubt every one of us occasionally wondered what made us carry on. I have

Deck carling raised from the *Mary Rose* in 1971, lying on the deck of the *Julie-Anne*. To the left of the ruler is the graving piece inserted by the Tudor shipwright to correct a wrongly-measured cut he had made. Photo: Alexander McKee.

no doubt at all that Alexander McKee, or 'Mac' to us all, was the man who held the team together with his mixture of optimism, realism and persistence. He first found the wreck that the 'experts' knew was not there and then proved that she and her uniquely-preserved artefacts were well worth raising.

We were only able to work periods of four days or more on suitable tides by calling heavily on people whose jobs enabled them to get out for a few hours on weekdays. Shift workers were particularly useful: men such as Ray McLaren who worked in Southampton Docks, and Mick Russell, Tom Smith and Ted Pearn of Portsmouth Fire Brigade: there were other firemen, too, from London and Gloucester. One morning Mick Russell lost a gold ring in the excavation. The chap who was supposed to lower a heavy weight for Mick and Tom to take slowly down to the bottom, for some reason or other let the rope run out freely. Mick and Tom ended up in a heap on the bottom with the operator of the airlift underneath them. What could have been a nasty accident resulted only in the loss of the ring which was worn and broken. Mick left the site early in order to go on night duty at Cosham Fire Station, and that evening a London fireman, who had been a guest diver that day, called in on his way home up the A3 to return the gold ring! As the excavation continued the ring had been found, causing great excitement! It was thought at first to be a valuable artefact from Henry VIII's time. On another occasion enough time elapsed for barnacles to grow on an object lost by Mick Russell.

I was duty standby diver ready for any emergency.

He died in the *Mary Rose*. Photo: Alexander McKee.

Airlifting was being carried out by Percy Ackland, but unknown to us on the surface he had just been dealt a severe blow in the mouth by the airlift, which had completely dismantled his demand valve, leaving him on the bottom with no air.

Being an excellent and well-trained diver Percy made a free ascent, arriving at the surface only slightly out of wind but in some degree of trouble. On seeing this, I was in the water in a flash, in my haste shedding one of my fins in the process. Percy only required a small amount of assistance, and the incident was soon forgotten.

But many months later, a diver surfaced from his shift and with some degree of ritual handed to me a well barnacle-encrusted fin, which to my absolute amazement was the one I had lost.

Where possible, the actual digging was done by hand—with ungloved fingers—the airlift serving merely to take away the disturbed soil. This was why it was possible for a light, tiny object like Mick Russell's gold ring to be found and recovered. Very often, however, the mud contained masses of old, sharp-edged oyster shells which could cut a bare hand very badly; and when the diver could stand it no more, he usually found an implement with which to excavate—an archaeological trowel, an oyster shell or anything else handy. I used to do this, and Mick did, too.

It was a standing joke that whenever I brought any bones to the surface, Margaret Rule would dismiss them—quite correctly—as animal bones thrown over the side from ships. One day I found a very useful piece of bone to use as a scraper with the airlift. I did two or three dives that day and each time I left my digging tool stuck in the mud for future use. But on the last dive, I thought I might as well try again and presented my bone to Margaret Rule for her opinion. I was amazed at her enthusiasm this time! She definitely identified my bone as a poor seaman's femur. I didn't tell her the use to which it had been put!

Reg Cloudsdale surfaced in the swirling eddies of the airlift and held up a dark, curved object like a lobster claw. It was the blackened top of a human skull, complete to the eye sockets. He had been excavating in the North Trench, exposing strangely splintered side-framing about four or five feet below the seabed, when his digging hand had touched a curved object in the mud; he had thought it was a round shot until his fingers told him that it was hollow and must be a skull.

We gazed at the find with melancholy disinterest. *Annie Moore* pitched and rolled, as she had been pitching and rolling for four hours; and would continue to pitch and roll for another four. Damp and dismal grey clouds raced overhead and now and then the rigging would emit a brief howling to warn us that although the wind was blowing at only Force 5, it was gusting 6 or 7.

Our suits stank from the clouds of macerated sewage that had swept across the site all week. Our

A human bone lying on the underwater sketch pad of the diver who recovered it. Photo: Alexander McKee.

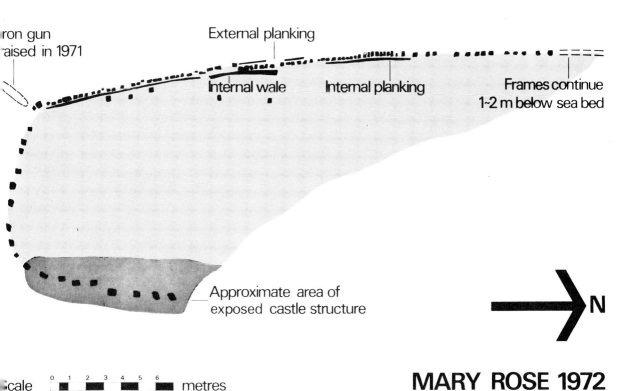

ron gun
raised in 1971

External planking

Internal wale

Internal planking

Frames continue
1~2 m below sea bed

Approximate area of
exposed castle structure

N

Scale 0 1 2 3 4 5 6 metres

MARY ROSE 1972

At the end of 1972 the 'outlining' process of a shallow excavation along frame heads had reached this stage. A deep dig had been made at one point only—between the 'internal wale' and the iron gun raised in 1971. It was not then clear that the rudder lay below the iron gun; this was revealed by deep excavation in 1975.

muscles ached from holding on, to stop ourselves being hurled from one side of the boat to the other. Holding on, that is, for every second of eight hours. The time spent underwater might have been luxurious relaxation in comparison, had it not been for the bitter cold sea below and the chilling wind above. There was no way to rest or get warm this side of bed. And it would be the same again tomorrow, for this was the eighth day of a nine-day operation carried out in the wind and water conditions of a particularly poor December. But it was not December, it was the first half of July, 1972.

The winds had stirred up the sediments so much that it took more than a brief calm spell to disperse the murk and darkness shrouding the *Mary Rose*. Even so, the excavations were going well—this trench was ruler-straight with strictly parallel, absolutely vertical sides, telling an accurate story. To the North, the ship's framing did not deviate eastwards—those were internal timbers—but ran on to the North where they went too deep for us under a high mud bank. There were signs here of a small local gunpowder explosion, probably Deane's, as indeed there were in the South

Trench where we found two lengths of twisted lead tubing typical of the underwater ignition methods preceding the use of electricity. We found no signs of damage to timbers, however.

The South Trench also progressed. By digging deeper around the timbers already 'outlined', a massive composite timber (on which another wrought-iron gun had been found and removed) began to appear, looking more and more like a transom fashion piece—the point of transition between a ship's side and its stern. This South Trench now led East, following the run of the eroded frame tops, and then North; and increasingly, this end of the ship seemed more like the stern than the bow.

On the eastern side everything changed. By digging down to five feet we discovered that the ship was built here in a quite different way. Previously we had been finding heavy frames, closely spaced a few inches apart, heavily planked inside and out in carvel fashion—the planks butted edge to edge. Now we saw smaller double-frames (technically, the outboard one was a 'wale'), spaced some three feet apart, and sandwiched between each pair of frames was a single

101

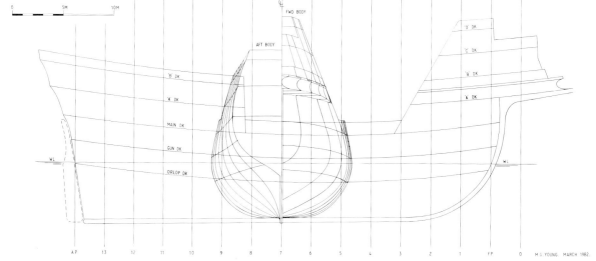

Conjectural sheer plan and body sections: originally drawn 1972 and updated to available information March 1982.

layer of light planking clinker-built—the planks overlapping each other. The whole structure was very light, not much heavier than my garden shed, just about arrow-proof and windproof, and was clearly castling from high up the hull of the *Mary Rose*. This type of construction was vaguely hinted at in old pictures familiar to me, but the details were unknown. Now we were actually seeing it. The fact that this side of the ship was so different, structurally, from the side we had first examined, indicated some degree of heel. Just how much, we still had to discover.

The associated finds included ammunition of stone and lead; two flagstaff tops (necessarily from the top of the stern castle); a wooden handle for a dagger; a wooden bowl with 'I.D.' carved on it in two places (presumably some Tudor seaman's initials); and a large number of human remains, among which I saw what I took to be fragments of a leather jerkin or 'jack'. From one small area nine inches square and only a few inches deep, two divers in 70 minutes digging recovered a group of related finds: 1 circular box base, 1 fine comb, 1 coarse comb, 1 thimble, 1 awl, 1 small knife, 2 spinning bobbins. As an ex-soldier, I recognised the sixteenth century equivalent of the Second World War issue canvas 'housewife' (pronounced 'huzzif'), and in the jerkin the remains of a government-given garment of a type I had myself worn in a war.

The corpses at this high level in the ship were quite clean and sanitized—unlike the dreadful wreckage of more recent fighting that I could remember from France, the Low Countries and Germany in 1944–1945. To some younger divers, the sinking of

the *Mary Rose* was an historical romance; to me it was real and the deaths of the men struck home.

In *The Silent World*, Cousteau describes the idea of finding human remains in a wreck as mythical, but I had always worked on the opposite assumption—that we might have not less than 200 corpses preserved to varying degrees, together with some of their clothing, weapons and personal possessions, thus giving a cross-section of Tudor military and naval society. We could almost, but not quite, bring the dead back to life. This, to me, was even more important than the unknown hull, unknown rigging, half-unknown armament.

The best preserved would of course be way down in the hull, lying sealed under as much as 25 feet of clay and mud, for this was a big ship deeply sunk into the seabed. How were we to excavate it? Even if we worked still more months without earning, the task seemed too immense. I had discussed the matter with Dr. George Bass, who excavated underwater off Turkey with teams from the University of Pennsylvania, and he wrote to me in 1970:

> We have never faced a situation remotely similar to yours—open sea, thick clay, poor visibility—so our experiences would be almost meaningless. We put down 16 to 20 divers twice a day, in pairs, 6 days a week, for three months at a time, but our methods wouldn't begin to dent your site and as our mapping methods all depend on photography now they would be of no use (we need to get 15 to 20 feet above the wreck to take the pictures).

George Bass was the world's foremost practitioner of this kind of operation, and if he could suggest nothing, who could?

Chapter 9

The Sixty Degree Factor

Disasters and Triumphs, 1973–1978

In 1973 British Petroleum were planning to scrap a diving platform, but before doing so they had the kind thought of offering to sell it to us, at a fraction of its true value. Slung on inflatable rubber sponsons, about 50 feet long by 30 feet wide, it would enable us to leave most of our heavy equipment on board, so reducing the two hours' loading time we wasted each day; we would also save on boat fees. We bought it for £5. It took time to make all the arrangements for lighting and mooring, and to obtain permission and agreement; so it was July before we were operating from the former *Seaclear* (which we renamed *Keepclear* because anything moored or anchored is an irresistible attraction to yachtsmen and other boating enthusiasts).

11 July was hectic. We logged 'More than two dozen wave-offs by McKee alone, starting with the Prime Minister'. Edward Heath's big yacht *Morning Cloud* was well up at the head of the pack in a race that morning, when they all decided the best course was to shave us as closely as possible. What they did not know was that we were not anchored, but moored to four buoys which pulled under when the tide ran fast. As *Morning Cloud*'s sharp bows came closer to the submerged obstruction, I could see Mr. Heath at the wheel. But there was no help for it and I gave the order for our lookouts to wave him off; if I had not, *Morning Cloud* would have gone to the bottom a year before she actually did.

We had now turned the Mary Rose Association into an organised Special Branch of the British Sub-Aqua Club. Apart from giving us third party insurance it enabled us to control diving on the site in accordance with the procedures we had worked out over the years. This was necessary because many different diving organisations, all with their own rules, wanted to dive with us; and some procedures, safe on other sites, would prove deadly on this one. We could lay down, and did, that divers who wanted to join had to reach a certain minimum logbook standard, but in addition we had to try them out—and let them see if they liked us—by asking them to come out at least three times before putting their prospective membership to a vote of the Branch. This policy produced a tightly integrated team of friends who are still together as a diving group.

I was Chairman of the Mary Rose Special Branch and the Director of Excavations for the Mary Rose (1967) Committee, whose membership now included half a dozen of the divers who were actually carrying out work on the seabed.

In May the Duke of Edinburgh paid us a visit and I was able to show him round the new *Mary Rose* rooms at Southsea Castle which Portsmouth City Museums had now devoted to our discoveries, as a kind of preview of the full-scale museum we hoped to build. When we ran out of money towards the end of that month, the Duke gave a personal donation which enabled work to continue.

Our object was to complete the excavation and survey of the starboard stern castling, in order to discover at what depth the light clinker construction joined the heavier main hull. We exposed a port, but with no gun in it; a broken castle panel where a heavy gun had crushed the flimsy clinker in its fall; and also a number of other concretions which were almost certainly guns, some quite small—bases or hailshot pieces—which we back-filled to await adequate conservation facilities. With money so tight, we had to concentrate on the possible rather than the desirable. On the other hand, confirmation that we had castling at the stern, meant that the hull must be preserved to some considerable height. But what height exactly? And what was the angle of heel? The castling lay at 45 degrees from the vertical, but would not have been vertical when the ship was afloat—it would have sloped inboard. That would indicate a greater angle of heel than 45 degrees; but had it

A christening with mead! *Right to left*: John Barber who bought the catamaran *Roger Grenville* for the project; Mrs. Gwen Holder, a descendant of Roger Grenville, the captain of the *Mary Rose*; and the author, Director of Excavations. Tony Glover is in the background. Photo: Portsmouth *News*.

perhaps, being so flimsy, bent over like a flattened blade of grass?

Keepclear worked perfectly as a diving platform. There was an internal ramp so that one could walk into the sea as if off a beach in protected water, and swim back in with equal ease. She was stable in rough water, when a normal boat would have put on a bucking bronco act. Our heavy cylinders and weight-belts could be stored in the twin towers which supported a high cabin where there was a useful chart table for drawing. But in case of accidents, I had moored her clear of the *Mary Rose* on the eastern side, normally the downwind—or downgale—side of the site. In fact, she easily weathered several gales, until on Sunday, 5 August, I noted an ominous change.

Severe Gale, Force 9, unprecedented in summer, with sea raging so high on Hayling beach that I and my storm-loving family for once did not go in the water for a swim or snorkel dive. It would have been suicidal. All the doors in the house kept opening of their own accord under the outside wind pressure. There was no let-up, no slackening of the gale.

The wind blew for three days at Force 8, 9 and 10 (12 is hurricane) with only one let-up of Force 6 to 7 for two hours on Monday, 6 August; and in that comparative lull, Percy Ackland and I made our bid to save the diving platform.

I rang round all the fishermen I knew who had big, seaworthy boats, but none were available. The Camber harbourmaster rang me: our Q.17 (a 17-ft.

open hard boat) was half full of water at the quayside. Gilkicker reporting station rang me: the platform was listing so badly that the compressor seemed likely to fall over the side. I rang Percy Ackland to meet me at the Camber with the Avon ($14\frac{1}{2}$-ft. inflatable) on the roof of the USG van; we would try to find a fisherman there who would be willing to take us out in his boat.

The wind dropped from Force 9 with torrential rain to Force 6, about ten minutes after I had left my house by Hayling beach. I drove to the Camber along Southsea front; the platform was still afloat but listing heavily. At the Camber, there was not a fisherman in sight, although all their boats were idle and in harbour.

We baled out the Q.17, which was undamaged, and set off. Both of us were wearing lifejackets, and I was also wearing a neoprene survival suit jacket and carrying distress flares and two underwater cameras (plus mask, snorkel and fins in case I had to swim). We took it in turns to drive, because our glasses got wet, and we had to creep round to the site in a half-circle in order not to be sunk by the waves. Two cargo ships of about 1,500–2,000 tons were anchored at Spithead, presumably sheltering from the gale. Gilkicker knew we were going out and one of the ships might pick us up if we sank.

Lacking engines, *Roger Grenville* had to be towed out to Spithead by Tony Glover's trawler *Julie-Anne*. The inflatable loaned by Avon acted as pick-up and rescue boat. Photo: BP Chemicals International Ltd.

We circled *Keepclear* to photograph the damage. She was listing about 30 degrees, the rubber sponson on the low side torn and collapsed for half its length; the other sponson was all right, but riding high on its compressed air. But if one more compartment tore open in the damaged sponson, *Keepclear* would go right over.

We had to board her on the high side, where there was a little lee; and we had to jump, not climb aboard. While Percy got the compressor going to pump tight the remaining airbags in the torn sponson, I photographed the damage. The metal platform slung between the two rubber sponsons was entirely underwater, the Atlas-Copco compressor for the airlifts washed by the waves but still firmly bolted. Percy's pumping produced some effect, but the situation was serious and there was no way of rectifying it immediately. We decided to remove all disposable top-weight, particularly a dozen or so aqualung

The Q.17 coming in to pick up a mooring in rough seas and driving rain. Diving continued in all weathers—even a Force 8 gale. Photo: Alexander McKee.

cylinders and two tool kits stored in the bases of the two metal towers.

Percy took the risk of going down into the narrow towers and handing up the cylinders to me. It was comparable to entering the conning tower of a sinking submarine, an impression heightened by the fact that the lower part of the first tower was filled with water to above the level of the cylinders stored there. I had the comparatively safe job of taking the cylinders off him and then walking with them uphill through the cabin to the head of the ladder we would use. Had just one more airbag ripped at this time and the platform in consequence capsized, there would have been no hope for Ackland. The tower top would have been upside down on the seabed and he would have been bottled up inside under fifty feet of water.

Transferring these weights to the Q.17 was not easy, but at last we had all the heavy cylinders, both toolkits, one bag of survey kit, two large coils of expensive rope, and one diving flag safely in the Q.17. We judged that this was as much as it would take, the wind now Force 7 again and increasing. The large diving flag I had left behind in the cabin, as untying it from its unwieldy metal pole took too long, and I thought I might be risking a lot for a little.

We moved off, very low in the water, feeling as though we were abandoning a sinking ship, took a few final pictures, and had a long, dangerous ride back into Portsmouth Harbour, frequently having to turn 90 degrees off course to take particularly dangerous waves, which seemed to come in groups. We wanted to go North, but had to steer East and then West for part of the time.

The gale continued at Force 9 all through the night and into the next morning, when *Keepclear* finally disappeared. The Portsmouth *News* reported an

11,000-ton tanker driven ashore in Wales, and its local headlines heralded one crisis after another: COWES RACING CALLED OFF; GALE RIPS CITY ROOFS; SEA RESCUE DRAMA IN WEEKEND OF STORMS; MYSTERY OF MAN'S BODY IN HARBOUR; ADMIRAL'S CUP SHOCK; RAIN-HIT SHOW AWASH WITH MUD. Off Hayling, the sea was solid for 50 yards out with ripped-off weed.

Keepclear had sunk on Tuesday, 7 August, and I had to wait until Saturday, 11 August, before diving. It took three dives to sort out everything. Briefly, when one rubber sponson finally tore away completely, the platform turned right over, and ballasted by the one-ton plus Atlas-Copco compressor, went straight to the bottom upside down, with all moorings still in place and no damage to the excavation, because of her position to the east of the *Mary Rose*, not directly

The author driving the Q.17 to the attempted rescue of the sinking diving platform in 1973. Photo: Percy Ackland.

The last of the diving platform. One rubber sponson is half-ripped; when one more compartment tears, the platform will roll over and sink. Photo: Alexander McKee.

above. Out of this disaster, I realised, we now had the unparalleled opportunity to observe a re-run of the sinking of the *Mary Rose* herself, for the seabed was the same, although the platform was lighter. Barely five days had passed since the sinking, yet the cabin top, the highest part of the platform, was already in a scour-pit, three feet below the seabed.

I could go into the cabin, by swimming down the seabed where the currents had scoured it away, and once inside look out through the large glass windows. The lowest few feet of the glass were black—that was the mud in which the cabin top was already buried. Above that was the dark green of the sea with pollack and pout swarming round. I was inside the glass bowl gazing at the fish circling me outside it. They had already taken up residence in the semi-darkness of the upside-down platform ramp, compressor and gang-ways. Five days later, mud had already drifted in through the open door and begun to build up inside the cabin, covering some of the debris lying there. From this tangle I recovered the large diving flag, the knots securing it to the metal flagpole still only half-untied where I had abandoned the task six days before. I manoeuvred it now, pole and all, out of the door, swam it up the scourpit to the level of the seabed which was engulfing the wreck, and finned along the aft end, finding the same burial process underway and a one-pound lobster in residence among the torn, rumpled fabric of a ripped sponson. I grabbed him behind the head and surfaced slowly, holding the lobster in one hand and the diving flag and its staff in the other.

On 26 August, three weeks after the sinking, I found other illuminating developments. Superficial-ly, the platform seemed to be shaking itself to pieces when the tide ran fast. The main structure was unaffected, but all the lightly-built parts, such as loose panels, doors and railings, were either falling off or waving in the current. In particular, the large, light items came down complete, soon to be covered with a light film of sediment, sufficient to inhibit the growth of many organisms. On the south side, a mass of dead

Left: The lower end of the diving platform, upside down on the seabed. Less than a month after sinking, it is not only well down into the mud, but already being covered over. This is the process that helped to preserve the *Mary Rose*. Photo: Alexander McKee.

Right: Trench at seabed level. Weed has caught in the marker pole. Photo: Alexander Mckee.

Left: The bottom of a trench after the winter. Crabs and fish have burrowed homes for themselves in the side of the excavation. Photo: Alexander McKee.

Right: A heavy concretion (probably an iron gun) has broken through one panel of the stern castling in its fall as the ship heeled over. Photo: Alexander McKee.

weed had collected. I kept a photographic record and had the scourpit surveyed each year, as a guide to where one might look for missing parts of the *Mary Rose* after the main hull had been lifted.

As a replacement for the diving platform a Hampshire businessman, Mike Coomber, offered to buy us a small ship 98 feet long; but we could not afford to run it and had to reject his generous gift. Instead, we accepted John Barber's welcome offer to fit out his catamaran *Roger Grenville* (which I had named after the captain of the *Mary Rose*); with two new engines given by Volvo, it was a better proposition than it had been as a nightmare tow for Tony Glover.

Cash to cover running costs was the main restriction in 1974, as in previous years. Weather was another. I planned to work 32 days, but in the event managed less than half that—only 15. It would have been reckless to open up the deep and difficult castle dig, so I began a shallow excavation outboard at the stern, to be extended and deepened in 1975.

Legally, things were looking up. In 1973 the Historic Wrecks Act had been passed, with the *Mary Rose* the second wreck to be designated. Underwater archaeology in Britain was now legitimate rather than eccentric. In January, 1974, a government buoy was laid at government expense to protect the site, and all new charts had the area circled and marked as that of an historic wreck. We had put the *Mary Rose* on the map, quite literally!

In July, there was an official State inspection of the work involving both London government and local government. The lads put on a brilliant show of efficiency, and two of the visitors went down to see for themselves. Margaret Rule escorted Alexander Flinder, an underwater archaeologist of great experience, while I took down a Member of Parliament, John Prescott. Both seemed impressed by the size of the ship and the degree of preservation, although there was not all that much to see. Most of the *Mary Rose* still lay hidden under the mud, a distant promise for the time when money would become available.

Nic Knights, a ship draughtsman from Southampton, who joined the team in 1975 when we were retagging timbers at the start of a new season, saw the site in a different perspective from those of us who had grown old with it. Furthermore, the timbers were in such excellent condition that they were in danger of being eaten by marine organisms, so I had filled in both the deep dig outboard and the stern castle trench.

Nic's first dive on the *Mary Rose* left a deep impression on him:

I took another plastic tag from the bucket and nailed it to one more frame top before my air supply dictated that I must return to the surface. Little had I imagined 12 years before, when as an apprentice I drove my first copper nail into oak yacht frames, that one day I might be putting nails into oak more than 430 years old and 50 feet below the surface of the sea.

This was my first dive on the *Mary Rose* and I had been given a tour of the site by Don Bullivant, shown how to operate the airlift, and had then been left to continue tagging frame heads. As we descended, my imagination took wing. Common sense and experience told me not to expect too much, but at the same time I could not stop myself hoping that when the seabed came into view I would see a recognisable ship laid out before me.

Naturally I was disappointed, when all I could see was a row of frame heads (like broken-off posts) sticking out of the mud. But it immediately impressed upon me what a dedicated group of amateur divers I was hoping to join. For ten years these people, largely at their own expense and in their own time, had patiently searched for and then uncovered what is undoubtedly a major discovery. After all these years, due to a lack of public support and shortage of finance, they did not yet know how much of the ship remained or whether it would ever be possible to salvage it intact. Still they persevered.

In the following two years I was lucky enough to be involved when major structural details were revealed, soon leading to greater financial and practical support. Salvage was no longer a dream and there was no shortage of volunteers to help excavate what had now been proven to be a worthwhile project. But, apart from the excellent state of preservation of the hull structure, it was the determination of those pre-1975 divers that I found most remarkable.

Early in 1975, as Director of Excavations, I proposed to the committee a continuation plan:

To complete the Stern Excavation (Areas 1, 2, 3) begun in 1974. Establish: centre-line of hull; angle of heel; height to which preserved; distortion of hull, if any, at weakest point. Method: excavate, examine and record the stern to a depth of six feet below tops of eroded timbers, the corners being dug to nine or ten feet until the structural questions are answered. Particular attention to be paid to the possibility of finding the rudder or an identifiable aperture to indicate the preserved height of the ship.

There was an understandably cautious element in the 1967 Committee which felt it to be wisest to hold back, keeping a financial reserve, rather than spend

The tops of two flagstaffs were recovered from the stern trench in 1975. The inset shows detail of the head of the left-hand finial. Photo: BP Chemicals International Ltd.

to the limit in the hope of obtaining a definitive result. They cropped my programme to end on 7 July. Had I accepted that verdict, the season would have ended in failure, but I pressed my case, and on purely archaeological grounds was able to obtain agreement for an extension to 5 August.

I had, however, another very good reason for continuing beyond 7 July. As early as 1973 the possibility of a visit by the Prince of Wales had been suggested to me, and when I had been introduced to him at the British Sub-Aqua Club's 21st Anniversary Banquet, the Prince, who was President of the Club, had assured me that he would like to dive the *Mary Rose* at the first opportunity. Now he had at last been able to give me a date on which he could visit the site,

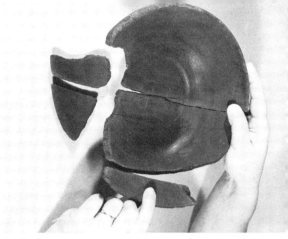

Left: Excavation at a high level in the stern, revealing a mix of artefacts: the base of a modern glass bottle next to a broken wooden plate from the *Mary Rose*. Photo: Alexander McKee.

Right: The wooden bowl re-assembled after conservation. The scribings on it are probably the personal mark of the owner. Photo: BP Chemicals International Ltd.

and that date was 30 July. I could not reveal the Prince's intentions, for I had been warned that if the news leaked out, the visit would be off. By refusing to acept 7 July as a cut-off date, we not only got a Royal tour of the site on 30 July, but also obtained our definitive result with one day to spare—on 4 August—the day before my extended programme had to end for lack of funds.

30 July was a splendid day, bright, warm and sunnily calm. As the divers drove up to the quay and began unloading their gear, they were surprised to find themselves 18 strong instead of about eight. Only now could I say that Prince Charles would be coming aboard *Roger Grenville* in half an hour.

No one now would imagine that the catamaran had been holed and half sunk on 11 July, one engine compartment flooded with filthy water, when unattended on her mooring. With a few telephone calls to the right people, I had managed to save her—for we had no paid staff any longer, since Percy Ackland had had to leave us because of financial and health problems. The submerged engine had to come out, be stripped down, all electrics replaced, and put back; with help from Vospers, our volunteers did it, notably Tony Barber, Mike Pritchard and 'Robbie' Robinson, working like slaves inside the hull in a heatwave.

Albert Kirby, who was to cox the close cover rescue boat, had a memorable day.

> It was a hot summer's morning and the 'cat' was a hive of activity. On arriving at *Vernon* we saw that the Navy had arranged a cluster of officers and men to receive the Prince. Gold braid was flashing everywhere, but the moment H.R.H. boarded, all the pomp went overboard

and it was just as if he had known all of us for years. He became one of the diving team, one of the lads, was speaking our language and telling us about his experiences of diving under the ice cap.

On site the water boiled for 45 minutes, as the two 'hooverers', Adrian Barak and Eric Sivyer, made sure that the heir to the throne would have something to see. They reported to me that all weed had been removed, but there was poorish visibility of about four feet on the seabed, much worse down in the excavation. Necessarily, there were many lines in it, for supplying and controlling the two airlifts. This was one hazard it was hard to avoid. I think it was one of Prince Charles's companions who said that if we lost H.R.H., we need none of us bother to come back.

I had an outer patrol boat (the Q.17) to ward off yachts; and a close cover boat alongside the cat, ready to go, with two kitted up divers aboard. On the cat were four back-up divers, two of whom, Pete Powell and Reg Cloudsdale, both ardent monarchists, would 'ride shotgun' on the Prince and myself, hovering in our bubbles. In poor visibility, at the bottom of a deep, dark pit, this could be easier said than done.

I had a site plan drawn on a waterproof board which we would take down with us. While briefing Prince Charles with its aid, about three minutes before entering the water, the colour of the sea gently flowing past us changed completely. It became bright and sparkling. Bottom visibility jumped to between eight and ten feet. What could have been dangerous became a doddle, probably the safest dive I was ever to make. Moreover it was apparent immediately that the Prince was a very good, unruffled diver.

Eric Sivyer parcelling up a gunport lid, 1976, ready for a safe journey to the surface: Photo: Alexander McKee.

After the usual guided tour of the run of main frames to the north, we turned and swam back to the stern where the port quarter was partly exposed with a loose gunport lying on it. We could not talk, but brief messages could be passed by writing them down on our waterproof wrist-pads. Here the dig had gone down six feet, exposing a remarkable curve of the timbers which still puzzled us. To see the hull, it was necessary to sink down between the scaffold poles of the grid, under the airlift lines, the airlift running ropes and all the survey tapes and general gubbins, and get in actually under the curve of the hull, so that it was above us—all without flippering up a cloud of impenetrable muck. But together we managed it. Then, as we floated up the stern to the top of the

excavation again, Reg Cloudsdale swooped down and politely lifted a thin survey line out of the Royal path.

Our guest was so obviously enjoying himself and longing for more, that I suggested he take a brief rest and then go down with Don Bullivant on an airlift shift, to see how the digging was actually carried out. Afterwards, the Prince declared himself 'delighted and fascinated' by what he had been able to see. It was almost exactly 430 years since Henry VIII had seen the last of the *Mary Rose*, and on just such a splendid July day as this. But whereas 29 July, 1545 (which 19 July would have been by our modern calendar) was a day of sorrow for the court, 30 July, 1975, had been a wonderful occasion for all of us; Royal recognition for our efforts in the most happy way imaginable.

Five days later Morrie Young at last cracked the mystery of the *Mary Rose*. Having started with my idea of a ship heeled 45 degrees from the vertical, so that one side would be largely preserved but the other side would mostly be missing, the initial results of our excavations appeared to contradict this theory, indicating instead a kind of English *Wasa*—a deeply-buried wreck, heeled only slightly, and preserved almost equally high up on both sides. All of us had this impression: historians, shipwrights, archaeologists. At the stern, on the port side, there was a very large composite timber which Morrie thought might be a

Left: Lifting another wrought-iron gun in 1977. Found near the bow, the broad arrow—the Government mark—was legible, and the earliest known. Photo: Alexander McKee.

Right: The gun went into this new hydrogen reduction oven for treatment. Photo: Alexander McKee.

transom fashion piece; if it was, we should be able to find its companion over on the starboard side. But no such piece appeared. Niggling doubts began to accumulate—certain parts of the structure had seemed to me (but I was not a real ship expert) to resemble parts of the hold of the *Victory*. In any event, as Morrie had long ago told us, the large composite timber must be a key piece, and now at last we had the time and money to dig it to a respectable depth and so reveal the truth.

On 4 August, 1975, I was just drying off after my third inspection dive of the day, when Morrie Young surfaced, came into the cabin and said something like: 'Sorry, Mac, it's not a fashion piece, it's the sternpost.'

Everything fell into place. You could almost hear the click! The fashion pieces are curved timbers which outline the transom stern, joining the sternpost which is a vertical timber. A measurement there would give the true angle of heel to within a degree or two. Instantly, I went down again, this time with Morrie—and found that he was absolutely right. Now that he had said it, we could all see. The sternpost it was, but the angle of heel was terrific—the *Mary Rose* must be lying right over on her side.

I had on board, in my 'portable office' folder, a copy of my 1970 interpretation of the 'W' feature as representing a buried wreck heeled 45 degrees. Now that we were back to square one again, I took it out and studied it, to work out the implications of a heel much greater than 45 degrees.

At home that evening, I converted an aircraft navigational instrument (which I still had from my pre-war Portsmouth Aero Club days) into an underwater angle measurer; and, using it on 5 August, our final day of the year, found that the angle was not less than 60 degrees and probably a bit more. That had tremendous implications.

We had already measured the angle the starboard stern castling made with the seabed—45 degrees. Allowing a reasonable 10 or 15 degree inclination inboard when the ship was upright, that meant that the castling might still be in its original position and not bent over like a flattened blade of grass. Now if the deck beams, when we found them, were all at 30 degrees, this would indicate with virtual certainty that the major part of the hull was structurally sound. But we still had to investigate the bow—with the stern, a main weak point of any ship—and measure the tread length of the keel.

But there was no more money to finance further diving in 1975. The stunning implications of Morrie Young's discovery, and deeper excavation of the hull, would have to wait until the following year.

I was abroad much of the autumn, lecturing in Stockholm and then researching in Greece. A minor heart attack landed me in an Athens hospital, and when I returned to England it was with strict instructions to spend the next three months resting and avoiding all stress. I would be able to start swimming again the following summer, and would recover completely in 12 to 18 months, but for the moment I could not deal with the political manoeuvrings that seem to become part and parcel of any major project like the *Mary Rose*.

In any case I found these undercurrents difficult to deal with. They had been growing steadily since, with Morrie Young and Percy Ackland, I had raised the first gun back in 1970, and I found them time-consuming and detrimental to the project itself; also, alas, they made me angry. I had looked on the steady uncovering of the *Mary Rose* as a fascinating study and loathed the unpleasant atmosphere that resulted when some people saw it as a 'property' for personal ambition. However my programme of work for the next two seasons, 1976–1977 (which was my most urgent concern), was passed by the committee, and in June I was aqualung diving again on the *Mary Rose*.

In this I was luckier than some of the team who had been forced to give up diving for medical reasons, especially trivially annoying ones such as ear and sinus troubles. Tony Barber, an engineer and photographer, was a case in point. Joining the team as a diver in 1973, sinus trouble made him give up in 1976. However, his skills as an engineer made him perhaps even more valuable in maintaining the boats and gear. A twin-hulled craft such as *Roger Grenville*, 40 feet long and 15 feet wide, with two engines and two compressors, was a handful. Further, she was not conveniently moored alongside the Camber quay but out over the water at Vospers pontoon where Tony went regularly to maintain her:

> Besides work on her at weekends, I found it necessary to pay two or three visits during the week. Each visit meant baling out a leaky dinghy and then paddling it, sometimes in vain, against a headwind in the dark. It's no joke struggling down a one-foot-wide catwalk at 45 degrees when the tide's out, with a heavy bag of tools, especially when it's slippery with frost. It's even less fun when, after working by torchlight for an hour, running

Left: A broken protractor found in a compartment under the fighting castle at the bow. Photo: Portsmouth City Engineer's Dept.

Right: the broken protractor was lying this side up, as shown by the shellfish that have settled there. Photo: Portsmouth City Engineer's Dept.

the engine to pump the bilges out, you perhaps have to manhandle a heavy duty battery up the same slippery catwalk with just a single rope to hold on to.

The craft had been built by an amateur in his garden as a sailing craft for cruising, not as a heavy-machinery workboat-cum-diving platform, and it had to be treated like a basket of eggs. Don Bullivant, an ex-submariner who used to take turns as cox, commented:

At the start everything worked perfectly, but how we cursed as the years passed and mechanical breakdowns started and made it very difficult to handle—rudders parting, gears not engaging, one or even two engines stalling—making it a nightmare for the coxswain.

Nevertheless, *Roger Grenville* served us well from 1971 to 1978, and she never did come apart in the middle and become two separate boats, as I some-times feared she would when we drove her back in a Force 8 gale. With up to 200 ships a day using Portsmouth Harbour in 1976, and more than 5,000 leisure craft berthed nearby, the Solent was no fun-fare for the feckless. For those who have never driven a boat, it must be added that in no way does it resemble a motor car in its handling; wind and tide can act powerfully on the hull and there is not the precise control one expects with a road vehicle. However, fog was probably the deadliest hazard, with ships belting along trusting to radar.

The financial side began to show definite improve-ment; it was no longer hand-to-mouth. The City of Portsmouth increased their stake so that our budget varied between £10,000 and £15,000 a year. The desperately improvised character of our operations disappeared. But to work a continuous programme of two or three months was quite beyond the resources of unpaid part-timers, mostly restricted to weekends. The extra divers came from the ranks of university students and graduates, particularly from the Uni-versity of Aston in Birmingham, while a marine biological team joined us from Bangor. They lived in primitive conditions, camping locally and doing much of their own cooking, and were paid only subsistence. There were also one or two professional archaeologists now, among them Keith Muckelroy from the University of St. Andrews, whose death in a diving accident a few years later was a tragic loss.

By August, 1976, we had got right down below the keel at the stern in a giant, right-angled pit more than a dozen feet deep; often, I had to clear my ears from the increasing pressure as I swam down the sternpost. In natural light the wood was black, but by torch or flashlight the timbers turned a rich brown, except for the lower strakes where they shone with a silvery, metallic sheen, perhaps part of the anti-fouling composition used in Tudor times. The rudder proved to be narrow-bladed and turned slightly to starboard, protected underneath by a skeg. Its iron hangings had vanished into concretions which preserved their shape. Apart from that, the stern appeared encourag-ingly intact. Nic Knights, our ship draughtsman, reported:

The structure in this area is obviously very sound. The planking seams, including the housing of the plank ends into the sternpost rebate, are still very tight without any indication of displacement or weakening of the internal structure. Trenail fastenings are still apparently secure,

A modern measuring instrument: a hand-held sonar 'gun' that records distances with precision and speed. Photo: Alexander McKee.

but any iron fastenings in the plankends will undoubtedly be suspect. I do not think there can be any dispute over the condition or structural integrity of this area of the hull.

By excavating to the keel at the stern, we had one firm starting point for measurement. The 60 degree angle of heel I had already taken the previous year before we had actually got down to the keel, so I at least was clear in my mind that the *Mary Rose* now lay right over on her side. There was, however, confusion in some quarters between 60 degrees and 30 degrees, and for some years diagrams showing only a 30 degree angle of heel actually appeared in the literature and in slide shows; how this occurred, I have never understood. It was not an academic point, because it vitally affected how much hull we had underneath the mud on the starboard side and consequently, not only the value of the remaining hull but the time it would take to excavate.

Another measurement along the keel from the sternpost indicated that the hull had reached the bottom not merely heeled right over, but stern down. That explained the misleading impression given by the Cowdray Engraving which showed only the two tallest masts rearing out of the water, one higher than the other; this I had assumed, wrongly as it turned out, to be the mainmast. The narrowness of the rudder blade confirmed that one or both of the mizzenmasts probably played an important part in steering a carrack.

The ship experts, both those who dived with us and those who advised us from abroad, were unanimous that the most important remaining measurement was the tread length of the keel—that is, the distance between the forefoot (where stem and keel join) and the sternpost. This would be the equivalent of measuring the spine of a man; it would give you roughly all the other measurements. It would even tell you in advance how large the ship hall of your museum had to be. Therefore, the next object must be to find the bow, identify the forefoot, and take the measurement.

In 1976, we discovered some damage at the bow, and in 1977 we located the forefoot. The stem itself was missing, probably fallen away to starboard in the scourpit. The archaeologists became concerned. I understood and respected their impeccable principles—that we should record the ship as if we were not going to raise her but destroy her (which is often the necessary result of archaeological excavations on land, where one building site overlaps another). But the ship experts became impatient when people were set to drawing the individual spike holes indicating where a plank had been 'hung' on the hull with iron nails before the fastenings proper, the trenails, had been inserted. This, they thought was a trivial measurement compared to the key length between stem and stern. At last the archaeologists produced a figure of 129 feet, which to the theoreticians seemed excessive; the *Wasa* was only 122 feet and the *Mary Rose*, they believed, would be somewhat less. Some years later, the archaeologists remeasured and announced a final figure of 105 feet as the tread length.

During 1977 and 1978 we dug across the hull at the bow in order to find the starboard side. The archaeologists thought the hull might be broken longitudinally and in any event must lie only about six feet down, whereas the ship experts thought the distance was double that—more than 12 feet to dig. And they were right. Consequently the excavation took two years instead of one which, in the context of the long history of the *Mary Rose*, was a matter of not the slightest consequence. I, with the nautical experts, did not believe that the hull—apart from the extremity of the bow—had broken. As the dig across the ship went on, I measured the angles at which the deck beams and bulkheads were emerging from the clay and had consistent results of about 30 degrees, which for a deck on a ship heeled 60 degrees, was of course exactly right.

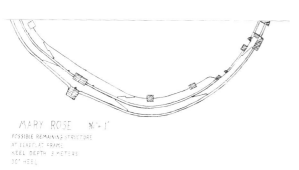

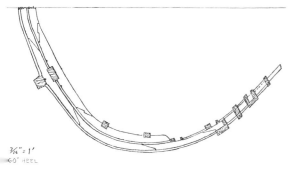

MARY ROSE 3⁄16" = 1'
POSSIBLE REMAINING STRUCTURE
AT DEADFLAT FRAME
KEEL DEPTH 3 METERS
30° HEEL

3⁄16" = 1'
60° HEEL

The immense difference between 30° and 60° angles of heel, illustrated by Edward Von der Porten on a theoretical section through the *Mary Rose*.

A new 6-inch airlift with a semi-flexible lower end to make digging easier. Ray McLaren and Adrian Barak lower it into the water, while two divers swim it down. Photo: Tony Barber.

Now, for the first time on a large scale, we were actually entering the ship; going inside her. It finally became apparent that the dig had cut across on the line of a bulkhead running along the aft end of the fighting castle at the bow. In one small compartment, under a ladder, a long grey wooden box lay on a steeply heeled deck. The dovetailing was perfect and it looked exactly like the sort of chest one might expect to find in one's grandmother's attic, sound but covered in cobwebs. One would never imagine that this furniture had been under the sea for more than 430 years, except that a gaming board, part of a protractor and a human bone lay upon it.

At last many important people were convinced that the *Mary Rose* had a future that must be not merely national but international; and the largest underwater excavation of all time began, designed to culminate in the raising of the hull and its display ashore in a purpose-built museum.

Chapter 10

The Prince as President

Full Excavation and Salvage, 1979–1982

When in the early years people asked me how long it would take to raise the *Mary Rose* and what it would cost, I used to answer, with the insouciance of one accustomed to dealing with pounds, shillings and pence (and more of the last than the first), 'Five years and five million pounds.' The actual salvage would not cost more than a fraction of that sum, but besides raising the hull a museum complex would have to be built around a shiphall where temperature and humidity could be controlled while conservation work was carried out. I saw the project as the equivalent of erecting a new school; and a Tudor Ship Museum such as I proposed would certainly be educational. We might not be able to bring back to life the soldiers and seamen who had died in her, but we would be doing the next best thing: re-creating for twentieth century eyes the surroundings and conditions in which men of the sixteenth century had lived and died.

Shortly after the formation of the Mary Rose Trust in 1979, Prince Charles agreed to become our President, making clear that he would like his involvement to be more than nominal; and indeed it was! He gave a great deal of his time to it, addressing many fund-raising functions and coming down each summer to dive on the *Mary Rose* again and see how work was progressing.

I became a member of the Trust's Executive Committee, which was in effect its board of directors, and also a member of the Site Development Panel responsible for planning and building the Tudor Ship Museum I had long envisaged. This was now as important as the work at Spithead because at least the ship-hall with its built-in controlled environment and some public viewing facility must be ready before the *Mary Rose* could be raised. In effect, there were now two *Mary Rose* sites, one at Spithead and the other ashore in Portsmouth, and work on them had to be dovetailed. Only one other Trustee, also a member of

the site team, the London architect Alexander Flinder, was an amateur diver familiar with the *Mary Rose*. The rest would not see the *Mary Rose* (except on television) until we raised her. I was still able to dive and inspect the progress of the work at Spithead, but no longer had any operational control or responsibility for it. This was now entirely exercised by the Archaeological Director, Margaret Rule, who also accepted 'special responsibility' for salvage, and much else besides.

Privately, I doubted the possibility of raising the ship in 1981, which some people expected. Speaking for the experienced divers, I warned that 'the time-scale will prove unrealistic', although 'it might be achieved by a year or two's extra work.' However, there was no denying that the feeling so widely generated, that the *Mary Rose* was about to surface any minute, had a most marvellously beneficial effect on fund-raising; people became desperately anxious to contribute.

Nevertheless, cash was still short, as it had always been. All that had changed was the scale. In the beginning, I was always wondering where the next four or five or ten pounds were coming from; then it was the next £50 or £100; in the last few years of the Mary Rose Committee the usual deficit was around £1,000. Now, it became a matter of the next £100,000, or even the next half million. But always, somehow, in the end we raised the money and paid the bills.

The Trust's programme was to empty the ship of guns, artefacts and ballast before salvaging what would be the empty shell of a one-sided ship; and parts of that ship, particularly the decks, were to be dismantled in order to allow safe access to the areas beneath. In the event, the process of full excavation lasted from the summer of 1979 to the summer of 1982.

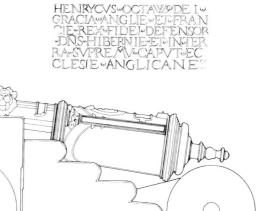

ROBERT·AND·JOHN·OWYN·BRETHERYN·BORNE
IN·THE·CYTE·OF·LONDON·THE·SONNES·OF·AN
INGLISH·MADE·THYS·BASTARD·ANNO·DNI·1537

HENRYCVS·OCTAVV·DE I·
GRACIA·ANGLIE·ET·FRAN
CIE·REX·FIDEI·DEFENSOR
·DNS·HIBERNIE·ET·IN·TER
RA·SVPRE·MV·CAPVT·EC
CLESIE·ANGLICANE·

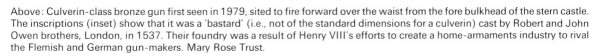

SCALE   0 _____ 1metre

Above: Culverin-class bronze gun first seen in 1979, sited to fire forward over the waist from the fore bulkhead of the stern castle. The inscriptions (inset) show that it was a 'bastard' (i.e., not of the standard dimensions for a culverin) cast by Robert and John Owen brothers, London, in 1537. Their foundry was a result of Henry VIII's efforts to create a home-armaments industry to rival the Flemish and German gun-makers. Mary Rose Trust.

Below left: No one knew what Tudor shipboard gun carriages were like until Eric Sivyer found this example in 1979, with a bronze gun mounted on it. Mary Rose Trust.

Below right: The lifting points on the 1979 bronze gun were very noble lions' heads. Mary Rose Trust

GUN CARRIAGE
RECONSTRUCTION

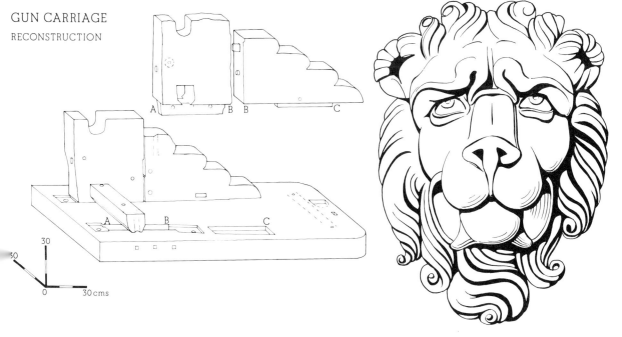

30

0   30cms

Another bronze gun being inspected at the headquarters of the Mary Rose Trust by work experience scheme youngsters and their supervisor, Peter Upton. Photo: Mary Rose Trust.

The entire ship, the hold, the gundecks and the cabins, were filled with clay and mud containing the most delicate artefacts—shoes, boots, wicker baskets. The excavation had to be carried out with great care. The system used was to divide the dig into small squares delineated by a grid system of scaffold poles. Each square was numbered and any digging there controlled by an individual supervisor. Many hundreds of amateur divers were used, but most saw only a tiny part of the *Mary Rose*—their immediate working area. On my inspection dives, however, I toured the whole ship at intervals over the years; and it *was* literally years before the entire hull could be seen.

Up to now we had deliberately avoided digging inside the hull unless absolutely necessary; our excavations had been directed towards the exposure of key parts of the ship's external structure. And because, as became apparent, we were dealing with a largely intact (if one-sided) hull, the finds had been minimal. They consisted mainly of items which had

fallen into the scourpit during the long period of decay and collapse of the upperworks and port side. Now that we were digging inside, however, spectacular discoveries came thick and fast. They consisted of displaced artefacts which had been in the castles but in the collapse stage had become trapped in the intact areas of ship below them; and of intact items still in place on the decks, more or less as they had been on 19 July, 1545.

On 3 June, 1979, after working on the project for twelve years, Eric Sivyer made a momentous discovery. 'Outlining' was still going on along the stern castle on the starboard side and the waist of the ship had not yet been found. The last frame I had had numbered there (back in 1973) was frame 186; now 189 had been found and numbered. Sivyer's task was to dig forward on the line of the framing to find the next one to the north and number it 190. Swimming to 189, he measured north the usual distance between castle frames (about 3 feet) and dug there, without result. Eric therefore veered a few feet inboard and began to dig again—and this time there was timber. He started to uncover the wood. If it was a frame, it was a very curious one, for it was stepped. Then, alongside and attached, a curved timber began to appear—a wooden wheel! Eric now dug on the opposite side of the stepped timber. A greenish metal tube with rings on it began to emerge. The colour instantly told him what his find must be—a bronze gun. It was the most thrilling moment for years—the discovery of the first such gun since those found by John Deane in 1840. He sketched his find and then surfaced to report to Jonathan Adams, the archaeological supervisor for this area of the ship. Jon asked: 'Did you find 190?'

'No, but I found something of interest', replied Eric. Showing the drawing, he added, 'Do you recognise this?'

Listed in the inventory were '20 hailshot pieces' with 'iron dice' as their ammunition. This is one found in the stern castle. It is a small, semi-portable gun with a wooden butt. The square dice would spread from the muzzle in a deadly scatter to mow down boarders. Photo: Mary Rose Trust.

Adrian Barak, who joined the project in 1971, with a longbow recovered ten years later. The 'pull' of such a weapon might be as much as 80 lbs. Photo: Mary Rose Trust.

'Oh, my God!' said Jon, and dived to have a look. Sure enough, there was a rose on the metal; it was indeed a Henry VIII gun.

I was particularly interested in the siting of this gun. I had, long years ago, made a crude model of the *Mary Rose*, trying to work out some of the problems presented by the only authentic picture, in the Anthony Roll, to see where the arrow slits for archers might be, and where the very mixed collection of guns might be mounted. This one came as a great surprise. A culverin-class weapon, very similar to one raised by Deane in 1836, it was lying along a deck in the stern castle, above the height of the ordinary gundecks, and its muzzle pointed north towards the bow. Firstly, it was a heavier piece than I would have expected to find at this height in the ship. Secondly, as excavation in the area went on, I became convinced that the gun had not rolled down here from somewhere else, but was still actually emplaced as it had been for battle—that is, it was not a broadside piece, but was mounted to fire forward over the waist and possibly off the bow to starboard. A bit of the breeching rope was still in position and a copper powder ladle found partially crushed under the outboard side of the barrel, so the gun had evidently tipped over on its carriage when the ship rolled to starboard and sank.

This was, incidentally, the first Tudor shipboard gun carriage ever seen. They were known only from a few ship sketches showing the armament at a very small scale indeed. That alone was exciting, but even more so was the appearance of a bulkhead alongside the gun, which gave the clear impression, to me at any rate, that there had been an aperture through which the muzzle of the culverin had originally protruded. The breech end of the barrel, which would have been inside the stern castle and decked over, was perfectly clean except for a thin concretion; but the muzzle and the few feet of metal just behind it were quite thickly encrusted with oysters. This would have happened very soon after the ship sank, although it would have taken three or four years for the spat which had settled there to grow to this size. One could visualise the hull heeled over, with the silenced gun muzzles, wreathed in oysters, pointing out into the slanting sunlight; and behind them, in the dark recesses of the covered decks and flooded cabins, the gunners, seamen and officers trapped there forever—until the moment when we came and exposed them to the sunlight again.

Excavation soon showed that this was indeed the

Above: Authentic items of archery were few and far between until the *Mary Rose* was excavated; from her decks and storage boxes have come thousands of these unknown or scarce artefacts. Shown here are longbows. Photo: Mary Rose Trust

Below: Ready-to-use ammunitiion: 24 arrows from a quiver, the shafts being held apart by a leather spacer. Photo: Mary Rose Trust.

forward end of the stern castle and that the upper gundeck lay below. On it, only a short distance from the culverin's muzzle, was the back end of a huge slide carriage which clearly held a monster wrought-iron gun whose muzzle, many feet down in the clay , would still be protruding through a port in the starboard side. In terms of excavation time, the muzzle was still two years' work away. However, the waist began to appear and, forward, what looked like the junction of waist and bow castle and concretions which might be catted anchors. On the gundeck between there were small gratings, with another gundeck lying below that, still filled with solid clay; there were many poles which were in fact boarding pikes lying on the steeply tilted upper deck; bows of various sizes gradually came to light, and arrows also, plus a complete quiver containing 24 arrows, the equivalent of the cartridge bandoliers and magazine pouches of the Second World War. Bones, too, were everywhere emerging from the clay. Some, like that silent culverin still peering out of the stern castle, had oyster valves growing on them.

What I judged to be spars and supports to hold boarding netting, together with ropes which appeared to be part of the netting itself, showed how the upper deck in the waist had been closed over for battle, dooming everyone on it when the ship sank. I jotted down in red in my rough logbook:

> Finds of spar deck, spars and boarding netting in waist show why bodies could not rise to surface and must remain in ship. THIS IS WHY SO FEW SURVIVORS. Only sailors in rigging and servants on poop deck stood a chance.

That day, 5 August, I had also seen, aft in the stern castle, what looked like the first actual body (as distinct from bones, scattered or otherwise). I recorded in my log:

> I went to the stern castle, swimming along the deck inboard, not over frame ends. Saw skull at once in good, clear visibility (in the morning it had been 2 feet clear, maximum 4–6 feet). Well excavated by Jonathan Adams in area where he found pike head. Saw pelvis beyond and higher, apparently half-buried in soil; and two big bones sticking up. I took flash pictures from all directions for at least five minutes. Then I realised there was a strip of fabric, like a belt, near pelvis, and pelvis was part of a *solid lump of something*. I touched it—*soft and rubbery* (so not concretion, weed or soil). Looked like a torso which had perhaps been clad in a jerkin: there was a curve to it (like a breastplate). The 'belt' was where the

Some of the thousands of arrows recovered—so many that they represent a real storage problem. Photo: Mary Rose Trust.

waist might be. It could be a strap, of course, not a belt.

I don't think any of the others at that time had ever seen anything like this. I had—in a farmhouse on the Dutch-German border in March, 1945, after the snows had melted away from the corpses of the soldiers who had died there many months before. One of the Canadians had no head, only the top of the spine sticking out; while the legs had mummified (and been booby-trapped). Such things had been the common coin of my generation. And because there were still live Germans in that area, I might have joined the ghastly dead. This was true also of diving on the *Mary Rose* where experience and skill were vital. Indeed it was in that same month that 'Robbie' Robinson came close to losing his life:

> It was my second dive of the day and it was about noon. The sky was overcast with a light wind, and the tide was just starting to run.
> I was briefed by the diver who had just come up that he had uncovered what he thought was a piece of leather. I checked my gear—I had on a life jacket belonging to the Trust. The day before I had had

Two angels carved on bone—possibly part of plaque. Photo: Mary Rose Trust.

trouble with my demand valve, but that night I had had it serviced and it had been all right on my first dive. I entered the water, taking with me a plastic carrier bag in which was a two pound lead weight. I swam down the shot rope that was attached to the diving platform suspended amidships on the starboard side of the diving ship.

When I reached the bottom I stopped and looked around. The visibility was good: around 15 feet. I followed the yellow scaffold pole leading to my working area. To my left was the level seabed, to my right the grid which covered the ship. The squares of the grid were numbered with tags on the yellow pole. My number was 6, the second one along this pole. It was about 10 feet square, and tied to one of the poles was the airlift. I attached my bag to the corner opposite the one where I was to work. I lay along the pole on which the airlift was tied and looked around. There was no other diver in the water at this time.

I looked at my working area—it was level and about a foot below the poles. There was a brown shape in the soft grey clay. I took a closer look and measured in from two of the poles and recorded it on my board. My first job would be to clear this object out of the way.

I now began to notice that I was having difficulty in getting air. I knelt up and tipped my head back (with a twin-hose demand valve this sometimes clears the obstruction). That did the trick.

I started to airlift around the object which, to my delight, proved to be a complete shoe. I carefully placed it in my bag and went on removing the clay. Once or twice I had to stop to clear my valve. Gradually it got worse until I had to stop work altogether. As I was tying the airlift to the pole, my air stopped. Panic!

I turned to find the yellow pole, but then remembered my bag with the shoe. I was not going to leave that behind. I swam over to where it was and untied it.

I began to feel pains in my chest. It seemed a long way back to the shot rope, but I remembered thinking that with the change in depth my valve would work when I neared the surface. At last I reached the rope. The water now seemed dark and menacing. I raced upwards, my lungs bursting. My brain was telling me I should be going slower: no faster than your bubbles—but I had no bubbles. At last I could see the surface. Just below it the shot line stretched to my left as far as I could see. I knew I would not make it if I followed the rope, so I let go about two feet below the surface. I thought that once on the surface I would be able to find it again. This was my first mistake—as soon as I let go of the rope it disappeared.

On the surface, I dropped my mouthpiece and gulped in a mouthful of air and water as I was hit by a large wave. Facing me a few yards away was the diving platform. On it I could see the standby diver. Still

Tudor warships carried musical instruments for conveying orders as well as for entertainment on board. This one, being examined by Debbie Fulford, senior illustrator in the drawing office, is a tabor pipe to be played at the same time as the drums. Photo: Mary Rose Trust.

spluttering and coughing I raised my right arm to signal that I was in trouble, and waved until I went under.

On coming up all I could see was the open sea. There was a loud clunk as my cylinder struck something and I was spun around: I had hit the ship's mooring cable. I clutched at the cable and held on, with my back to the waves and the diving platform. I tried to pull myself up on the cable but I was too exhausted. If only I could get two good lungfuls of air I would be all right.

I did not panic, but my brain seemed to slow down and become detached from my body. I seemed to talk to myself.

'You have a lifejacket, why don't you blow it up?'

I opened the cylinder. There was a noise as the air entered the jacket.

'Now you're all right', I said, so I relaxed and promptly sank. I coughed and spluttered back to the surface.

'Why not breathe from the jacket?'

I found the mouthpiece. It was then I noticed that the tube had come away from the jacket and there was now a large hole in the jacket, which filled with water.

I waved the hose in the air with contempt to show the standby diver what had happened.

I heard myself say: 'You are not going to make it. This is going to be the end.'

I thought of my wife, the house we were in the process of buying. We would not get that now, but the insurance would pay off the mortgage on the old one. I thought of my two children. They would miss having a father.

I had now given up the struggle. It was not worth it—why not relax and get it over? It was the thought of my wife and children which brought me back. 'Have one more go.'

I knew, if I let go of the cable the next wave would sweep me away. The engine on the inflatable rescue boat was not working properly, so by the time it was started I would be lost. With what seemed great reluctance, I let go of the carrier bag containing the shoe. With the two pound weight inside, it sank. After the next wave, I would let go of the cable and try to undo my weight belt. This meant holding what breath I had, as I would go under. If I could not do it, I would not come up again. I let go.

At the same time something grabbed my cylinder and I was moving backwards but underwater. The next thing I remembered, I was lying on the diving platform stripped of my gear and feeling sick.

Drowning is supposed to be an easy way to go. 'Robbie' didn't find it so, nor had I when some years before I had been trapped for a few minutes without air, down on the *Mary Rose*, and had begun to breathe water before being saved by Reg Cloudsdale. I thought I knew very well what the last moments of the dead men aboard her had been like, hopelessly doomed and helpless.

Towards the end of August a second bronze gun was found in the castle near the first, but this one was muzzle down, so all one saw in 1979 was the cascable, the breech end of the barrel and part of the wooden carriage. Like the wrought-iron gun in the waist, the gun port through which it still glared out as if at the French, lay many feet down and two years away.

When the concretion was knocked off the culverin Eric Sivyer had discovered, I noted with surprise that the barrel was blue. One knew that guns were often painted in bright colours in Tudor times, but underwater, with pinkish-red seaweed drifting past and a crab hiding in the blue muzzle and another sitting on the blue cascable, it made a highly unlikely picture. A readable inscription showed that it had been cast by the Owen brothers in 1537, the year after the re-

Little was known about Tudor rigging. The 'parrel' is often mentioned in connection with the masts and spars of carracks, and here is one—an elaborate assembly of wooden ball bearings. Photo: Mary Rose Trust.

The earliest known mariner's compass in the world— recovered from the *Mary Rose*, and not all that different from a modern one. Photo: Mary Rose Trust.

building of the *Mary Rose*. A concretion containing a small swivel gun which I had found in the early 1970s and then backfilled, was raised in 1979 and when opened some years later, proved to hold a hailshot piece loaded with iron dice. This must surely have been a close-quarter anti-personnel weapon.

We no longer used a diving boat which went out and came back every day. We had the luxury of a ship moored on site all round the clock for the entire season—spring to autumn and sometimes into the winter. A paid crew manned the ship and a nucleus of paid divers controlled the masses of volunteers from the sub-aqua clubs who swarmed in, giving up a week or two—or more—of their holidays to work on the *Mary Rose*. To begin with, they had to be trained, for most had never done any archaeological work of this nature before and had never handled an airlift. This was a sore point with the old hands of the Special Branch who had been working on the site for between 8 and 12 years; for they were put on the same basis as everyone else and not allowed to work at weekends or indeed at any time at all unless they could afford to give up at least nine continuous days. This even applied to the people who had made the original airlifts. Only four of the experienced divers were willing or able to give the time required, so the Branch was unable to control the diving any longer. This was formally recognised at a Branch meeting held early in 1980, and from that date the Branch's responsibility ceased.

Those members of the Branch who did continue to go out on site, despite or perhaps because of their great experience, were often given the technically difficult and strenuous manual tasks, while the in-experienced newcomers were put to the delicate work of excavation. There were other changes, too, per-haps inevitable, as Don Bullivant recalled.

> The close, friendly atmosphere disappeared, and the whole show became more and more military: super-visors we did not know, new divers all very serious, mostly too nervous to take the jokes we used to play on each other.
>
> But the project started to go into the big time, and I decided to go along with it. We made every attempt to keep the original team together. Eric Sivyer, 'Robbie' Robinson and myself became known as the Pickfords Removal Team, no job too large for us. One dive I recall was to remove a carling (a very large and heavy timber running fore-and-aft through the centre of the ship). It had to be removed to enable excavation to be carried on into the hold. With the help of a lifting bag secured to one end, Robbie and I shunted the timber backwards and forwards, pumping more air into the lifting bag until a neutral buoyancy was obtained; carefully walk-ing across the wreck; and eventually laying it outside the ship.

A small pair of navigational dividers from the stern castle. Photo: Mary Rose Trust.

Going back to investigate the area where the timber had been removed, I found a large partition and, protruding from under it, a skeleton; one leg, one arm and part of the rib cage.

After the usual measuring and recording, I removed the partition, exposing the whole skeleton: leather shoes, leather around the ribs, and the skull lying on its side grinning. The whole lot lay across a large box which turned out to be full of arrows. In fact, three boxes of arrows were eventually excavated.

On 2 July, 1980, Miss Louise Mulford, a 21-year-old volunteer from Reading with three years amateur diving experience, was making her fourth dive on the *Mary Rose*, working an airlift in one of the grid squares. She had taken to the work quickly and was happily working away when a supervisor passed by on an inspection tour. Some minutes later a super-visor on the ship saw what looked like a pair of fins floating just under the surface. The standby diver was into the water in a flash, inflating her lifejacket; and the rescue boat was pulled out on a line within seconds. Louise was taken on board and resuscitation started; within 15 minutes a helicopter was clattering overhead to take her to the R.N. hospital at Gosport, two miles away. But it was all useless, Miss Mulford was dead.

The day had been perfect, a flat calm sea with no wind and an underwater visibility of 10 feet. Miss Mulford's airlift was properly tied off to the grid, as if she had just completed her shift when something happened. Her mouthpiece was in place and her air cylinder held 30 ATS, the normal safe margin a diver leaves to take care of emergencies on the way back to the shot rope leading up to the diving platform at the side of the ship. The inquest showed

A carpenter's plane recovered in 1981. Photo: Mary Rose Trust.

Personal possessions, standing out with a very human aura among the ship's gear and obviously government issue items. Photo: Mary Rose Trust.

Here the work seemed to have been first class. All the barber surgeon's medicine bottles and instruments were recovered; even his cap, a badge of office very different from the one my father had worn, was found, excavated, conserved and put on display. It was most impressive. What we had here were not a few medical items collected from diverse sources, but an actual Tudor ship surgery complete, with everything of the same date and undeniably authentic. Working conditions must have been better than in Nelson's *Victory*, where the doctors worked deep down in the bowels of the ship. If the *Mary Rose* were upright this surgeon's cabin would be full of light and air.

Just above it a third bronze gun had been uncovered, apparently trapping a corpse. This man too had been wearing a leather jerkin or 'jack', the front part of it as stiff as a breastplate. One thigh bone stuck out, with curious fish nosing up past it.

A peppermill in such perfect condition that one might almost sell it as new in a modern shop. Photo: Mary Rose Trust.

that the poor girl had vomited underwater, suffering the same serious trouble that had nearly killed Percy Ackland ten years before, on the morning the timbers of the *Mary Rose* were seen for the first time. He had been able to struggle back to safety; she had not. The most terrible aspect of the whole sad affair was that the standby diver who had gone to Louise's rescue was her fiancé.

In August I went out for four days, diving twice a day, looking particularly at the fastenings of the ship, the standing, hanging and beam knees—large wooden brackets which tie the sides to the decks. Alas, they had been iron-fastened and the iron had rusted away, just as it had in the *Wasa*. I did a 37-minute all-in tour of the entire site, bow to stern and both sides. Then I went into the doctor's surgery—a poignant moment, as my father had been a Surgeon-Commander, R.N. This was located on the starboard side just inside the stern castle. Visibility was at best two and a half feet, my torch flooded on the way down, and the excavation here was deep and black. I sank slowly down into it, hardly finning; waited some minutes at the bottom for my eyes to accustom to the darkness, and then explored the clay in the barber surgeon's cabin with the skin of my fingers. Brushing lightly, I felt a little ointment pot. I noted in my log:

> I don't know how the novices manage. Vis. very poor and you dive into a black hole, about 14–15 feet deep, inside the ship, not knowing what to expect, and fearful of damaging delicate areas. You just let yourself sink down gradually. But how is it for the inexperienced? A test of nerve, with some hazard. And damage to artefacts? They can hardly see what they are doing.

126

Underwater visibility in the summer of 1981 was amazingly clear, with bright light. On one August day, lying in the water by the diving platform and about to swim down the shot rope, I could see more than 40 feet below me the faint yellow gleam of the painted poles of the grid. The seabed, being dark, was invisible. Even so, even with the airlifts working to stir it up, once on the bottom I could see for 20 to 25 feet in any direction. And now, for the first time, one could see almost the entire ship. The excavation was exposing almost all of the decks and had also gone down outboard on the heeled starboard side. My dream of finding a half-intact ship with real guns on real gun decks was beginning to come true as layer after layer of clay was carefully stripped away.

'Robbie' Robinson, recovered from his accident and taking time off from his job as a french polisher, vividly recalled one dive that same August.

The day was overcast with the sun hidden behind a cloud as I swam down the shot line. I followed the ground lines through the gloom until I came to the stern trench. I lay on the seabed and took my bearings. To my right I saw the airlift disappear into the black void of the trench. Just then the sun came out like someone switching on a floodlight. The trench was filled with light, and an amazing sight lay before me.

The face of the trench had been cut straight down and was about 10 feet square. On the seabed at the top of the face were bundles of pike handles, about a dozen in all, each bundle still tied around with cords. Lower down on the left of the face was a round leather disc with holes in it; through some of these holes were broken arrows. A little way to the right, two longbows were protruding about three feet from the face. At the bottom of the trench lay a large bronze cannon. It must have been at least six feet long, with its muzzle disappearing into the face.

On the right side of the trench halfway up the side was a human skull. The mud had been cleared from around it but not from underneath. It was if the skull were on a mud shelf. The lower jaw was missing, or was still buried

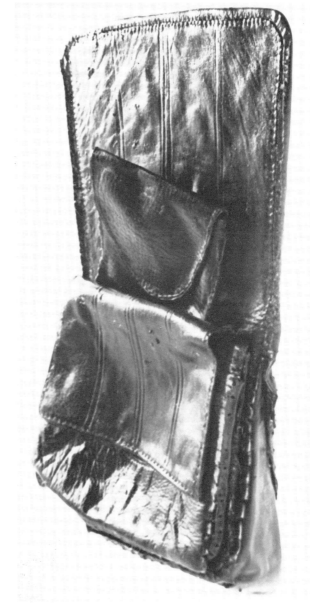

A leather satchel and purse. Photo: Mary Rose Trust.

in the mud shelf. The skull was light brown in colour but the upper teeth were white. It seemed to stare at me from the empty eye sockets. I wondered if he could have been a gunner still at his station, or perhaps an archer. Just then the light began to fade. Slowly, as if an unseen hand were drawing a curtain, the skull faded into the gloom and I was left looking down into the black void.

Douglas J. Barnard, a civil engineer and diver from West Sussex who had been with us for ten years, often took three weeks off at a time to work at Spithead, with the odd week or two at intervals. In 1981 he was

An officer's knee boot. Photo: Mary Rose Trust.

127

A typical shoe from a dead man's foot. Light and serviceable, the slits would make the leather even more flexible and suitable for shipboard life. Photo: Mary Rose Trust.

not so well situated but was able to offer nine days in September.

Friday, 4 September, was the beginning of a short diving session between biggish spring tides. The area now being excavated was the midships section of the deck below the

A pocket sundial, no larger than a modern wrist watch. It includes a compass. Photo: Mary Rose Trust.

main gundeck—the 'orlop'—which previously had been thought to contain only ship's stores and food supplies, and was found to hold very different things indeed.

Immediately forrard of the section I was to work in was a high bulkhead and partition separating the galley from the ship's stores. Here there was an enormous copper and bronze cauldron six feet across, four feet high, for cooking hot meals for the crew—bowmen, sailors, gunners, and probably ship's officers. Around this big cauldron was the complete brick hearth. But because the ship had a heel of 60 degrees to starboard, the whole lot had collapsed, fallen on its side, the cauldron completely turned upside down.

Not only had the ship fallen right over on her starboard side, she had gone down sternfirst as well. The skeg, which projected aft from the sternpost to prevent ropes fouling the rudder, had acted like a ploughshare, cutting a path for the ship into the hard clay like a knife-handle through butter, stopping with a jolt that displaced many items in the hold and on the decks.

A finds assistant on the base ship *Sleipner* cleans an artefact prior to conservation. Photo: Mary Rose Trust.

Doug was able to see the results of that sudden, jarring halt:

The jolt had affected the big sections of timber stacked in piles each side of the galley cauldron hearth. They were just rough tree trunks and branches about four feet long and up to nine inches thick. These burst through the relatively thin bulkhead partition and tumbled down onto the ship's stores and larder area where piles of

barrels were stacked one upon the other—small barrels of salted meats, jointed pork, mutton, and larger barrels of beef sides. Some barrels were intact and not crushed. Very few escaped complete. One of the first things one has to remember about any shipwreck is that animal protein and fats will not just lie there forever, waiting to be covered with silt to encapsulate everything until discovered by divers 400 years later.

Far from it! Within a very few hours of the ship going down the human skin would become white, wrinkled and softened. After the initial clouds of silt had dispersed in the tide, the seaweed in the water would catch on to the obstructions. The anti-boarding netting would have 200–300 drowned bowmen, gunners and sailors caught like fish in a net. After one or two days these would float up in the netting, being first attacked by fish. Then, as the corpses settled, the shoal fish would invade the wreck. They would remove the extremities first—that is, fingers and toes. Gloves would not have been worn by plain bowmen and seamen. Also, most sailors would be barefooted; few would have worn shoes. Those shoes that have been found are heel-less—flat soles with a single one-piece upper over the toes. Only a few

A consignment of artefacts emerging from the freeze-drying chamber in the conservation laboratory ashore in Old Portsmouth. Photo: Mary Rose Trust.

elaborate boots have been discovered, with laces, or thonging up each side.

The ship was intended to be manned by 415 men but was probably over-manned to try to even the odds. There were about 36 survivors. And to this date 93 skeletal remains had been recovered. Most are handless and footless except for those who had armour on, that is, leather gloves, worn by the officers or a few bowmen.

What I found, lying in square o6, was a 99 per cent complete human being, or its remains. He was lying on his back, feet towards the side of the ship, against the partition adjoining the galley cauldron. He was lying on a straw palliasse. Re-assembly of the main bones revealed that he was of substantial stature, in excess of six feet tall and probably 12 to 14 stone in weight— perhaps a bowman injured early in the battle. Beside him but six feet further aft, two more bodies were discovered, but I did not excavate these and have no details.

Big fire logs had thundered down the deck, roughly parallel, confirming that this compartment was empty apart from the barrels of meat, and was used as a sick bay. This bowman died instantly, his rib cage crushed, collar bones and shoulder bones broken, and tips of five vertebrae broken off. The only parts of him I was unable to recover were the hands and feet—but not far away six right-foot and two left-foot bones were found. One can

Large timber items are held in 'deep freeze'—in refrigerated freight containers. Photo: Mary Rose Trust.

easily imagine crabs scurrying around in the gloomy green darkness, seizing a finger or two, and disappearing to hideaway holes between the broken barrels.

The first part of the man I discovered was the 'U' bone of the underside of the jaw. I gradually felt around the hard bone, easing the soft, cold surrounding silt to the suck of the airlift. It made a shudder go right

A finds assistant drawing a tiller from one of the ship's boats. Photo: Mary Rose Trust.

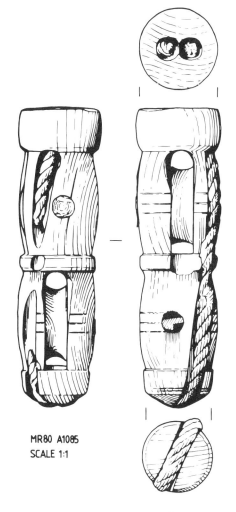

MR80 A1085
SCALE 1:1

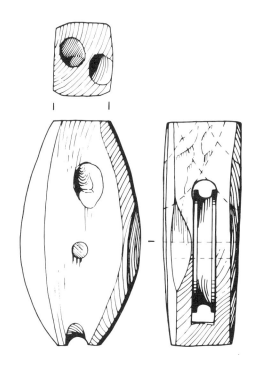

Blocks from the rigging of the *Mary Rose*. The largest are more than 5 feet long; many are similar to modern blocks. Photo: Mary Rose Trust.

through me, even though I had found skeletal remains many times before. This wasn't just a piece of bone. It was the skin of a soul lost while keeping England a free country.

Easing out those bones from beneath the firelogs took a long time—five days and 13 dives lasting between 22 and 45 minutes. All bones were placed in large grey plastic boxes with red lids tied on, to prevent anything being lost on the way up. His leather garments were sorted out separately and put into larger boxes, and only brought to the surface when the waves abated.

Doug worked in the usual way, cutting a vertical face 12 inches high, leaving a horizontal bed of mud and silts behind. After recovering the skeleton of the sick or wounded man who had been crushed by the falling firelogs as the ship sank sternfirst, he now found random barrel staves from several shattered barrels which had also been crushed by the cascade of logs. The contents of the barrels were also put into grey plastic boxes with red lids, weighted with 4lbs of

lead. Up to now, Doug had been working 20 feet below the seabed underneath the main deck beams angled at 30 degrees over his head and behind him. Then the 'dismantling team' removed them.

This allowed much more gentle green light into the work area. Immediately above me in square M6 was a beautiful 24-lb bronze cannon, still on its carriage with its muzzle right through its gunport. That dark green opalescent water sometimes cleared enough to see 12 to 15 feet, and on freak tides and water conditions, on an afternoon of bright sun, for about 20 minutes there was 25 feet.

I could see that the pork bones from the broken barrel still actually had meat on! As I lifted two handfuls at a time, my fingers went through the meat, and white globules and tears of fat came free and adhered to my mask. But trying to wipe fat off my mask in cold water just made the glass smeary. The contents of one barrel filled two-and-a-half plastic boxes measuring 24″ × 18″ × 9″. I think it must have been so well preserved and

131

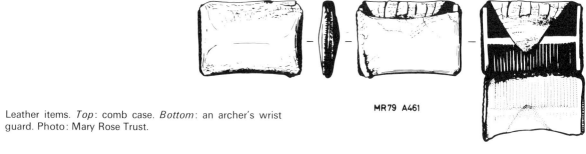

Leather items. *Top*: comb case. *Bottom*: an archer's wrist guard. Photo: Mary Rose Trust.

MR 79 A461

MR 79 A1224

Miscellaneous finds: a linstock head for igniting the gunpowder in the touch hole; some unexplained pieces resembling weights; bronze buckles; wooden knife sheaths. Photo: Mary Rose Trust.

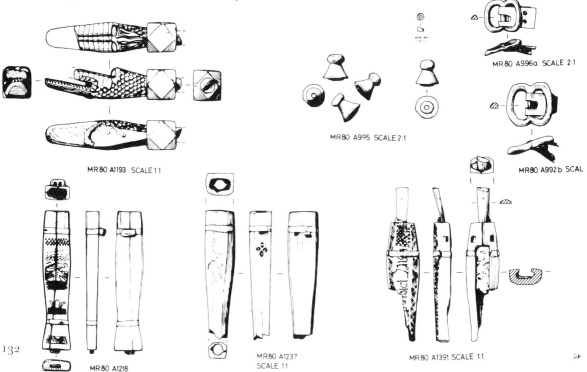

MR 80 A1193 SCALE 1·1

MR 80 A995 SCALE 2·1

MR 80 A996a SCALE 2·1

MR 80 A992 b SCAL

MR 80 A1218
SCALE 1·1

MR 80 A1237
SCALE 1·1

MR 80 A1391 SCALE 1·1

132

Enough to make a sick man shiver: some of the medicine bottles and instruments from the barber-surgeon's cabin, including a wicked-looking bronze syringe. Photo: Mary Rose Trust.

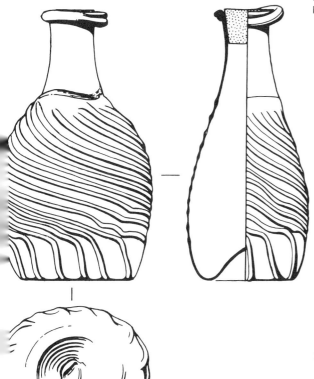

Glass bottle from the barber-surgeon's cabin. Photo: Mary Rose Trust.

so salty, that the meat had lasted all this time. But no one wanted me near them when I surfaced because of the really evil smell of rancid fat more than 400 years old. I could even taste it in the water through the sense organs in my lips.

The barrel staves were in excellent condition: clean-shaped, sharp edges. The bungs were still in place. The ends were made from three pieces butted side-by-side; the hoops from what looked like 'D'-section willow or hazel branches.

The texture of the muds and silts changed considerably. Some was coarse hard clay that I could pull away with my hand, leaving four finger-grooves. Some soft silts were so cold that it felt like putting a hand into a bag of cement—heavy, but fluid and cold. Going on past experience, the hands tell the brain what the hands have found, and the mind runs away with itself. I found an octagonal piece of hardwood two inches across, and inches away another similar piece. My hands told my brain that it felt like a small folding stool, so I continued excavating. But there was no stool. The 'legs' of the stool turned out to be dipsticks for measuring liquid levels in casks or barrels.

My wildest imaginings had become reality. In 1962, now unbelievably twenty years back into the

133

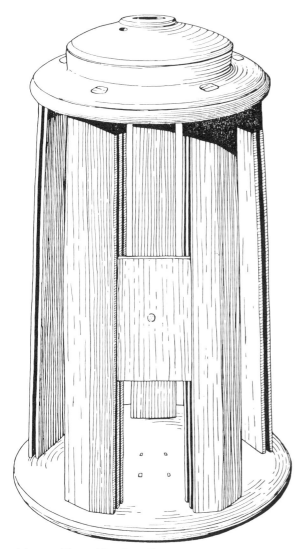

A lantern. Photo: Mary Rose Trust.

time and its height now in the reign of Elizabeth II; and to use this on site for briefing divers. Now it had come true, except that the 60 degree angle of heel had preserved more of the castle than I had bargained for. These were the bold and risky predictions, where I might well have been wrong, as so many had thought. But as for the condition of the wood, the leather, the organic remains and so on—that had always been obvious, given the nature of the soil. There can hardly be a better preservative than clay. Peter Throckmorton had long ago predicted that even paper might survive in that soil—and, lo, in 1981, at last, we had paper! Not very much, but undeniably part of a book someone had been reading in 1545.

By July one could swim inside a recognisable ship. One day starting at the concreted, catted anchor at the bow, I swam south along a real gundeck with real guns on it, their ammunition and gear and dead gunners lying around them. No one will ever quite see that again, even when the ship is raised. Those moments were unique. The first gun I came to, in

Selection of personal possessions: a spoon, a shoe, a folding pocket knife, a comb, a dagger handle. Photo: Mary Rose Trust.

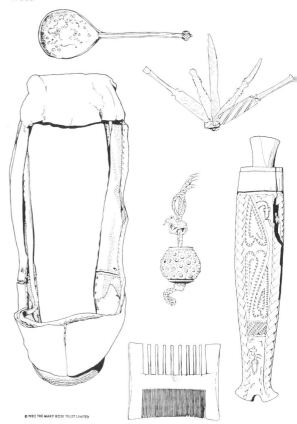

© 1982 THE MARY ROSE TRUST LIMITED

past, I had begun enquiring where the *Mary Rose* wreck might be because I had become aware from personal exploration that the Solent Area was most favourable for the preservation of wooden warships. In 1970, after extensive invisible trenching by sonar, I had become convinced by actual digging that we might have an open doll's house of a ship, preserved on one side to the upper gundeck and perhaps part of a castle above that, and on the other side preservation only to the turn of the bilge, approximately, below the position of the gun batteries. I was confident enough to sketch out a hypothetical section, based on a 45 degree heel and some informed guesswork as to the relationship between the seabed level in Henry VIII's

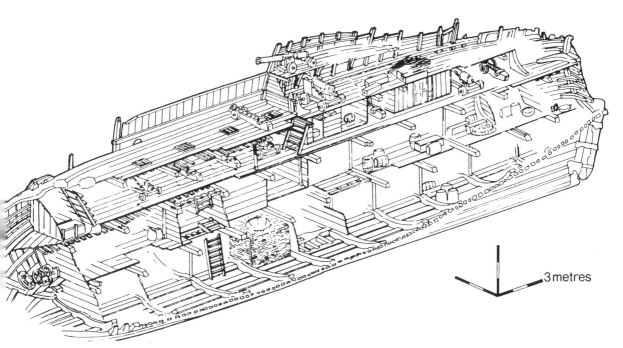

An isometric sketch of the surviving structure of the *Mary Rose* as revealed at the end of the 1981 diving season. The white areas in the ship represent mud and clay to be removed in 1982. Some missing parts of the hull may lie buried under the seabed not far away. Photo: Mary Rose Trust.

3 metres

firing position through its port, was a heavy wrought-iron breech-loader on a slide carriage; the next, also in firing position, was a very heavy bronze piece on a truck carriage, possibly a cannon royal, with vent-cover in place, maker's plate and Tudor Rose; then another wrought-iron gun in position through its firing port, but instead of the slide or bed being flush with the deck, it was mounted at the outboard end on big field wheels as used in land battles; and above this, where the deck and the bronze gun that had stood on it had been lifted out of the way by the 'removal team', there was a now-empty gunport which was not square, not even rectangular, but U-shaped; and dipping down onto the main gundeck again, I swam on past another bronze gun, violently displaced and angled, with under it a skull with white teeth, a pelvis and a shoe; and beyond that a sizeable concretion with a longbow at one end and a sliced off skull (I think it was) at the other; then a large wheel; then the wing transoms at the stern; and turning sharply right to follow the line of the transom, the rudder and sternpost, newly re-excavated.

Back I came, but not along the side; instead through the centre of the ship, peering down into the orlop and the hold. I passed over panelling which I

took to be the door to a cabin not yet excavated in Area 9; a stool or trestle among jumbled wreckage and bulkheads in Area 6/7; a long box, contents unknown but possibly arrows; and at the bow, heaped field wheels for big guns in pristine condition which had been found in a store nearby and were now gathered for the attentions of the removal men. At one point, I had noted oyster shells attached to the underside of the main deck (technically, the deck-head of the orlop); and I wrote: 'Bones all over: layer of bodies mostly in bits?'

By August, there was more yet as the excavators began to clear the last few feet down to the ports. Now, two anchors could be seen, catted, at the bow; now, there was a small port aft of the empty gunport in the castle deck; now a small bronze swivel gun was half-exposed aft—by it there was a half-broken wheel. Where the decks were slanted steeply upwards at the breech end, the loading tray was empty but, incongruously, there was a spade with pristine handle and of identical design to a modern garden implement, and an arrow, and a jumble of objects out of which stuck a pelvis. Dropping down that steep slope of planking, one came to the actual breech, which had only now appeared in the clay, and on that level the top of

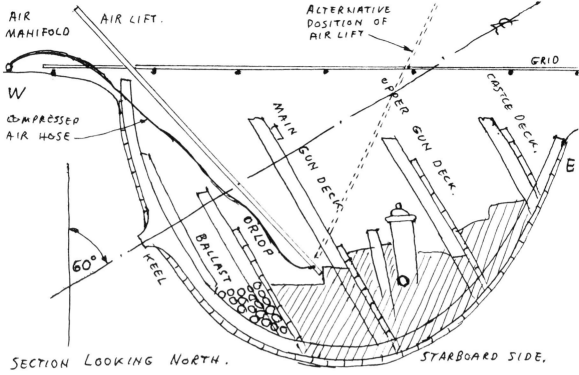

AIR MANIFOLD

AIR LIFT.

ALTERNATIVE POSITION OF AIR LIFT

GRID

W

COMPRESSED AIR HOSE

60°

KEEL

BALLAST

ORLOP

MAIN GUN DECK.

UPPER GUN DECK.

CASTLE DECK.

E

SECTION LOOKING NORTH.

STARBOARD SIDE.

Pages from Doug Barnard's log, September 1981.
a) Doug's working area on the orlop deck, indicated by the airlift tethered by the 12-inch face he is cutting through the clay.
b) Complicated debris including human remains emerging from the clay where the fire-logs have broken through the partition, crushing some of the food barrels and also a wounded man lying in the sick bay.

someone's cranium was just beginning to be exposed. The gun muzzle and the side of the ship lay several further feet down, hidden from us as yet.

The pelvis and the cranium might have belonged to one man or to two, and one or both might have been a gunner. But there was no doubt about the man who had been found some weeks before, lying in the waist at the break of the stern castle. He was lying on a sword and in his pockets were gold coins. An officer, his last order given. And as I came back to the shot line I saw Adrian Barak working on a complete body lying there in a leather 'jack' or jerkin, which was brought up shortly after; and minutes later another diver brought up bones and a skull found lying under a wheel which had been removed in the morning.

There was so much to see on a complete tour that one could hardly take it all in: the step for the foremast; the barrels in the hold piled high to the

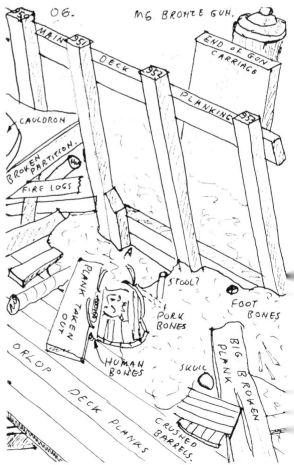

O6.

MG. BRONZE GUN.

MAIN DECK PLANKING

END OF GUN CARRIAGE

CAULDRON

BROKEN PARTITION

FIRE LOGS

STOOL?

FOOT BONES

PLANK TAKEN OUT

PORK BONES

HUMAN BONES

SKULL

BIG BROKEN PLANK

ORLOP DECK PLANKS

CRUSHED BARRELS.

When the author first found the site of the *Mary Rose,* there was nothing to see but seabed—some 5 feet above the level of the scaffold poles of the grid. Now a great ship with massive decks is exposed to the light. August 1981. Photo: Alexander McKee.

deckhead; the huge diameter wooden pump fitted horizontally; the tame fish, including a violent-pink wrasse, swarming everywhere around me; the lobsters and the crabs peering out of the homes they had found as the excavation went on, soon to be evicted.

Until recently, the seabed had been level with the frame heads on the starboard side (it had been much higher when we began, but such a vast excavation had lowered it around the ship by some five feet locally). Now, however, the dig had gone down outboard on this side and been carried down until the gunports and the gun muzzles glaring through them were exposed, and below that the attachments for the standing rigging—the chain plates—beautifully preserved. I shall always remember coming up from inside the ship, swimming over deck after inclined deck, and then finally rising up over the castle deck, and then dropping down the other side—the starboard side outboard.

The side of the *Mary Rose* was heeled right over above me, held by a single metal support put in by the diving team, so that one sank down underneath and most of the light was shut out; one had to wait and accustom to darkness. And there, at last, it was: the port-lid—up and open. One could see the rows of small concretions marking where the nails in the flanged lid had been, and see the ring which the gunner would grasp to close the port when the gun had been withdrawn.

But this gun had never been wheeled back, this port had never been closed after battle. This was where the water had rushed in that had sunk the *Mary Rose.*

By June, 1982, the excavation—the emptying of the ship of its contents prior to salvage—was nearly complete. There were a few thousand bricks (from the oven hearth) and a few hundred tons of ballast to come. And here, because so low down in the hull and soon silted over, there were artefacts in a parti-

A dense shoal of pollack circle over the heeled ship. Photo: Alexander McKee.

Right: Writing materials from the *Mary Rose*—quills, an inkpot and a seal 'G.C.' For George Carew? Also recovered were two pewter plates marked with the arms of Lord Lisle, who entertained Henry VIII and Carew at dinner the day before the battle. Photo: Mary Rose Trust.

Below: A gunport high up the hull. The deck below it has been removed. 1981. Photo: Alexander McKee.

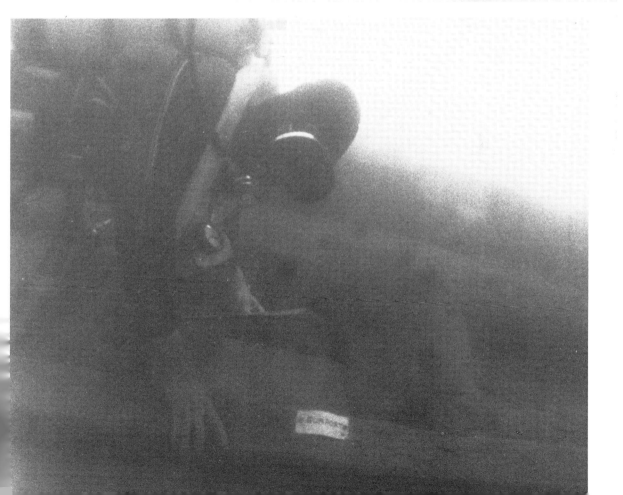

At last, in 1982, the ship's bell was found; and it was dated 1510. Photo: Mary Rose Trust.

On 14 June, 1982, the lifting frame to be positioned on the seabed above the *Mary Rose* by divers of the Royal Engineers, was towed to Spithead suspended beneath a barge. Photo: Mary Rose Trust.

cularly fine state of preservation. So far, some 80 identifiable individuals had been found, plus the remains of many others, totalling in all some 160–170 men. Officers, gunners, seamen, bowmen, pikemen, servants. In the *Wasa*, from the skeleton of one young lad, the pathologists had been able to show that he had undergone three separate periods of malnutrition in his short life; which said volumes about Sweden in the 17th century. But only some two dozen bodies had been found in and around the *Wasa*. From the near 200 still in the *Mary Rose* a very positive picture of life in Tudor times will eventually emerge, when all the remains have been studied by highly-qualified people. And then, one hopes, they will all be buried

together and a memorial placed above them, to commemorate the sad day when the *Mary Rose* went down.

In September or October this year it is hoped that the *Mary Rose* will be raised. The strengthened hull will be hung from a lifting frame before the last clay is cut away from underneath, thus avoiding the suction (or 'stiction') effect which would otherwise place great strain on the structure. Then a floating crane will transfer the hull underwater to a cradle fixed to a pontoon placed on the seabed. Bearing the *Mary Rose*, the pontoon will be lifted to the surface, carrying the ship on her last journey back to Portsmouth dockyard where she was built, 472 years ago.

The giant crane-barge *Tog Mor* (Gaelic for 'Big Lifter'), ready, before dawn on 10 October to attempt to raise the *Mary Rose*.
Photo: Alexander McKee

Epilogue

It was 4.50 on the morning of Sunday, 10th October, 1982. A clear, fine night with a chill breeze blowing gently over the water. Tony Glover's big new trawler *Sand Julie* (successor to *Julie-Anne*) lay alongside the slipway at the Camber, from where we had sailed so many times to Spithead. The boat was packed with original *Mary Rose* team divers ('a few years older and a few stone heavier', as Ann Clarke remarked) and their wives. Astern of her lay John Barber's fast cruiser *Margaret Anne*, twin engines growling, and just coming in, mast bobbing, was Mike Coomber's tall yacht *Ronar M*. Both of these boats, too, were loaded with members of the early team and their supporters. Yet another boat, Mick Aitken's *Snow Goose*, would be sailing round from Hayling Island to rendezvous with us at Spithead.

None of us had slept much—I think I managed an hour—but the excitement kept all weariness at bay.

By five o'clock it was time for Tony to lead the little flotilla out of Portsmouth Harbour—more than fifty people gathered to witness the raising of the *Mary Rose*. Less than six hours later we were back in harbour, the *Mary Rose* still below the surface of Spithead and the whole lifting operation in jeopardy. It seemed that my worse fears had come true.

It is easy to be wise after the event, but in fact I had been anxious about the salvage operation for some time. Back in January, 1979, when the Trust was being formed, I had pointed to a major weakness in the plan of organisation: 'Engineering and salvage are plainly regarded as low grade.' In November, 1980, I had warned:

> There is still a risk that the *Mary Rose* will be broken by the lift, or the salvage fail in some spectacular way, simply because there seems constant resistance to all suggestions for a salvage expert to be appointed.

What was missing was, not expert advice, but an expert with directional powers. I had made a close study of the *Wasa* operation in Sweden, where the salvage director, who actually owned the company carrying out the lift, had been forced into 'mutiny': either he would be allowed to get on with the job in his own way or he would pull out and let the rest of them get on with it. I did not want the same thing to happen to us, but we had no salvage director and I had no way of enforcing my views. The result was a series of delays which brought the date of the lift dangerously late in the year, to the period of the big spring tides and frequent long spells of bad weather.

The final plan, excellent in itself, involved two specially designed and engineered pieces of equipment: an underwater lifting frame and a cradle. For her rise to the surface into air the *Mary Rose* was to be sandwiched between the two on the 'locked box' principle, so that the steel cradle, and not the Tudor hull, took the strain. The frame was like a giant bedstead with four legs on which it would sit above the *Mary Rose* while the wooden hull was attached to it. Divers from the Trust and from the Royal Engineers would make the attachments underwater and cut away the clay from under the hull. The connection with the seabed would be broken gently.

The tailored cradle would be lowered alongside and the frame, with the *Mary Rose* suspended, would be moved up and along until it was over the cradle; then it would be gently lowered, the four legs of the frame fitting smoothly into four funnel-shaped 'stabbing guides' built on to the cradle. In effect, the cradle was the bottom and sides of a meccano-like box, the frame being the lid. The *Mary Rose* was the contents.

The intricate tasks of actually fitting out the cradle were the responsibility of the Royal Engineers under Captain John Brannam; the heavy lifts would be carried out by the giant floating crane-barge *Tog Mor*, loaned by Howard Doris.

DIVISION RENFREW TIPTON AND GRAVESEND

After 437 years, the *Mary Rose* rises to the surface on 11 October, 1982. What look like wooden posts are deck beams. In the background is part of the stern castle. Photo: Alexander McKee

What was required for success was calm weather, weak tides and plenty of time to fit the frame 'lid' to the cradle 'box'. This also had to be co-ordinated with a vast promotional and publicity exercise, to be carried out on a specific date under the eyes of the Prince of Wales, and with media men and women converging on Portsmouth from all over the world. This side of the operation was conducted with great skill, even when equinoctial gales turned the Solent into a frothy mud-bath and caused the postponement of the transfer of the *Mary Rose* to her cradle—originally planned as a ten-day manoeuvre.

The new lifting date had to be planned for the next neap tide, Sunday, 10 October. So, on Saturday the 9th, as more than 500 media representatives from the

United States, France, Germany, Brazil, Canada, Australia and many other countries, swarmed into the Press centre at Southsea Castle, the divers and engineers, prevented by bad weather from making the transfer to the cradle before that, were trying to accomplish in that one day and night what should have taken them ten.

Where 437 years before a vast encampment of tents had arisen to house the assembling English army, its commanders and its King, now stood twentieth-century prefabricated buildings and an array of TV and radio aerials above the mobile caravans of the outside broadcasting units. One BBC programme was watched by nearly three million people. Three TV networks were showing to the United States. The lift

The stern of the *Mary Rose* riding higher. The girders at water level are part of her cradle. The lifting frame above her is locked to the cradle by four legs, one of which is shown here, correctly positioned inside the funnel-shaped 'stabbing guide'. Photo: Alexander McKee

was timed for the first slack water on Sunday morning—7.30 am. As the darkness faded and the ring of bobbing red and green lights became visible as the inner screen of 50 boats of which ours were part, so did the cameras begin to roll, with the world watching.

Up to 7.20 am I had kept filed securely away, so to speak, all thoughts of what it might be like on the day the *Mary Rose* came to the surface. For twenty years I had kept my attention fixed on the next stage, and the next, and the one beyond that, and never allowed myself to become excited. But with ten minutes to go to the start of the lift, tension began to build; I had to will my fingers to keep still.

Ray McLaren, whose trade is lifting heavy weights into and out of ships at Southampton Docks, watched it all with professional attention:

When we arrived on site, *Tog Mor* was bathing the sea with her lights. Boats small and large, their mastlights bobbing and swaying, surrounded her as far as one could see. Very little activity, though. *Tog Mor* looked silent, her great mast angled to the night sky, the four lifting wires angling downwards to the locating posts just visible. As the morning grew brighter a diver could be seen hanging onto one of the posts. He was watched with great attention by everyone on board *Sand Julie* as he carried out whatever task had been allotted to him. After finishing he swam to *Tog Mor* and shortly afterwards Prince Charles arrived. The lifting suddenly com-

The hull of the *Mary Rose* was caulked and tight. It leaked slightly in three places only, so that four pumps had to be used to remove the water inside. Photo: Alexander McKee

'Mad Mac' and the *Mary Rose*—up at last after seventeen years' diving. Photo: Associated Newspapers

menced. Slowly, very slowly, inch by inch, the lifting wires moved upwards, then suddenly stopped. All eyes strained to see the slightest movement. I noticed that *Tog Mor* was listing heavily to starboard and the port side lifting wire closest to her had gone slack.

There were several possible explanations. The most probable was that the lifting frame had separated from the lifting cradle. Yes, this would explain it. I expressed my misgivings to Mac and at this time two divers were sent in to investigate. Shortly afterwards the lift was suspended.

Pete Smith of the Portsmouth *News*, a journalist who had been covering the *Mary Rose* story since the 1960s when we were small beer indeed– one boat and a dozen men—was with us now as *Sand Julie* steered for the Camber.

Never once, as our small boat steamed back into Portsmouth Harbour, did the man who found the *Mary Rose* look back at the giant marine crane holding her suspended under the sea.

For an agonising two hours, he had grown visibly more anxious as it became clear that something, unseen to him, had gone wrong. He did not know whether the *Mary Rose* had been irreparably damaged or whether some slight hitch had caused a minor delay. When it became obvious that nothing was going to happen that day, his mind switched to the immediate future. Occasionally, he could not contain his fears. 'She's left there exposed. She's at her most vulnerable,' he said. 'It's what I feared most.'

Ashore, many new volunteers had been on duty since 6.30, selling souvenirs from fifteen trading posts, or out with information leaflets and collecting boxes (for we were £300,000 short of our four million pound target), and also trying to keep the Press happy when nothing whatever seemed to be happening. Gaile Matchan, their organizer, recalled:

The disappointment caused by the delays was obvious everywhere, but the patience and understanding of all the people I spoke to was really amazing. Throughout this long day I never heard a single grumble.

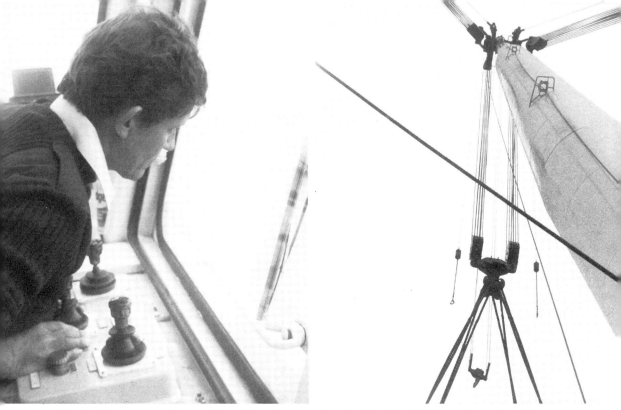

Left: John Studdes, master and crane-driver of *Tog Mor*, assessing the risks of the lift. Photo: Alexander McKee
Right: The crane-jib of *Tog Mor*, capable of raising loads of nearly one thousand tons. Photo: Alexander McKee

When we got ashore we were all surprised to realise that it was only 10.30 am, so slowly had the hours of waiting passed. The Trust had announced a postponement until the following morning, but we were so sick with disappointment that organising a trip for Monday seemed hardly worth while.

What had gone wrong that Sunday morning? In the hurried compression of fitting and testing the frame and cradle, to make all ready for the lift by 7.30 am, one of the frame legs had been damaged, and when lifting began it had been unable to take the strain, causing the whole contraption to lurch. That afternoon—and all the following night—the Royal Engineers worked without sleep to burn off the damaged leg and rig up a makeshift system of wires that would, in theory, hold the frame steady for the next attempt.

Concern for 'our ship' got the better of us by the next morning, and we all packed into *Sand Julie* for another night ride out to Spithead. The sea was still

calm, but a gale was forecast, and there were other changes, too, as Ray McLaren recalled:

This time the arena looked empty; the boats which had ringed the site the day before were absent. Cold rain beat down from an overcast sky promising possibly worse weather to come. This time there was instant activity to be seen; figures scurried about on the great barge which was to receive the lifting cradle and an army assault craft was fussing about the lift, shepherding divers. It was obvious we were watching the completion of the night's work. We settled down to wait, wiping binoculars and camera lenses to remove the rain beating into us. Suddenly *Tog Mor* was taking up quickly, unlike the previous day; it was almost as if the *Mary Rose* had decided she couldn't trust those present to bring her once more into the air but had decided to give her a hand.

The large yellow tubes appeared first, a slight pause as the tubes vented and then up again, the lifting wires festooned with lighter wires attached to the tubes. I noticed that at least two of the lifting wires were out of place and that the lifting frame was tilted at an alarming angle. Checking with binoculars, I saw that the tilt was due to the missing section of docking leg now replaced by wire straps. What I had thought were misplaced lifting

The barge is manoeuvred underneath the cradle holding the *Mary Rose*. Photo: Alexander McKee

wires were in fact the actual arrangement, except for the starboard outer which was wrapped around the lower part of the leg.

A few minutes before, with the lift imminent, a Dockyard Police launch on guard duty had obscured our view. We did not know his radio frequency, so my elder son (an ex-Royal Marine who had come out to join us in his single-seater canoe) paddled over to ask politely if the Police would move over. His craft looked like a tiny water-beetle silhouetted against the giant floodlit bulk of the 5,479-ton *Tog Mor*. The Police shouted to him and he shouted back, that Alexander McKee ('my dad') was in the big trawler over there with all the early *Mary Rose* team divers, and that the Police boat was blocking their view. Would they please move 20 yards? After a momentary 'er-um', they obliged. But they must also have reported the incident, for the loudspeaker in *Sand Julie*'s cabin began to crackle a message for me to come over to *Tog Mor*. Tony Glover started his engines and let go the buoy. I went up the side of *Tog Mor* just as the *Mary Rose* was appearing.

Part of the starboard stern castling and the main deck beams showed first. Then I found myself looking at the port side aft and could recognize the frames I had first seen and then dug in 1971. The hull lay on its side in the cradle just as she had in the seabed below, but as very slowly the *Mary Rose* was lifted clear of the sea, only three tiny streams of water spurted out beneath. Almost all her seams and caulking were still tight after 437 years; and four pumps had to be placed inside the hull in order to empty it of water. What struck me were the beautiful lines by which the midships section, which curved one way, was subtly altered to a curve in the opposite direction as the planking was run in to the sternpost. Those nautical historians who talked about clumsy 'round ships' were wide of the mark. The *Mary Rose* looked good.

The same could not be said of the lifting frame. From the bridge deck of *Tog Mor* it seemed a shambles, tilted and twisted, two of the three remaining legs bent—one badly—and the fourth missing altogether where the REs had had to burn it away underwater. It looked as if a hurricane had struck it. The air and water bags which were meant to cushion the hull against the steel girders of the cradle below were in disarray, many having burst. Sick at heart, I turned away.

Then occurred a bang which, thanks to more than a score of 'live' microphones, literally went round the world. The whole vast steel bulk of *Tog Mor*, so big that one hardly noticed the helicopters landing on the pad at the other end, shook under my feet. With Prince Charles apparently about to board the *Mary Rose* from the other side, the frame had slipped with a crash down the badly bent leg, nearly, but not quite crushing the hull flat; her timbers must have flexed a full five feet under the impact. A salvage engineer touched me on the shoulder and pointed: the frame was now prevented from falling further and utterly destroying the hull by a single, buckled $1\frac{1}{2}$-inch bolt. And so it remained for hours, literally hanging by a thread of metal.

The time passed in a haze of unreality. I remember the Prince of Wales chatting to me about the *Mary Rose*, and afterwards REs of all ranks coming up to shake my hand. Then I was invited to climb sixty feet up the mast to the control cabin of the crane where, to the murmur of quiet, professional voices, the final drama was being played out.

The Cuxhaven barge *TOW I* had to be moved under the cradled *Mary Rose*, still hanging in air high above the sea, and when both barge and cradle were precisely aligned, the crane operator had to bring his cargo to within a foot or so of the barge's deck and then gently lower her on to it. Due to the mechanism of the crane, there was a 22-second delay between pulling the lever and the order being carried out— and meanwhile the barge was shifting in response to the combined onslaught of wind, tide and wave. Even more hazardous was the fact that the load was not hanging square and horizontal: it was monstrously distorted, so that one of the four corners tended to touch first and throw everything out; and all this weight was hanging at one corner on a single, thin bolt. It was not merely a matter of the safety of the *Mary Rose* but of the lives of the men manning the barge.

John Studdes, crane operator and master of *Tog Mor*, who, I was told, had not slept for 21 hours, was patiently dealing with each shifting crisis as it arose, talking quietly to his colleagues below as the load moved slowly above their heads. Only when it was exactly right and likely to stay right for half a minute, could he take a decision. A wrong one, I think, might have capsized the barge and sent the *Mary Rose*, cradle and all, upside down to the bottom of Spithead.

Back on the buoy, in *Sand Julie*, Ray McLaren was anxious.

We waited and watched as water and large pieces of mud cascaded from the hull. With great difficulty the barge was placed in position; then lowering took place and due to the grotesque angle of the hoist resulting from the various mishaps, more problems faced the Trust who by now must have been living on their nerves. Finally the *Mary Rose* was secured and the request came through to pick up Mac. Upon arrival, we were all invited aboard *Tog Mor*. I made straight for the control room, where the air weight was still registering on the panel: 637.9 tons. Questioning revealed that initial lift was about 210 tons. I could not find out what had been the Trust's estimated weight. I noted that the cushioning bags placed on framework designed to protect the *Mary Rose* were burst or splayed out; they had obviously burst because too much weight had been placed upon them. How close did the *Mary Rose* come to disaster that day? I believe very close.

In fact, she was by no means safe until the next day, when the Dockyard put in some urgent work to prevent the frame from slipping further and crushing her flat.

Ashore, the suspense of the long-drawn operation was felt by the anxious spectators, too. Gaile Matchan wrote:

Raining! Still the people came to watch and wait for another uncertain day, wrapped in plastic and patience. Southsea Castle field had become a muddy quagmire, but still a few sturdy kiddies leaped about excitedly. The trading point at the RN War Memorial was lashed with wind and rain, but still the gallant band of volunteers sold pencils and cards. Newsmen were looking tired and resigned in the Press centre, each with the inevitable cup of coffee. Mrs Frances Handley, our most dedicated street collector ready to go out in the rain, this remarkable pensioner raised £151,96 by her own efforts. Truly amazing! My impression of those two long days is that the people of Portsmouth were tightly united with the people of the world in this extraordinary drama, and for a moment *were* all one. I am proud and privileged to have been a small part of those 48 hours—a witness to this historic occasion.

When we left *Tog Mor* and headed back to the Camber, we were damp, hungry, thirsty and jubilant. It was only a step from the quay to the pubs on 'Portsmouth Point', where generations of Navy men—including Nelson's after Trafalgar—had caroused. Morrie Young wrote:

There had been times for celebration before. The day when the first dozen or so of the 'old girl's' timbers were exposed to our gaze for the first time standing barely

The barge is now correctly positioned under the cradle. Photo: Alexander McKee

inches above the seabed. Then came the artefacts: a pewter wine flagon, lead shot, dagger handles of wood and a seaman's 'ditty box' containing hand-made cotton reels, a comb, a bradawl and thimble. But above all was the ship. To me as a shipwright there was nothing to surpass her. Now the *Mary Rose* has felt the wind on her cheek for the first time since 1545 and in so doing has touched the hearts of thousands of people. I am very proud of my association with the *Mary Rose*, Alexander McKee and the diving team he still leads, and if my cheering and my slightly inebriated condition caused offence as that lovely old warship was towed slowly back into Portsmouth Harbour later that evening, I make no apology.

When the tow began, only a handful of men were on the barge that held the cradled hull, among them Colonel Wendell Lewis, The Trust's Director of Recovery:

At the entry to the deep channel leading to the harbour entrance I could see lights at Eastney—cars putting on their headlamps and giving a few little toots on their horns. As we neared Southsea Castle and Portsmouth the volume of traffic grew—a traffic jam ashore with many headlights and cars sounding their horns. Then ships started blasting their sirens and playing searchlights on

Four of the 'marauders': Don Bullivant, Pete Powell, Tony Glover, Maurice Young. Photo: Alexander McKee

us; more and more people on the sea wall; fireworks going up into the night, and a gun was fired—I don't know where it came from.

As we came level with the pubs on 'Point' I heard clearly from the shore: 'Three cheers for the *Mary Rose*!'

I sent a signal to the Port Admiral: 'We request permission for *Mary Rose* to re-enter Portsmouth Harbour after a rather long commission of 437 years.'

What I was looking forward to above all was the feeling of actually tying her to a buoy up the harbour.

Our little group of original *Mary Rose* divers came out of a pub on 'Point' to watch the arrival. She came in very slowly, preceded by a tug. Orange flares exploded overhead. There were roars of cheering taken up by ships' sirens, echoing over the still, black water cold under the lights. Crowds of people came running onto 'Point' from further along the walls—as many as for the homecoming of the carrier *Invincible*

from the Falklands, I was told. Some of them knew who we were and came up to shake my hand or ask for autographs. My eyes went damp.

The *Mary Rose* was an eerie sight under the lights, half-hidden by the crazy wreckage of the wildly tilted lifting frame.

Nevertheless, I felt a wave of utter relief.

That night, I telephoned Tessa Harrow in London. Tessa had edited this book with a mixture of sympathy, encouragement and enthusiasm which alone had kept me going as I slaved to complete the writing in a race against the recovery date. Tessa had been out with us in Tony's boat the day before, eager to meet the men whose contributions to the book she had read, and to see the ship they had worked to save. But she had missed this day. I think my voice was hoarse. All I could say was: 'She's home at last, in harbour with the *Victory*.'